ENERGY FOUNDATION 能源基金会
本项目由能源基金会中国可持续能源项目支持

The Road to Rule of Law in Environmental Protection
A Study Report on the Thoughts of Revision of the Environmental Law of PRC

通向环境法治的道路

《环境保护法》修改思路研究报告

杨朝飞 主编

中国环境出版社·北京

图书在版编目（CIP）数据

通向环境法制的道路 ：《环境保护法》修改思路研究报告／杨朝飞主编．--北京：中国环境出版社，2013.8

ISBN 978-7-5111-1484-6

Ⅰ．①通… Ⅱ．①杨… Ⅲ．①环境保护法－研究报告－中国 Ⅳ．①D922.684

中国版本图书馆CIP数据核字(2013)第126223号

出 版 人 王新程
责任编辑 赵惠芬
责任校对 唐丽虹
装帧设计 彭 杉

出版发行 中国环境出版社
（100062 北京市东城区广渠门内大街16号）
网 址：http://www.cesp.com.cn
电子邮箱：bjgl@cesp.com.cn
联系电话：010-67112765（编辑管理部）
发行热线：010-67125803，010-67113405（传真）
印 刷 北京中科印刷有限公司
经 销 各地新华书店
版 次 2013年8月第1版
印 次 2013年8月第1次印刷
开 本 787×960 1/16
印 张 20 彩插1
字 数 290千字
定 价 60.00元

编委会

主　编：杨朝飞

副主编：袁　伟　唐大为

编　委：（按姓氏笔画排序）

王　曦　王灿发　孙佑海　许国栋　李启家

李庆瑞　李艳芳　汪　劲　别　涛　赵立建

《环境保护法》修改思路研讨

项目简介

《中华人民共和国环境保护法》(以下简称《环保法》)历经1979年、1989年两次修订，至今已23年。2002年以来，修法呼声越来越高，全国人大已经连续7年，每年都有代表建议修改《环保法》。2004年至今，修法建议和提案已近百件。2012年8月全国人大常委会审议了《环保法》的修订草案，与会代表认为全国人大常委会环资委向会议提供的现草案很不成熟，既造成了与现行法律法规的重复和矛盾，又脱离了环境保护的主战场，应当进一步研讨。为了进一步理清《环保法》的修改思路，提高修法质量，推动修法进程，中关村汉德环境观察研究所（以下简称汉德研究所）组织召开了系列研讨会，收集学术界、NGO和相关机构、组织的建议，计划形成综合报告并提交决策者。能源基金会为本项目提供了资金支持。

汉德研究所分别于2012年12月20日、2013年1月15日组织召开了《环保法》修改思路专家研讨会和《环保法》修改思路社会组织建言会。会议由中国环境科学学会副理事长杨朝飞主持，环境保护部政策法规司司长李庆瑞、副司长别涛、副巡视员韩敏及上海交通大学教授王曦、北京大学教授汪劲、中国政法大学教授王灿发、中国环境资源法研究会副会长孙佑海、中国人民大学教授李艳芳、武汉大学教授李启家、武汉大学副教授柯坚、中国政法大学副教授胡静、全国工商联环境服务业商会监事长许国栋、中华环保联合会环境法律中心督查诉讼部部长马勇、美国环保协会中国项目负责人张建宇、全球环境研究所执行主任金嘉满、公众与环境研究中心副主任王晶晶、中外对话北京办公室副总编辑徐楠、阿拉善基金会资助项目官员王小颖、汉德研究所特约研究员李伟和环境法研究中心主管王社坤等近40位专家参加了研讨。与会专家围绕《中华人民共和国环境保护法》和2012年《中华人民共和国环境保护法修正案（草案）》，就“有关环境的政府行为和政府责任、污染者责任、监管体制、环境权益、信息公开、公众参与、公益诉讼、民事赔偿、司法保障”等议题展开了讨论并提出了修法建议。

2012 年 12 月 20 日《环境保护法》修改思路专家研讨会开会场景

2012 年 12 月 20 日《环境保护法》修改思路专家研讨会合影

2013 年 1 月 15 日《环境保护法》修改思路社会组织建言会开会场景

2013 年 1 月 15 日《环境保护法》修改思路社会组织建言会合影

Report of Research Program on the Thoughts of Revision of the Environmental Protection Law of PRC

A Brief Introduction of the Research Program

The current Environmental Protection Law of PRC, which was formulated in 1979 and amended in 1989, has been effective for 24 years. Since 2002, there have been increasing voices suggesting a revision to the law. During the recent 7 years, the representatives of the National People's Congress ("NPC") have submitted motions for revision to the law every year and there are nearly one hundred motions since 2004. In August 2012, the NPC Standing Committee reviewed the revised draft of the Environmental Protection Law put forward by the Environment Protection and Resources Conservation Committee ("EPRCC") of the NPC Standing Committee. The attending delegates hold the view that the draft was quite premature. It would cause unnecessary duplication and contradiction to the current law and was not with the right focuses of environmental protection work. Therefore, a further discussion should be carried out. In order to clarify the thoughts, improve the revision quality and promote the revision process, HD Institute of Environment Observation ("HD Institute") organized a series of seminars to collect suggestions from the academia, NGOs and relevant organizations to formulate a comprehensive report to be put forward to the decision-makers. This research program is sponsored by the Energy Foundation.

An expert seminar and a social organization meeting on thoughts of the revision of the Environmental Protection Law were organized by HD Institute separately on December 20th, 2012 and January 15th, 2013. These meetings were presided over by Yang Chaofei, the Deputy Chairman of Chinese Society For Environmental Sciences and nearly 40 experts attended the discussions including the following:

Li Qingrui, Director, Department of Policies, Laws and Regulations of the Ministry of Environmental Protection,

Bie Tao, Vice Director, Department of Policies, Laws and Regulations of the Ministry of Environmental Protection,

Han Min, Deputy Inspector, Department of Policies, Laws and Regulations of the Ministry of Environmental Protection,

Wang Xi, Professor, Shanghai Jiao Tong University,

Wang Jin, Professor, Peking University,

Wang Canfa, Professor, China University of Political Science and Law,

Sun Youhai, Vice chairman, Chinese Society for Environmental and Resources Protection Law,

Li Yanfang, Professor, Renmin University of China,

Li Qijia, Professor, Wuhan University,

Ke Jian, Associate Professor, Wuhan University,

Hu Jing, Associate Professor, China University of Political Science and Law,

Xu Guodong, Chief supervisor, China Environment Chamber of Commerce of All-China Federation of Industry and Commerce,

Ma Yong, Director, Department of Inspection and litigation of Environmental Law Center of All-China Environment Federation,

Zhang Jianyu, Project leader, China Project of Environmental Defense Fund,

Jin Jiaman, Executive Director, Global Environmental Institute,

Wang Jingjing, Deputy Director, Institute of Public and Environmental Affairs,

Xu Nan, Deputy Editor-in-chief, Beijing Office of the China Dialogue,

Wang Xiaoying, Funding Project official, SEE Foundation,

Li Wei, Guest Researcher, HD Institute of Environment Observation,

Wang Shekun, Supervisor, Environmental Law Research Center of HD Institute of Environment Observation.

The experts discussed on the current Environmental Protection Law and the 2012 revised draft of the Law regarding the topics of "Government's Action and Responsibility of Environmental Protection, Polluters' liability, Supervision and Regulation Mechanism, Environmental rights, Information Disclosure, Public Participation, Public Interest Litigation, Civil Compensation, Judicial Indemnification, etc". Experts put forward their proposals and suggestions of the revision to the law.

Seminar on Thoughts of Revision of the Environmental Protection Law on December 20th, 2012.

A Group Photo of Experts Attending the Seminar on Thoughts of Revision of the Environmental Protection Law on December 20th, 2012

The Social Organization Meeting on Thoughts of Revision of the Environmental Protection Law on January 15th, 2012

A Group Photo of the Social Organization Meeting on Thoughts of Revision of the Environmental Protection law on January 15th, 2012

目　录

CONTENTS

绪　论

多年来，由于经济发展的高速和超常规的增长，我国虽然取得了举世瞩目的成就，但是也付出了非常沉重的环境与资源的代价。当前我国面临的环境压力比世界上任何国家都大，环境资源问题比任何国家都突出，解决起来也比任何国家都困难。环境形势可以概括为：局部有所改善、总体尚未遏制、形势十分严峻、压力继续加大。

当前，我国的环境形势还有一个新的特点，就是环境风险上升、环境事故频发、群体性事件增多、环境损害加重。高发的环境群体性事件也呈现出四大分布特点：一是大中城市基础设施建设引发环境群体性事件越来越多，包括交通、电力、垃圾焚烧厂等；二是在小城镇、农村的违法排污（暗管、私倒）引发的环境群体性事件居高不下，特别是重金属、有毒废物的污染等；三是大型企业由于安全生产事故导致的流域性、区域性的污染事件引发的环境群体性事件增多，如紫金矿业污染事件等；四是现代化工业建设项目引发的环境群体性事件大增，如什邡事件、启东事件、镇海事件等。

媒体与公众越来越关注环境保护。每一次污染事故和群体性事件发生之后，媒体与公众总是提出一系列的质询和质问，一是要质问被污染企业，二是要质问当地政府及有关部门，三是要求追究有关人员的责任。

我一直在思考一个问题：关于严厉追究责任，我们喊了那么多年，又处理了那么多人，但是污染事故和事件却依然与日俱增。各地投入了大量的资金和精力，但收效甚微。各类污染事故和事件的发生原因、过程、形式、结果大体相同，实际上我们每时每刻都在复制着一个相同的污染事故和事件。山西有污染事故，广西有污染事故，吉林、黑龙江、甘肃、陕西、福建、广东、湖南、湖北、江苏、浙江、四川、云南、河南、江西、安徽等地，也都有污染事故，几乎没有一个地方没有发生过污染事故和群体性事件的。而每一个污染事故与事件的过程都很简单，事故发生之前，企业为了降低成本、追求利益，大量偷排、漏排污染物；在事故发生之后再去花大钱消灾。各级政府也是如此，在事故发生之前，为了快速发展经济，都在大力招商引资，而且大都是在走一条牺牲环境发展经济的道路；在事故发生之后，又不惜血本拿着财政资金去清除污染，恢复社会秩序。这些官员们的目的非常简单，事故发生之前，就是要通过发展 GDP 为升官铺垫；事故出来之后，又不惜财力，拿老百姓（纳税人）的钱，去清污，为个人消灾保官。无论是群体性事件还是污染事件，都在不停地重复着过去的老路，复制着几乎相同的事件。

近年来，每一次事故都要处理一大批的人，被处理的人真是前赴后继，一个接一个。几年下来，被处理的干部、职工人数与日俱增、急速膨胀，不仅葬送了个人的发展前程，殃及和危害了家属，也给国家和社会造成了巨大的损失。我们处理、处分、处罚的那些人员，都是工作在第一线的个人，但是有谁去追究在事件产生背后的机制、体制问题呢？如果我们不下决心改变导致这些问题的机制和体制问题，总是止步于处理具体的个人，我们就会进入一个无休止的恶性循环，其结果只会使事情变得越来越严重。我们的法律和纪律虽然不算非常严厉，但是这些年处罚的人已经不少了。我们靠处理这些许许多多的具体的个人，能不能改变环境问题的现状？能不能缓解污染事故和群体性事件的发生呢？显然是不能的。核心的问题、根本的问题，就是必须要从机制和体制上，找到正确处理经济发展与环境保护之间关系的出路。

正确处理经济发展和环境保护的关系是非常重要的。发达国家在处理经济发展和环境保护关系的时候，首先是从规范政府行为入手，通过建立行之有效的机制和体制，确保政府不会放纵牺牲环境换取经济发展的错误倾向。只有规范了政府行为，环境保护和经济发展的关系才能真正走向和谐和统一。在此基础上再采取综合措施，进一步规范企业行为、规范公民个人行为，进而实现由现行的恶性循环走向环境保护的良性循环。只有这样才能使被处罚的人数越来越少，环境问题也才能得到真正改善。如果政府行为规范问题不解决好，法律越严厉，被处罚的人就越多。到那时，财政就只能拿出更多的钱，为此去兴建劳改所和监狱。这就是我们现在应该思考和解决的问题。

通过修改《环境保护法》规范政府行为，妥善解决环境保护和经济建设的协调发展问题，是人们认识上的一个飞跃和进步，也是《环境保护法》最应该解决的问题。

当然，通过修法，明确《环境保护法》的重要地位，对于我国环保事业还具有其他一些非常重要的基本保障作用：一是为环保事业奠定法律基础和组织保障；二是为环境保护规定一般性的环境监管制度提供依据；三是纠正现行《环境保护法》与其他环境保护法律法规的重复功能，从而理顺环境保护法律体系的内部关系等。

人们对修改《环境保护法》寄予了很大的期望。

杨朝飞

2013 年 4 月 3 日

《环境保护法》修改思路研究报告

关于《环境保护法》几个重大问题的建议

一、紧紧抓住《环境保护法》的修法有利时机

1. 修改《环境保护法》成为当务之急。尽管我国环保事业取得了长足进步，但是环境总体恶化的趋势尚未得到根本遏制。当前我国环境污染依然严重。在这种形势下，修改《环境保护法》为环境保护工作提供法理依据就成为当务之急。

2. 修改《环境保护法》成为众望所归。《环境保护法》于1979年制订，1989年修订，至今已经24年。对于是否有必要保留并修改《环保法》，一直存在很大争论。但是2002年以来，要求保留并修改《环保法》的呼声越来越高，已经连续7年有全国人大代表建议修改《环保法》。2004年至今，有关《环保法》的修法建议和提案已近百件。2012年8月，全国人大常委会审议了《环境保护法（修正案）草案》，并公开征求意见，期间共收到11 000多条建议和意见。可见，修改《环保法》已是共识，并被寄予了很高的期望。

3. 修改《环境保护法》应当坚持质量第一。一是要认识到《环保法》在我国环保法律体系中应有的基础性地位及其对保障我国环保事业顺利开展的不可或缺的作用，因此我们要从战略上看待《环保法》的修改工作，不能满足于小修小补，不能用“有限的修改目标”束缚人们的思想，不能为了表现政绩去修法，而应当解放思想、实事求是地进行较大的修改，修法进度一定要服从质量。二是认真总结之前在修法的过程中暴露出来的问题，认真地参考和吸取社会各界特别是环境法学专家的建议。三是要充分总结实践经验。近年来，环境管理方面的实践是丰富多彩的，有很多被证明相对有效的手段需进一步上升到法律层面，为进一步制定法规、规章、

规则提供应有的依据。例如，环保经济手段、公众参与程序、环境公益诉讼等。四是必须统筹处理好经济发展与环境保护的关系，一定要与时俱进地吸收科学发展观及党的十八大关于生态文明建设的新理念、新原则和新要求，在总则增加诸如科学发展理念、环境优先原则、风险防范原则、不得恶化原则等有关重要原则。五是一定要避免因过多地关注环保部门的制度需求、过少地关注社会公共利益的选择而导致的权力和权利的失衡问题，一定要强调国家行政权力和社会环境保护公共事务权利的结合。六是要注意妥善使用“环保优先”的概念，环保优先并不是不计条件、任何条件下的优先，而是经过比较和选择的利益优先，是有限度的优先。具体的法律条文设计应该有两个层面：一个层面是明确宣布在发展经济、社会和科技的同时，必须首先要明确兼顾环境保护；第二个层面是当经济社会科技发展对环境有严重不良影响或者危害的时候，才应当强调必须要“环保优先”。

二、准确定位《环境保护法》

从法律功能上看，《环境保护法》是为我国环保事业提供法律保障的一项特殊法律，具有基础性、综合性的特点，其功能和任务与防治污染、保护自然资源等专项法律的功能和任务有很大的不同。环境保护的各个专项法已经分别覆盖了环境要素或监管领域的具体方面，较为齐全。但是有些事项是不宜由这些法律来规定的。例如“环境”的法律定义；环境保护工作的基本理念和原则；国家环境保护行政管理体制；公民、法人和其他组织的环保权利和义务；一般性环境管理制度或措施，如国家环境监测制度、污染物排放收费制度和环境经济手段等；以及有关环境保护的法律责任。这些事项都是涉及国家环保事业法律基础的事项，宜集中由《环保法》来规定。此外，规范和制约有关环境的政府行为也是一个环保事业中的一般性问题，不宜由专门的污染防治法或自然资源保护法来规定，而宜由《环保法》来规定。这也是美国、日本等发达国家的成功经验。发达国家在处理经济发展和环境保护之间的关系时，首先就是规范有关环境的政府行为。

由此看来，我国的《环保法》有两个基本的功能和任务，一个是为环保事业奠定法律基础，另一个是规范和制约有关环境的政府行为。因此《环保法》的修改应聚焦于这两个基本问题。

从《环保法》与其他环境保护类法律的关系上看，《环保法》的功能和任务是规定环保事业的法律基础和规范、制约有关环境的政府行为，而其他环境保护类法律的功能和任务则主要是规范和制约企业行为，分别从防治污染、保护自然资源和生态系统，以及一些专门事项如环评、清洁生产、防沙治沙、循环经济等方面做出规定。因此，从规范对象上看，《环保法》与其他环保类法律是基础与“上层建筑”的关系和互补的关系。前者奠定环保事业的法律基础和主体框架，后者涉及在此基础之上的具体环保领域；前者管政府，后者管企业。二者互相配合，互相补充，各司其职，相得益彰。在明确了《环保法》的功能和定位之后修改《环保法》，就可以理顺环境保护类法律的内部关系，避免法律、制度之间的重叠、矛盾和空缺，从整体上改善我国环保类法律的实施效果。

三、严格规范政府环境行为

《环保法》是调整有关环境法律关系主体的行为规范，环境法律关系主体包括排放污染物的企业、社会公众与政府。目前，我国环境单项法以排污的企事业单位为其主要调整对象，对政府责任的规定不明确、不充分且可操作性差，而一些政府在环境保护方面的不作为或违法作为又助长了环境恶化的趋势。《环保法》的重要功能之一应当是规范和制约政府环境行为，促使各级政府能够自觉运用法治方式、法律思维执政，真正做到依法行政、依法保护环境。

1．预防为主，为政府建立有关环境的科学决策制度。我国各级政府面对环境保护具有双重的身份。他们既是“裁判员”，又是“运动员”。在管理企业排污行为时，他们是管理者，即“裁判员”，在招商引资、规划地方产业发展时，他们是“运动员”，即经济活动的直接规划者、参与者和推动者。这种规划、参与和推动，如果搞得不对，就会带来严重的环境问题。很多地方的环境污染事故和环境群体事件表明，其所在地方的政府没有平衡好发展经济与环境保护的关系，重经济发展，轻环境保护。为此，需要通过对《环保法》的修改，在法律上建立有关环境的政府科学决策制度，在政府决策阶段以环保优化经济发展。这类制度主要有“环境与发展综合决策制度”、“政府环境保护部际联席会议制度”和“环境咨询委员会制度”。其中，环境咨询委员会的成员主要由政府以外的人士担任，如人大代表、政协委员、专家学者、居民代表、环保团体代表或其他德高望重人士、有公益心之人士。环境咨询委员会有权列席政府有关环境的问题决策过程。建立这种“环境咨询委员会”的好处，一是可以让政府有听到政府以外的意见和建议的固定渠道，从而预防决策失误；二是把有关环境问题的社会矛盾由体制外转到体制内解决，避免因环境问题引起社会的动荡。建立这种社会咨询机制，也是发达国家和我国港澳台地区的成功经验。

2．建立政府环保履职的监督制度和机制。一是加强政府的内部监督，在明确各级政府的环境保护职责、科学制定跨部门制衡机制的基础上，一方面加强中央政府与地方政府之间和地方政府上下级之间的环境保护履职监督，另一方面强化环保部门对其他部门的制衡，让其他职能部门能够自觉遵守环境保护法律法规。二是加强诸如社会、公民、公民全体人大、政协、司法机关、媒体等的外部监督，为其提供应有的监督政府的机制、制度和专门途径。“把权力关进笼子”，一靠政府内部的监督和制约，二靠政府外部对政府的监督和制约，二者缺一不可。

3．用契约的方式在中央政府与地方政府之间建立正当的博弈机制。地方政府具有双重角色，一方面是地方利益的代表，另一方面也是中央利益在地方的代表。在环境立法中，应该肯定地方政府作为地方经济利益代表的正当性。因此，在处理中央和地方之间的关系时，地方政府不仅要服从中央政府，而且应当有机会与中央政府在法律规定的范围内进行正当博弈。立法就是要让地方和中央的博弈公开化、明朗化，从法制、机制和体制的建设上真正解决“上有政策、下有对策”的问题。契约的方式是中央和地方利益博弈的基本途径和必然结果。即便是单一制国家，中央和地方的契约精神也是必要的。中央政府对地方政府的管理，不仅要有“大棒”——依法行政，而且还要有“胡萝卜”——经济激励，如可以通过财政转移支付的手段，引导和鼓励地方政府自觉执行《环保法》，自觉做好环境保护工作。

四、切实保障公民环境权益

环境权是人与生俱来的天赋权利，在法治社会中必须将这种天赋权利从应有权利变成法定权利和实有权利，《环保法》的修改为这种转变提供了很好的契机。要实现这种转变，《环保法》在修改中应当做到三点：一是通过公益诉讼来保障环境权，包括民事公益诉讼和行政公益诉讼两种方式；二是通过民事诉讼和行政诉讼的方式来推动公民私益环境权利的保护；三是在环境权实现的过程中，应当充分发挥民间环保组织的作用。

关于环境权的两个具体的法条的建议：第一，在总则的部分规定：公民享有在良好环境中生活的权利；各级人民政府对本辖区的环境质量负责，依法采取措施维护环境权；任何单位和个人，不得违反国家环境保护规定，从事污染或者破坏环境的行为。第二，在法律责任部分，应该针对侵害环境权的行为赋予救济途径：对于污染或者破坏环境的行为，公民或者环保组织有权向行政机关举报，接到举报后，应该在特定时间，如60天之内反馈处理结果，如果行政机关接到举报之后在特定时期内，没有采取措施，公民可以委托或者授权环保组织，向人民法院提起诉讼，请求停止这种污染或者破坏环境的行为。在负有环境保护管理职权的行政机关，没有依法履行环保职责的时候，公民或者环保组织可以向法院提起诉讼，请求行政机关依法履行职责。

五、加快推进环境信息公开的进程

信息公开是知情权、参与权、表达权、监督权、建言权、诉讼权实现的前提条件，也是公民实现环境权的重要保障。目前，我国关于环境信息公开的规定存在法律位阶低、内容分散、责任缺位或处罚偏轻等问题。针对上述问题，在《环境保护法》修改中应当：一是将环境信息公开制度作为一项基本法律制度在《环境保护法》适当的位置加以明确规定，以提高制度效力；二是整合现有法律、行政法规、部门规章中的成熟规定，在《环境保护法》中加以整体规定；三是增加企业环境信息公开的义务性规定，特别是强化上市公司等企业的环境信息强制公开的义务；四是对违反政府信息公开和企业强制信息公开义务的法律责任作出明确规定；五是在公开的内容上特别应当强调对环境影响信息的公开，对上市公司环境信息公开义务进行特别规定。

总之，《环境保护法》要在总结现有的做法和经验的基础上，对环境信息公开主体（政府和企业）及公开方式、程序、范围、监督与法律责任等，作出明确的、可操作的规定。

六、有力推动公众参与的制度建设

公众是环境保护中不可或缺的主体。环境法律关系是一个政府、企业、公众的三角关系，公众是三角关系中的重要环节。环境保护工作的目的就是要保护公民的环境权益，而公众参与又是推动环境保护的重要力量。因此公众参与既是对政府监管污染者的补充和延伸，又是对政府环保工作的监督。当前，在资源环境约束仍在加剧的情况下，我国公众对参与环境保护事业表现出很高的热情。《环境保护法》应当全面、系统地规定公众参与的方式、途径和制度保障，从而真正推动公众成为参与环境事业的主力军。

社会组织可以为公众参与环境保护提供有力的支持，因为无论是在经济实力，还是在专业技术方面，社会组织相对于分散的公众个人来说，都更加强大。因此应当保护和鼓励公众在环保社会组织方面的结社权。

社会协商是公众参与环境保护的重要形式。污染企业不仅应当公开环境信息，而且应当与利益相关的社区居民进行平等的对话，向群众说明情况，认真听取群众的意见；政府应当参与和推动企业与利益相关的社区居民进行平等协商与对话，帮助解决相关问题。

七、积极倡导环境保护的经济手段

环境保护不仅非常需要强制性的行政管制手段，同时也非常需要经济手段。环境保护经济手段主要是通过调整人们的经济利益，调动其环境保护的积极性，进而推动人们自觉地参与环境保护，已经在世界各国广泛使用，发挥着不可替代的、正向的鼓励和激励的作用。近年来，我国在使用市场手段保护环境方面做了不少有益的尝试，积累了较丰富的经验。因此修改《环境保护法》的一项重要任务就是为环境保护经济手段提供法律依据，解决其合法性问题，从而保证其名正言顺地推行。

环境保护经济手段主要包括现在实行的绿色财政、绿色税收、绿色信贷、绿色保险、绿色证券、绿色贸易、绿色产业、生态补偿政策等措施。这些问题都不是环保单行法或其他法律法规所能够解决得了的，由此应当在修改《环保法》的过程中明确其应有的法律地位。

八、进一步明确法律责任的基本问题

《环境保护法》和单项法的很大区别就在于只对环境法律责任的一般性问题做出规定。《环境保护法》的法律责任部分应当重点解决好以下问题。

1. 建立环境责任终身追究制度，让污染者为其违法行为付出高昂代价。 一是严格明确污染者必须承担污染治理全部费用的责任；二是企业经营者及产权拥有者的环境责任将是一种终身责任；三是要求在污染企业发展中的所有曾经获益者，都必须承担共同的连带责任。事实上，这是一种无限责任，即如果污染责任方无力负担其依法应偿付的污染清理费用和损害赔偿费用时，有关控股或参股的组织和个人，向其贷款、借款及销售过保险的组织和个人，均有可能成为被追究责任的对象。

2. 明确以环境损害为重要内容的民事责任。当前环境事故高发、环境纠纷激增，因开发建设、社会生活各个方面引发的环境矛盾不断激化，成为影响社会安定的重要根源。因此在修改《环保法》时，不仅要加强行政调解措施，还要通过修法把更多的环境矛盾、环境纠纷引导到法庭解决，拓宽司法救济途径。一是应当从两个层面明确公众的环境民事权利，一方面明确规定污染环境、破坏环境或者其他使环境质量下降、使环境质量受损或对环境有严重不良影响的行为，应当承担减轻、消除危害及修复环境损害的责任；另一方面明确规定受害者有权要求减轻、消除危害及赔偿损失。二是应当规定如果污染者、破坏者已经不存在或者无法确知的情况发生，政府要承担赔偿责任。三是除了规定对私益损害的赔偿责任条款之外，还应规定生态损害、环境损害索赔的相关规则，同时还应当规定造成环境不良影响和增加环境风险的也要承担必要的民事责任。四是应当规定环境污染损害赔偿诉讼的特别诉讼时效，为环境民事诉讼提供便捷、有利的条件。五是应当强调环境损害鉴定与评估在实现民事赔偿诉讼与审判工作中的重要性，环境司法鉴定应当引入专家证人，请专家到庭作证，推动司法鉴定制度的突破。

3. 明确以严厉追究重大环境损害责任为重要内容的刑事责任。司法作为社会秩序与稳定的基石，是解决社会纠纷的重要防线，也是解决环境问题的重要手段。发达国家解决环境问题的成功经验，就是建立了严格和完善的环境法律体系以及完整、有效的司法模式，采用以行政调解和司法裁决相结合的法律手段，惩处环境违法行为。司法保障必须强调法律的有效性：一是司法机关必须担当起严厉打击严重危害环境质量的恶意违法行为的重任，如违规设置排污口以及私设暗管排污的、违法排放有毒有害物质的、暴力抗法的、擅自涂改污染数据的、销毁污染证据的及排污单位故意不正常使用水污染物处理设施，或者未经环境保护部门批准、擅自拆除或闲置水污染物处理设施的、排放污染物超过规定标准的、造成重大污染事故的等。二是执行救济穷尽原则，司法保障是所有法律保护的最后屏障，不应当频繁使用，是在其他救济手段不能发挥作用的前提下才采用司法保障，应当充分考虑环境纠纷的行政救济。三是司法保障发挥双头鹰功能，一方面要监督制约企业，另一方面要监督制约政府，在设计和考虑司法保障的时候，千万不要把司法保障变成行政系统的附庸，变成单方面巩固政府权威或者行政行为的延伸。

4．明确以解决“违法成本低”为目的的行政责任。一是确立“先制裁违法的自然人（人身罚），再处罚违法的单位”的新理念，从目前双罚制中以处罚单位为主转变到以处罚自然人为主，提高法律的震慑力；二是行政制裁要和刑法处罚衔接，建立人身罚中的治安管理处罚、拘役、有期徒刑有机衔接的人身罚制裁制度，并采取列举适用治安管理处罚和刑事处罚的主要情形，给执法和司法实践提供可操作的指引；三是从目前以罚款为主到行政指导和训诫为中心，采用“按日计罚”的执行罚手段；四是不仅要在修法的过程中创新处罚制度，将来还可以通过司法解释来创新处罚制度，建议环保部门可以和最高法、最高检、公安部联合发一个通知，将治安管理处罚与刑事处罚制度有机组合起来，这样就会取得事半功倍的监管效果。

九、细化环境公益诉讼的具体规定

环境公益诉讼是公众参与的重要途径，对于保护公共环境和公民环境权益起到了非常重要的作用。2012 年 8 月，新的民事诉讼法专门加强了公益诉讼的内容：“对污染环境、侵害众多消费者合法权益等损害社会公共利益的行为，法律规定的机关和有关组织可以向人民法院提起诉讼。”但这只是原则性的规定，《环保法》修改中，应对环境公益诉讼作出细化规定。具体建议如下：

1．扩大受案范围。一是环境污染不必是结果，针对进行当中的环境污染行为也可提起环境公益诉讼，要求其承担预防性的民事责任，请求法院发布禁令，然后再通过行政或其他方法解决；二是环境公益诉讼不仅仅局限于污染，还可以扩大到生态破坏，同时兼顾渐进性环境损害的诉讼。

2．扩大起诉主体。民诉法规定环境公益诉讼的主体为“法律规定的机关和有关组织”。最高法院的民四庭以高民智名义发表的《关于民事公益诉讼的理解与适用》，认为“法律规定的机关和有关组织”中的“有关组织”不受“法律规定的”限制，这对社会组织提起公益诉讼有利，但其对“有关组织”的资格条件规定得非常严苛。但同时，文章也表示如果《环保法》修改后，作出了相关规定，再依照特别的规定受理。而“法律规定的机关”的含义是可以提起公益诉讼的机关，要有明确的法律依据。这个依据不仅要求机关的设立和职能由法律规定，其可以提起公益诉讼的权利也要由法律明确规定。因此，《环保法》的修改可以通过明确规定“法律规定的机关”和“有关组织”来扩大公益诉讼主体。

3. 明确规定诉讼请求种类。《民法通则》规定了十种民事责任承担方式，有很多都是预防性的，公益诉讼可以请求停止侵害、发出停止令等。恢复原状的责任方式具体到环境领域，可以有替代、修复、期间损失等方式。

4. 在诉讼费用上作出对公益诉讼起诉主体有利的规定。环境公益诉讼利益归属于社会，诉讼成本应当由社会承担。因此，原告起诉时可缓缴诉讼费。若判决原告败诉，则应免交诉讼费；若判决被告败诉，则应判决由被告承担。原告胜诉，则让被告支付由于公益诉讼产生的证据费用、鉴定费、律师费等费用。

5. 规定环境损害赔偿金的归向与使用。民事公益诉讼的性质决定了原告不能通过诉讼获得私利。原告代表国家提起诉讼，人民法院判决责任人承担赔偿责任的，一并判决原告受领赔款后向国库交纳。原告申请人民法院执行有关生效判决时，人民法院应当要求其提供财政部门指定的收款账户专门接受判决赔款。按照公益诉讼目的，建议国家应当设立专门的基金，将环境公益损害赔偿的资金纳入基金，由法律规定的相关方依法管理，专款专用，并接受由有关各方组成的机构的监督。

十、公开昭示协同减排温室气体的意愿

我国是温室气体排放大国，随着全球温室气体减排谈判的逐渐深入，

我国的国际减排压力也日益加大。控制温室气体不仅仅是国际减排义务的履行方式，更重要的是也可以促进经济发展方式的转变，实现经济可持续发展。

1．在温室气体控制立法模式争执不下的情况下，先行确立立法的必要性。目前关于是在《大气污染防治法》中规定温室气体减排的内容，还是单独起草气候变化应对法，不同部门、不同专家都各执己见。尽管争执难下，而且各方都在朝不同的立法模式努力，但是各方都认为应当通过立法确立温室气体减排的法律地位。《环境保护法》作为一部综合性的环境保护法律，具有宏观指导性，可以就一些具体细节搁置争议，是推动温室气体立法的最好选择。因此，有必要在该法中就温室气体控制作出方向性、原则性的规定。

2．明确规定协同控制制度，协调温室气体控制与其他污染物控制目标之间的冲突。其他污染物的控制在很多情况下可能导致温室气体排放增加，比如火电厂脱硫可能导致 1%～2%的电力损耗，这些损耗意味着要排放更多的二氧化碳。因此，如何协调温室气体控制与传统污染物控制目标之间的关系，实现协同，既具有环境意义，又具有经济意义，有必要在《环境保护法》中作出明确规定。

（本文由丁媛媛整理）

Recommendations regarding the major issues of the Environmental Protection Law

1. The favorable opportunity of the revision of the Environmental Protection Law should be firmly seized.

(a) Revising the Environmental Protection Law has become a top priority. Although China's environmental protection has made a great progress, the tendency of general environmental degradation has not been stopped yet. Environmental pollution is still in a severe situation in China, which makes it highly necessary to revise the Environmental Protection Law to provide legal foundation for the work of environmental protection.

(b) A revision of the Environmental Protection Law is welcomed by all walks of society. The current Environmental Protection Law, formulated in 1979 and amended in 1989, has been effective for 24 years. There have long been great controversies on whether the Law should be maintained and amended again. Since 2002, there have been increasing voices suggesting a revision to the law. During the recent 7 years, the NPC representatives have been submitting motions for revision and there are nearly one hundred of them since 2004.In August 2012, the NPC Standing Committee reviewed the revised draft of the Environmental Protection Law and opened to the public for commenting. During the commenting period, over 11 000 pieces of suggestions and advices were received. It shows that revising the Environmental Protection Law has become the public consensus and is granted great expectation.

(c) Quality should come first in the work of revision of the Environmental Protection Law. First, it should be recognized that the

Environmental Protection Law plays a fundamental role in our environmental legal system and is essential for the sound development of China's environmental protection. Therefore, we should tackle the revision of the Environmental Protection Law in a strategic way, other than making minor repairs and supplements, also we should not bound our thoughts with goals of "limited amendment", or aim at showing off political achievements. Major changes should be made based on the principle of emancipating the mind and seeking truth from facts and the quality of the revision should come before the speed. Second, the problems revealed during the revision should be elaborated, suggestions and advices from the public should be considered, especially those from environmental law scholars, should be taken into consideration. Third, we should learn from previous practice thoroughly. In recent years, there are plenty of practices in environmental administration. Many measures proved to be relatively effective, such as economic measures for environmental protection, procedures of public participation and environmental public interest litigation. They all could be taken into legislation to provide a better legal basis for the further formulation of ordinances, regulations and rules. Fourth, we must co-ordinate the relationship between economic development and environmental protection. New ideas, principles and requirements of scientific development perspective and the construction of ecological civilization brought up by the 18th CPC National Congress should be accepted. Important principles such as scientific development perspective, principle of environment protection prevails, risks prevention, deterioration prohibition etc. should be added in the section of general rules. Fifth, the imbalance between political power and public rights, which is generated by the excessive attention to the institutional requirements of the environmental department and improperly inadequate attention on public interest of the society, should be avoided. The combination of state's administrative power and the rights to protect the environment of the social community should be stressed. Sixth, the concept of "environmental protection prevails" should be used properly. The priority granted to environmental protection is not unconditional, but with comparison and selection, which is a priority under certain limitation. There should be two layers in the legal design. For one thing, it should be clearly stated that environmental protection must be taken into consideration with the development of our economy, society and technology. For the other thing, only when the development cause severe negative impact or causing damage to the environment should the environmental protection prevails.

2. The Environmental Protection Law should be accurately positioned.

Speaking of the legal function, the Environmental Protection Law is a special legislation which provides legal safeguard for China's environmental protection with certain characters such as fundamentality and comprehensiveness. The function and goals of the Environmental Protection Law are quite different from specific environmental protection legislations of pollution prevention and control and natural resources preservation. Those specific environmental protection legislations have already covered various specific aspects of different environmental elements or the environmental regulation. However, there are still some matters which are not appropriately regulated by these legislations. For example, the legal definition of "environment", the fundamental ideas and principles of environmental protection, the administrative mechanism of the national environmental protection, the environmental protection rights and obligations of citizen, legal persons and other organizations, the general environmental regulative mechanism or measures such as national environmental monitoring, charging on pollutants emissions and economic measures of environmental protection, etc., and legal liabilities of environmental protection. All the above issues are fundamental to the legal basis of national environmental protection and need to be provided by the Environmental Protection Law. Besides, regulating government activities in environmental protection is also a general issue, which is better to be included in the Environmental Protection Law other than the specific laws of pollution preventions or natural resources preservation. These legislation experiences are from developed countries such as the United States and Japan. When developed countries handle the relationship between economic development and environmental protection, the first thing they go to is regulating government actions relating to the environment. In this case, there should be two basic functions and goals of China's Environmental Protection Law: one is to establish the legal foundation of the environmental protection; the other is to regulate and restrict the government actions relating to environmental protection. These two basic issues should be the focus of the revision of the Environmental Protection Law.

From the relation between the Environmental Protection law and other environmental legislations, the function and goal of the Environmental Protection Law are to establish legal basis for environmental protection and to regulate and restrict on government actions relating to environmental protection while other environmental protection legislations should mainly focus on regulations and restrictions on enterprises' behaviors with provisions regarding prevention pollution and preservation of natural resources and ecological system and certain specific areas including environmental impact assessment, clean production, anti-desertification, circular economy and so on. Therefore, in terms of the objects of these regulations, the relationship between the Environmental Protection Law and other environmental legislations are like the relationship between the foundation and the superstructure, also they are complementary to each other. The former establishes the legal basis and general framework for environmental protection, the latter, based on the foundation of the former, regulates various specific areas of environmental protection; the former concerns the government and the latter concerns enterprises. They are coordinated with and supplementary to each other, bringing out the best in each other. The revision of the Environmental Protection Law should be carried out with a clear understanding of its functions and positioning so as to rationalize the internal relationship of environmental protection legislations, and to prevent from overlaps, contradictions and absences of legislations and regulations, which will lead to an overall improvement of the implementation effect of environmental protection legislations.

3. Government's environmental actions should be strictly regulated.

The environmental protection legislations are code of conduct for the subjects of environmental legal relation which include enterprise emitting pollutants, the public and the government. Currently, the specific environmental protection laws mainly focus on the enterprises emitting pollutants while there are no clear, adequate or operational provisions regulating the government authorities. Meanwhile, some of the government authorities' omissions and unlawful act led to the environmental deterioration. Therefore, one of the most important function of the Environmental Protection Law is to regulate and put restrictions on the government actions, procure the ruling by law of government of all levels.

(a) A scientific decision-making mechanism for the government in environmental protection with focus on prevention should be established. China's government at all levels are both "referees" and "athletes" in environmental protection. In other words, they are supervisors, i.e. "referees" when regulating the pollution-emission by enterprises; they are the direct planners, participants and promoters of economic activities, i.e. "athletes" when attracting investment and planning for the development of local industries and serious environmental problems might be brought up if such planning, participation and promotion are not properly carried out. Many environmental pollution accidents and environmental disputes showed that many local governments haven’t keep a balance between economic development and environmental protection, paying much more attention to the economic development while neglecting the environmental protection. So it is necessary to establish a scientific decision-making mechanism so as to optimize economic development by environmental protection in the revision of the Environmental Protection Law. Such mechanism should mainly include “integrated environment and development decision-making mechanism”, “inter-ministerial joint conference of environmental protection” and “advisory council on the environment”. The members of the Advisory council on the environment should be non-governmental people such as the NPC representatives, CPPCC members, experts and scholars, representatives of the residents, representatives of environmental groups or other respected persons and persons care for the public interest. These members should be entitled to attend the process of environmental decision-making. On one hand, such advisory council may provide a channel for the government to hear about comments and suggestions from outsiders in case making wrong decisions; on the other hand, such council may help settle the social conflicts within the administrative system so as to avoid the social unrest originated from environmental problems. Such society consulting mechanism is also learned from successful experiences in developed countries and regions such as Hong Kong, Macao and Taiwan.

(b) A supervision systems and mechanisms of the government’s **performance in environmental protection should be established.** First, the internal supervision of the government should be strengthened. Based on clarification of environmental protection responsibilities of governments at all levels and scientific design of balance among various departments, on the one hand, the environmental protection performance supervision between central government and local governments, and between various local governments at all levels should be strengthened, on the other hand, the counterbalance power of the environmental protection departments toward other government authorities should be strengthening to ensure the abidance by environmental protection laws and regulations of them. Second, it is necessary to strengthen the external supervision by social community, citizens, NPC, CPPCC, the judicial authorities, the media etc. Relevant system, mechanism and channel supervising governmental actions should be established. Both internal and external supervision, and constrain forces should work together to "cage the power".

(c) A legitimate game mechanism between the central government and local governments should be established. The local governments are not only the representatives of local interests but also the representatives of the central government's interests in local places. In this case, the legitimacy of the local governments' actions for the local economic interest should be affirmed in the revision of the law. The local governments should not only comply with the orders of central government, but also should be granted opportunities to have a legitimate game with central government within the limitations prescribed by law. The legislation is to make the game open and clear, to solve the problematic situation of "where there are policies there are countermeasures" through development of legislation, administrative mechanism and system. Contractual spirit is an essential approach and inevitable result of the wrestling between central and local interests even in a unitary state. The management of central government to local governments should be carried out not only with "stick", i.e. administration according to the law, but also with "carrot", i.e. economic incentives such as financial transfer payment encouraging local governments' abidance by the Environmental Protection Law and active implementation of environmental protection.

4. Environmental rights of citizens should be effectively protected.

The environmental rights are inherent and natural, which should be transformed into legitimate and actual rights in a society governed by the rule of law. The revision of the Environmental Protection Law has provided a favorable chance for such transformation. To achieve such transformation, the revision of the law should: (i) protecting the environmental rights by the system of public interest litigation, both civil and administrative; (ii) making full use of both civil and administrative litigation to promote protection of environmental rights for individuals; (iii) bringing the best of non-governmental environmental protection organizations in the process of exercising environmental rights.

There are two specific suggestions regarding provisions of environmental rights. First, it should be prescribed in the general rules of the law that citizens are entitled to the right to live in a good environment; governments at all levels are responsible for environmental quality of their jurisdictions and taking measures to protect environmental rights according to the law; no unit or individual should violate state regulations on environmental protection, nor engage in conduct polluting or damaging the environment. Second, remedies against infringement of environmental rights should be prescribed in the section of legal liability. For example, citizens and environmental protection organizations may report to administrative authorities of such infringement, if any, and after receiving such report, the authorities should feedback the results within a particular time, such as 60 days. If the authorities fail to do so, citizens are entitled to authorize or entrust environmental organizations to file lawsuits to the people's court, requesting for stop of such pollution or damage to the environment. Citizens or environmental organizations are entitled to file lawsuits against the authorities who is responsible for environmental protection but fail to perform their duties, and request the authorities to perform their duties in accordance with the law.

5. The process of environmental information disclosure should be accelerated.

Information disclosure is not only a prerequisite for realization of citizen's right to be informed, to participate, to express, to supervise, to suggest, to appeal, but also an important safeguard of citizens' environmental rights. At present, there are problems such as a relatively low position in legal hierarchy, fragmented contents, absent of responsibility and relatively light penalties in the provisions of environmental information disclosure. In this case, the revised Environmental Protection Law should: first, specify the environmental information disclosure system as a fundamental legal system in order to improve effectiveness of the whole system; second, integrate developed provisions of the current laws, administrative regulations and rules as a whole; third, strengthen environmental information disclosure obligations of enterprises especially of listed companies; fourth, clarify legal liabilities of failure in performing information disclosure obligations; fifth, emphasis disclosure of environmental impact information and put particular requirement on environmental information disclosure for listed companies.

All in all, the Environmental Protection Law should provide clear and feasible requirements on the parties (government and corporate), methods, procedure, scope, supervision and legal responsibility of obligation of information disclosure based on current practices and experiences.

6. The development of public participation mechanism should be strongly promoted.

The public is an integral party in environmental protection as it is an important part of environmental relation which is a triangular relation among the government, enterprises and the public. Environmental protection is to protect environmental rights of citizens and public participation is an important power in promoting environmental protection, so public participation as both a complement and an extension to the government's regulation upon polluters, and as a supervision power over the government's environmental protection work. Currently, while the constraints from resource and environment are still increasing, the public remains very enthusiastic towards environmental protection. The Environmental Protection Law should systematically provide methods, ways and institutional safeguard of public participation in order to help the public become a main force in environmental protection.

Social organizations may provide strong support for public participation in environmental protection, as they are more powerful than individuals in both economic and expertise abilities. So right of association of the public in environmental protection should be protected and encouraged.

Social consultation is an important form of public participation in environmental protection. Enterprises polluting the environment should not only disclose environmental information, but also take dialogue with community residents on an equal footing to explain the situation to the public and to listen carefully to views of the public. The government should participate in and promote consultation and dialogue on an equal footing between enterprises and community stakeholders and provide solutions for relevanting problems.

7. Economic measures in environmental protection should be actively encouraged.

Environmental protection is not only in a great need for the mandatory administrative control means, but also for economic instruments. Economic measures in environmental protection motivate the public to participate in environmental protection by influencing their economic interests. Such measures have been adopted worldwide. In recent years, China has carried out a lot of useful attempts in the use of market-based instruments to protect the environment and has accumulated rich experiences. Therefore, one of the important tasks of the revision of the Environmental Protection is to provide legal basis for using economic means in environmental protection.

The economic measures in environmental protection mainly consist of green finance, green taxes, green credit, green insurance, green securities, green trade, green industry, ecological compensation policy and so on. These measures can't be handled by the special environmental law or other laws and regulations but should be specified its legal status in the revision of the Environmental Protection Law.

8. The fundamental issues of legal liability should be further clarified.

One of the differences between Environmental Protection Law and the special laws is that the Environmental Protection Law only regulates general issue of environmental liability. The liability section of the Environmental Protection Law should be focused on solutions to the following problems:

(a) A lifelong tracing system of environmental liability to make the polluter pay a high price for its violations should be established. First, it should be expressly provided that the full cost of pollution abatement should be borne by the polluter. Second, it should be clarified that environmental liability will be a lifelong matter for business operators and property owners. Third, it should be required that enterprises polluting the environment, all the parties that have obtained beneficiaries during the business operation must assume a common joint and several liability. In fact, this is an unlimited liability, that is, if the liable party of pollutions can not afford clean-up costs and damages costs in accordance with the law, then relevant controlling shareholders or other shareholders, creditors, debtors or insurer, whether entities or individuals, may become accountable parties.

(b) Civil liability for environmental damage should be clarified. Currently, an increasing number of environmental accidents, environmental disputes environmental conflicts due to development and construction and different aspects of social life have been greatly intensified and became a major factor of social instability. Therefore, the revision of the Environmental Protection Law should not only strengthen administrative mediation measures, but also solve environmental conflicts, environmental disputes in the courts:

(i) The environmental civil rights of the public should be clarified in two ways: a) by regulating that the behaviors polluting and damaging/ deteriorating/ putting serious adverse impact on the environment should be liable for reducing and eliminating hazards to the environment as well as repairing the damages; b) by regulating that the victims should be entitled to reduction and elimination of hazards to the environment as well as compensation for losses. (ii) It should be provided that the government should be liable for the damages if polluters or destroyers no longer exist or uncertainty occurs. (iii) Applicable rules of ecological damage and of claims for environmental damage as well as necessary civil liabilities for behaviors causing adverse environmental impacts and increasing environmental risks should be provided. (iv) Special limitation of action should be applied to environmental pollution litigations so as to provide convenient and favorable conditions for environmental civil action. (v) The importance of forensic expertise and assessment of environmental damage in civil actions should be emphasized, and expert witnesses should be introduced to forensic expertise in environmental protection cases.

(c) The criminal responsibility with the punishment of material damage should be clarified. Judicial system, as a cornerstone of social order and stability, is an important safeguard resolving social disputes as well as an important method to solve environmental protection problems. Developed countries have established a rigorous and comprehensive environmental legal system as well as effective judicial system to punish violations of environmental laws by legal measures combining administrative mediation and judicial rulings. The validity of the law should be emphasized by judicial system in the following manners: (i) The judicial authorities should severely crack down on malicious offenses to the quality of the environment, such as illegal setting up sewage outlets or underground pipe sewage, illegal discharge of toxic and hazardous substances, violent resistance against the law, unauthorized alteration of pollution data, destruction of evidence of pollution, sewage disposal units deliberately not using sewage treatment facilities, removal of idle sewage treatment facilities without approval of environmental protection department, discharge of pollutants exceed the prescribed limits or causing significant pollution incidents. (ii) Apply the principle of exhaustion of remedies. The judicial system is the last safeguard of all legal protections and should not be used frequently unless other remedies cannot be used. Also we should take full account of administrative remedies to resolve environmental disputes. (iii) Judicial system should supervise enterprises as well as the government. Judicial system should not become a vassal of administrative system or an unilateral extension of consolidating government authority or administrative actions.

(d) The administrative responsibility aiming at solving the problem of "low cost of breaking the law" should be clarified. First, a new idea of "sanction natural persons (individual penalty) first, and then punish illegal entities" should be established. It is necessary to shift from current dual sanctions mainly focusing on legal entities to natural persons in order to increase deterrent effect of the law. Second, administrative sanctions and criminal penalties should be linked up. Administrative penalties for public security and criminal penalties including detention and imprisonment should be well connected in the individual penalties. Typical scenarios applying to such administrative penalties or criminal penalties should be exemplified so as to provide practicable guidance to law enforcement and judicial practice. Third, the focus of executive measures should be shifted from fine to administrative guidance and admonition and the fine should be calculated on daily basis. Fourth, it is necessary to create an innovative system of penalties not only in the revision of the law but may also in judicial explanation in the future. It is suggested that environmental departments and the Supreme Court, the Supreme People's Procurator, Ministry of Public Security may jointly issue a notice combining the social security sanctions with criminal penalties, which would achieve a multiplier effect.

9. The detailed provisions of the environmental public interest litigation should be refined.

Environmental public interest litigation is an important way for public participation in environmental protection and plays a very important role for protection of the environment and citizens' environmental rights. In August 2012, provisions on environmental public interest litigation were included in the newly amended Civil Procedure Law of PRC as follows: "For conduct that pollutes environment, infringes upon the lawful rights and interests of vast consumers or otherwise damages the public interest, an authority prescribed by law or relevant organization may institute an action in a people's court". However, this is only a principle provision and there should be more specific provisions on environmental public interest litigation in the revision of the Environmental Protection Law. The suggestions are as follows:

(a) The scope of environmental public interest lawsuits should be enlarged. First, it is not a prerequisite for litigation that serious consequences of pollution have been caused. A plaintiff may raise litigation against ongoing environmental pollution activities, and require the polluters to take preventive civil liabilities, or apply for a court injunction before the problems is solved through administrative measures or other ways. Second, environmental public interest litigation is not limited to pollutions, and ecological damages and the progressive damage to the environment may also fall within its scope.

(b) The scope of the plaintiff should be enlarged. Pursuant to the Civil Procedure Law, "an authority prescribed by law or relevant organization may institute an environmental action in a people's court". An article of "Understanding of Applicability of Public Interest Litigation" (reference: Gao Minzhi) published by the fourth civil court of People's Supreme Court puts forward that among the "authorities or relevant organizations", "relevant organizations" should not be subject to what have been "prescribed by law" which is favorable for organizations to file lawsuits. However, the requirements on the qualification of "relevant organizations" are very strict. Meanwhile, it is stated in this article that the qualification of "relevant organizations" should be subject to the specific provisions formulated after the revision of the Environmental Protection Law, if any. On the other hand, the "authorities prescribed by law" means that there should be a clear legal basis for the authorities' capacity of bringing public interest litigations. Such legal basis should require that the establishment and functions of the authorities should be specified by law, and their right to bring up public interest litigation should also be clearly prescribed by law. Therefore, the Environmental Protection Law may expand the scope of plaintiff for public interest litigation by explicitly providing that "the authority prescribed by law" and "relevant organizations".

(c) Claims of public interest litigation should be clearly defined. Pursuant to the General Principles of the Civil Law of the PRC, there are ten types of civil liabilities, many of which are preventive. The plaintiff of public interest litigation can request the court to stop the infringement by the polluters or to issue an injunction. The restitution responsibility can be specified as replacement, repair and so on in the environmental cases.

(d) Favorable provisions on cost of litigation to the plaintiff of public interest litigation should be made. The benefits of environmental public interest litigation will be finally vested in the community and the litigation costs should be borne by the society. Therefore, the plaintiff may apply to the people's court for postponement of litigation fees. If the plaintiff loses the case, the litigation fees should be waived. If the defendant loses the case, then the litigation fees should be borne by it. If the judgment comes out in favor of the plaintiff, the defendant should pay the costs of evidence collection, appraisal fees and attorney fees due to the litigation.

(e) The flow and use of the environmental damages should be prescribed. The nature of public interest litigation results that no profit should be obtained by the plaintiff through the litigation. The plaintiff brings the lawsuits on behalf of the state, so if the people's court rules that the responsible party should assume any liabilities of paying compensations/damages, the compensations/damages should be first paid to the plaintiff and then transferred to national treasure. If the plaintiff applies for the people's court to execute any valid judgment, the people's court should require it to provide an account designated by financial departments to receive the reparations. For the purpose of public interest litigation, it is recommended that the state should set up a special fund and include the damages of environmental public litigations into the fund. The management of the fund should be undertaken by the parties prescribed by law. The fund should be used for specified purposes and supervised by an organization composed by relevant parties.

10. The willingness of cooperation in reduction of greenhouse gas emissions should be clearly expressed.

With the development of the negotiation on reduction of global greenhouse gas emissions, China, as a big country for greenhouse gas emissions, is under increasing international pressure to reduce greenhouse gas emissions. Controlling the greenhouse gas emissions is not only a way of implementing obligations of international emissions reduction, but more importantly a promotion for transform of economic development pattern and realization of economic sustainable development. The suggestions are as follows:

(a) When there are disputes over legislative mode of greenhouse gas control, the necessity of legislation should be clarified first. Different departments and experts have different views on whether provisions of greenhouse gas emissions control should be specified in the Atmospheric

Pollution Prevention Law or should be formulated in a single law of response to climate change. Despite the disputes and the situation that various parties are striving on different ways of legislation, all parties agree that the government should enact the legal status of reduction of greenhouse gas emissions by legislation. As a comprehensive law on environment protection, it is the best option to promote greenhouse gas legislation that the Environment Protection Law provides a general guidance while leaving alone controversial details. Therefore, it's necessary to establish policy and principle rules about greenhouse gas control in the law.

(b) A coordinated control system should be specified to harmonize the conflict between objectives of greenhouse gas control and that of other pollutants. The control of other pollutants, in many cases, may increase emissions of greenhouse gases. For example, the process of desulfurization in coal-fired power plant could lead to 1%～2% power loss, which results in more carbon dioxide emissions. Therefore, it is necessary to make it clear in the Environmental Protection Law on how to coordinate the relation between control of greenhouse gas and that of traditional pollutants for the purpose of environmental benefits and economic benefits.

（This article was organized by Ding Yuanyuan）

《中华人民共和国环境保护法》修订建议稿

2013年3月16日

执笔：上海交通大学环境资源法研究所王曦、卢锟

（注：各条标题括号中的文字，仅用于说明条文内容，并非法律条文的组成部分。）

目录

第二章　科学民主决策

第 16 条（环境与发展综合决策）

第 17 条（政府环境保护联席会议）

第 18 条（环境咨询委员会）

第 19 条（政策建议的环境影响评估）

第 20 条（有重大环境影响的行政决定和规划备案制度）

第 21 条（主体功能区划）

第 22 条（环境功能区划和生态功能区划）

第 23 条（重点区域、流域生态保护规划）

第 24 条（规划环评）

第三章　环境监管制度

第 25 条（环境基准）

第 26 条（环境质量标准）

第 27 条（污染物排放标准）

第 28 条（环境监测）

第 29 条（污染物排放总量控制）

第 30 条（排污许可）

第 31 条（排污申报）

第 32 条（环境质量状况评价指标体系）

第 33 条（累积污染、复合污染和二次污染管理）

第 34 条（被污染场地的再利用）

第 35 条（土壤污染治理资金保障）

第 36 条（生态环境保护）

第 37 条（温室气体控制）

第 38 条（行政限批）

第 39 条（环保基础设施建设和监管）

第 40 条（工业开发区环境监管）

第 41 条（限期治理）

第 42 条（环境应急管理）
第 43 条（企业环境信息公开）
第 44 条（公布严重排污者）
第 45 条（企业环保信用信息管理）
第 46 条（排污者与环保部门会商改正方案）
第 47 条（联合执法）
第 48 条（跨界环境污染防治和监管）
第 49 条（环境污染风险与损害评估）
第 50 条（排污交易）
第 51 条（环境保护综合名录）
第 52 条（“绿色信贷”——信贷的环境风险防范）
第 53 条（“绿色证券”——上市公司环保核查）
第 54 条（“绿色证券”——上市公司环境信息披露）
第 55 条（“绿色采购”——政府优先采购环保标志产品）
第 56 条（环境税）
第 57 条（生态补偿）
第 58 条（绿色保险）

第四章　政府环保履职监督

第 59 条（政府环境信息公开）
第 60 条（公开听证会）
第 61 条（人大监督）
第 62 条（约谈和环保履职行政建议）
第 63 条（上级政府督办和代办）
第 64 条（行政机关和国有企业领导成员环境保护工作实绩考核）
第 65 条（环境公民诉讼——督促政府履行环保职能的特殊手段）
第 66 条（举报和投诉）

第五章　纠纷处理、责任与问责

第 67 条（环境纠纷处理和跨区污染责任）

第一章　总　则

第 1 条　（立法目的）

根据《中华人民共和国宪法》有关保护环境和资源的规定，保护和改善生活环境与生态环境，防治污染和其他公害，保障人体健康，规范有关环境的政府行为，制定本法。

第 2 条　（适用范围）

本法适用于中华人民共和国领域和中华人民共和国管辖的其他海域。

第 3 条 （科学发展理念）

环境是人类生存和发展所依赖的基本物质基础。

为了满足当代人及其子孙后代的利益，经济、社会和科学技术的发展不应当损害环境。

科学发展符合人民的当前和长远利益。

必须在科学发展观的指导下，以环境保护优化经济发展，加快发展方式和生活方式的转变，加快建设资源节约型、环境友好型社会。

第 4 条 （政府环境保护职责）

保护环境是政府公共职能和政府各部门的共同责任。

国务院对全国环境保护工作负责。地方各级人民政府对其管辖范围内的环境保护工作和环境质量负责。

各级政府应当依法保障公民在良好的环境中生活的权利和公民有关环境的知情权、参与权、表达权和监督权，督促公民、法人和其他组织履行环境保护义务，严格执法。

地方各级人民政府应当积极组织、参与和推动有关环境问题的社会协商，为公众、企业和政府之间的平等协商提供平台和服务。

第 5 条 （企事业单位的环保权利和义务）

企事业单位享有依法从事生产、经营等活动的权利，同时负有保护环境的义务。企事业单位应当积极预防和治理其生产、经营等活动造成的环境污染和生态破坏，依法对其造成的环境污染或生态破坏承担修复、治理、赔偿等法律责任。

企业应当依法向政府报告并向社会公开其生产、经营活动的环境影响，接受政府和公众的监督。

第 6 条 （公民和社会组织的环保权利和义务）

公民享有在良好的环境中生活的权利，同时负有保护环境的义务。公民应当选择和践行资源节约、环境友好的生活方式。

公民和社会组织享有依法从政府获取环境信息，参与政府环境决策，监督政府环保履职，就污染和生态破坏事项提出申诉、检举的权利。

公民和社会组织有权依据本法第62条的规定，对负有环保职责的地方各级人民政府提起环境公民诉讼。

第7条 （国务院环保行政体制）

国务院环境保护部门负责全国环境保护工作的综合管理，对国务院各部门和地方人民政府的环境保护工作进行监督、指导、协调和服务。

国务院环境保护部门可以设立区域性环境保护派出机构，协调和督促地方人民政府的环境保护工作，协调解决跨行政区环境纠纷。地方人民政府应当支持区域性环境保护派出机构的工作。

国务院其他有关主管部门依照本法和有关法律的规定对环境保护工作实施监督管理。

第8条 （地方人民政府环保行政体制）

县级以上地方人民政府环境保护部门负责本辖区环境保护工作的综合管理，对本级人民政府各部门和下级人民政府的环境保护工作进行监督、指导、协调和服务。

县级以上地方人民政府其他有关主管部门依照本法和有关法律的规定对环境保护工作实施监督管理。

乡镇人民政府对本辖区的环境保护工作实施监督管理；县级人民政府环境保护部门，可根据需要在乡镇设立派出机构，行使其委托的环境管理和监督职责。

第9条 （行政职责的检查和调整）

国务院和省、自治区、直辖市人民政府应当分别要求国务院各部门和省、自治区、直辖市人民政府各部门对照本法，检查其现行职责和行政程序同本法的一致性。对检查所发现的现行职责和行政程序同本法的不一致之处，应提出将现行职责和行政程序同本法保持一致的整改建议。国务院各部门和省、自治区、直辖市人民政府各部门应就此项检查分别向国务院和省、自治区、直辖市人民政府做出报告。国务院和省、自治区、直辖市人民政府应当将该报告汇总后抄送国务院环境咨询委员会并听取其意见。

省、自治区、直辖市人民政府应当要求省级以下各级地方人民政府开展前款规定的检查，并提出检查报告。省、自治区、直辖市人民政府应将该报告汇总后抄送省、自治区、直辖市人民政府的环境咨询委员会并听取其意见。

国务院和省、自治区、直辖市人民政府应当在本法生效后 24 个月内完成此项检查和整改。

第 10 条 （财政保障）

国务院环境保护部门和县级以上地方人民政府环境保护部门应当会同同级人民政府有关主管部门，制定并实施本级政府的环境保护规划和年度计划。

县级以上人民政府应当将环境保护规划和年度计划纳入本级政府国民经济和社会发展规划和财政预算。县级以上人民政府应当将环境保护投入列为本级财政支出预算的重点内容，并逐年增加投入。

各级人民政府应当加强环境保护机构建设，落实其编制和经费。

县级以上人民政府环境保护部门应当邀请同级环境咨询委员会参与本级政府环境保护规划和年度计划的制订，征求其意见和建议。

县级以上人民政府环境保护部门应当依法公开环境保护规划的制定程序，公开征求公众对环境保护规划的意见。

第 11 条 （财政激励）

为促进地方各级人民政府依法履行环保职能，国务院发展与改革、财政等部门应当通过同省、自治区、直辖市人民政府签订环保行政合同的方式，将财政转移支付与地方各级人民政府履行环保职能的绩效结合起来，使地方各级人民政府履行环保职能的绩效成为影响中央财政转移支付的一个因素。

国务院环境保护部门应当对国务院发展和改革、财政、金融等部门通报地方人民政府履行环境保护职责情况。该通报作为这些部门安排中央财政转移支付和经济开发或建设项目资金时的参考依据。

对不依法履行环境保护职责或履行不力的省、自治区、直辖市人民政府，国务院发展和改革、财政部门应当酌情减少中央财政转移支付并减少、暂停或终止为其安排经济开发或建设项目和资金。

地方各级人民政府环境保护部门应当对地方各级人民政府的发展和改革、财政部门通报下级地方人民政府履行环境保护职责情况。该通报作为这些部门安排对于下级地方政府的财政转移支付和经济开发或建设项目和资金时的参考依据。

对不依法履行环境保护职责或履行不力的下级地方人民政府，地方各级人民政府的发展和改革、财政部门应当酌情减少财政转移支付或者减少、暂停或终止为其安排经济开发或建设项目和资金。

第 12 条 （环保科技）

各级人民政府应当鼓励环境保护科学技术事业的发展，加强环境保护科学技术的研究和开发，提高环境保护科学技术水平。

第 13 条 （环境教育）

各级人民政府应当组织开展环境保护宣传教育，普及环境保护科学知识。

学校和其他教育机构应当开展环境保护科学知识教育。

报纸、广播、电视、网络等媒体应当加强环境保护科学知识宣传和环境保护公益宣传。

各级人民政府应当鼓励社区和社会组织开展环境保护科学知识宣传活动和环境保护公益活动。

第 14 条 （奖励）

对保护环境成绩显著的公民、法人和其他组织，由人民政府给予奖励。

第 15 条 （国际合作）

国家参与环境保护国际合作和交流，维护国家的环境与发展权益，严格履行承担的国际环境保护义务。

第二章　科学民主决策

第 16 条 （环境与发展综合决策）

县级以上人民政府各部门在做出可能对环境产生重大影响的决策之前，应当书面征求本级政府的环境保护部门的意见。环境保护部门在做出涉及经济社会发展问题的决策之前，应书面征求本级政府相关部门的意见。各部门之间应相互协商，共同促进环境与经济、社会的协调发展。如经协商，决策部门的意见与环境保护部门的意见没有达成一致，决策部门或者环境保护部门应将争议的问题和解决问题的建议提交本级政府环境保护联席会议审议。环境保护联席会议应当针对所审议的问题提出对策建议，报请本级人民政府决定。

国务院各部门在做出可能对环境产生重大影响的决策之前，应当书面征求国务院环境咨询委员会的意见。县级以上地方人民政府在做出可能对环境产生重大影响的决策之前，应当书面征求省、自治区、直辖市人民政府环境咨询委员会的意见。

第 17 条 （政府环境保护联席会议）

县级以上人民政府应当建立环境保护联席会议制度。

国务院环境保护联席会议的职能是：

1. 研究审议国家环境保护法律、法规、政策、标准、规划和计划的草案；

2. 研究审议国家环境保护法律、法规、政策、标准、规划和计划的贯彻和执行情况；

3. 研究审议由国务院部门提请审议的事项；

4. 研究审议国务院交办的其他事项。

县级以上地方人民政府环境保护联席会议的职能是：

1. 研究审议本行政区环境保护法规、政策、标准、规划和计划的草案；

2. 研究审议国家和地方环境保护法律、法规、政策、标准、规划和计划在本行政区的贯彻执行情况；

3. 研究审议由省、自治区、直辖市人民政府部门提请审议的事项；

4. 研究审议国务院和本级政府交办的其他事项。

县级以上人民政府环境保护联席会议应当邀请同级环境咨询委员会列席会议。

县级以上人民政府环境保护联席会议由本级政府的环境保护部门负责

召集。

县级以上人民政府环境保护联席会议下设秘书处。秘书处的工作由本级政府环境保护部门承担。

国务院环境保护联席会议的成员单位、议事规则等，由国务院环境保护部门会同有关部门制订，报国务院批准后施行。县级以上地方人民政府成员单位、议事规则等，由县级以上人民政府环境保护部门会同有关部门制订，报县级以上人民政府批准后施行。

第 18 条 （环境咨询委员会）

国务院设立环境咨询委员会。

国务院环境咨询委员会是国务院的顾问机构，其职责主要有：

1．对国务院提供关于国家环境状况和环境保护工作的意见和建议；

2．参与国务院环境保护部门的环境区划工作和规划和建设项目的环境影响评价工作；

3．应国务院或国务院环境保护部门的委托，对环境问题和事项开展调查研究，提出调查报告；

4．列席国务院环境保护联席会议。

国务院环境咨询委员会由赞同本法，具有高度的社会公益心和社会责任感，具有丰富学识和经验，有能力对环境保护政策、法律、法规、规划、计划和项目做出评价和建议的德高望重之政府官员、专家、学者、社会组织代表和其他人士组成，其中政府官员不得超过委员会成员总数的三分之一。

国务院环境咨询委员会的委员人数、章程和议事规则，由国务院环境保护部门提出方案，经国务院批准后施行。

省、自治区、直辖市人民政府设立环境咨询委员会。省、自治区、直辖市人民政府参照本法关于国务院环境咨询委员会的规定来规定本级政府环境咨询委员会的委员人数、章程和议事规则。

第 19 条 （政策建议的环境影响评估）

县级以上人民政府及其部门在提出政策的建议之前，应当由本级政府环境保护部门对该建议的环境影响进行评估，并提出环境影响评估意见。政策的环境影响评估意见应当抄送相应级别的环境咨询委员会并征求其意见。

政策建议的环境影响评估应当分析和说明该政策如付诸实施将会对环境带来的影响。政策建议环境影响评估意见应当作为政府和有关部门作政策决策时的参考依据。

政策建议的环境影响评估办法，由国家环境保护部门起草，报国务院批准后施行。

第 20 条 （有重大环境影响的行政决定和规划备案制度）

国务院有关部门做出的可能对环境带来重大影响的行政决定、经批准的综合性规划或专项规划，应当报国务院环境保护部门备案，并抄送国务院环境咨询委员会。

县级以上地方人民政府及其有关部门做出的可能对环境带来重大影响的行政决定、经批准的综合性规划或专项规划，应当报同级政府环境保护部门和国务院环境保护部门或派驻当地的国务院环境保护部门派出机构备案，并抄送省、自治区、直辖市人民政府环境咨询委员会。

第 21 条 （主体功能区划）

国务院发展与改革部门应当会同有关部门，编制全国国土主体功能区划。全国国土功能区划经国务院批准后施行。

县级以上地方人民政府应当依据全国国土主体功能区划，根据本地资源禀赋、环境容量、生态状况、人口数量以及国家发展规划和产业政策，明确本行政区内不同区域的功能定位和发展方向，分别实行优化开发、重点开发、限制开发和禁止开发。

县级以上地方人民政府应当邀请省、自治区、直辖市人民政府环境咨询委员会参与本行政区主体功能区划的制定，并向社会征求关于本行政区主体功能区划的意见。

全国国土功能区划和县级以上地方人民政府国土主体功能区划应当向社会公布。

县级以上地方人民政府制定的国土功能区划，不得与全国国土功能区划相冲突。

全国国土功能区划和县级以上地方行政区域的国土功能区划应当作为国家和地方制定国民经济和社会发展规划和计划的依据。

第 22 条 （环境功能区划和生态功能区划）

国务院环境保护部门应当根据科学发展的要求和国家主体功能区划，编制全国环境功能区划和生态功能区划。全国环境功能区划和生态功能区划报国务院批准后施行。

县级以上地方人民政府应当根据科学发展的要求、国家主体功能区划、全国环境功能区划和全国生态功能区划，编制本行政区的环境功能区划和生态功能区划。

环境功能区划应当包括环境功能区划的指导思想、基本原则、区划方法与依据、环境功能分区、环境功能区的主导环境功能、环境功能区的环境质量目标、污染物排放控制目标和环境功能区实施保障措施等内容。

生态功能区划应当包括生态功能区划的指导思想、基本原则、区划方法与依据、生态功能分区、生态功能区的主导生态功能、生态功能区的生态功能保护目标和生态功能区实施保障措施等内容。

城市总体规划、土地利用规划和各专业规划、专项规划和区域开发利用规划应当与环境功能区划和生态功能区划相协调。开发建设、生产和生活活动应当符合环境功能区划和生态功能区划的要求。

环境功能区划和生态功能区划由县级以上人民政府环境保护部门会同有关部门制定。

国务院环境保护部门应当邀请国务院环境咨询委员会参与全国环境功能区划和全国生态功能区划的制定，并向社会征求关于全国环境功能区划和全国生态功能区划意见。县级以上地方人民政府环境保护部门应当邀请省、自治区、直辖市人民政府环境咨询委员会参与本级行政区环境功能区划和生态功能区划的制定。

县级以上地方人民政府制定的本行政区环境功能区划和生态功能区划，不得与全国环境功能区划和全国生态功能区划相冲突。

全国环境功能区划、生态功能区划和县级以上地方行政区域的环境功能区划和生态功能区划，应当作为国家和地方制定国民经济和社会发展规划和其他规划、计划的依据。

第 23 条 （重点区域、流域生态保护规划）

县级以上人民政府环境保护部门应当会同有关部门，根据全国国土主体功能区划和全国环境功能区划、全国生态功能区划，制订重点区域、流域的生态保护规划，并将重点区域、流域的生态保护规划纳入国民经济和社会发展规划和财政预算。

县级以上人民政府环境保护部门应当邀请相应级别政府的环境咨询委员会参与本级政府重点区域、流域生态保护规划的制订，征求其意见。

第 24 条 （规划环评）

县级以上人民政府环境保护部门应当邀请相应级别政府的环境咨询委员会参加法律规定的规划环境影响评价工作，听取其对规划的环境影响评价工作和环境影响评价文件的意见和建议。

除法律规定需要保密的以外，规划的批准部门应当在批准前将规划中有关环境影响的篇章、说明或环境影响报告书予以公布，接受社会评议。接受社会评议的期限不得少于 30 个工作日。批准部门在批准规划后应当将规划的环境影响评价文件的审批结果及相关说明，包括对社会评议意见是否采纳以及采纳或者不采纳的理由，及时予以公布。

第三章　环境监管制度

第 25 条 （环境基准）

国务院环境保护部门组织制定环境基准。国家环境基准是制定国家环境质量标准和国家污染物排放标准的依据。

第 26 条 （环境质量标准）

国务院环境保护部门制定国家环境质量标准。

省、自治区、直辖市人民政府对国家环境质量标准中未作规定的项目，可以制定地方环境质量标准，并报国务院环境保护部门备案。

第 27 条 （污染物排放标准）

国务院环境保护部门根据国家环境基准、国家环境质量标准和国家经济、技术条件，制定国家污染物排放标准。

省、自治区、直辖市人民政府环境保护部门对国家污染物排放标准中未作规定的项目，可以依据国家环境基准、国家和地方环境质量标准，制定地方污染物排放标准。对国家污染物排放标准中已作规定的项目，省、自治区、直辖市人民政府环境保护部门可以制定严于国家污染物排放标准的地方污染物排放标准。地方污染物排放标准须报国务院环境保护行政主管部门备案。

凡是向已有地方污染物排放标准的区域排放污染物的，应当执行地方污染物排放标准。

第 28 条 （环境监测）

国务院环境保护部门对全国环境监测工作实施统一管理，建立国家和地方环境监测网络，实行国家统一制定的监测标准和环境监测资质审查制度，并负责组织环境监测人员的技术考核工作。

环境监测可由经环境保护部门认定的环境监测机构实施，并接受环境保护部门的监督。

国务院环境保护部门应当会同有关部门和县级以上地方人民政府建立跨行政区的环境监测信息共享网络，并建立环境事故应急监控和重大环境突发事件预警监测体系。

各级财政部门对非赢利性的公益性环境监测网络应当提供财政保障。

县级以上地方人民政府环境保护部门所属环境监测机构应当接受公民、法人和其他组织的委托，依法提供环境监测服务。

第 29 条 （污染物排放总量控制）

县级以上地方人民政府应当对本辖区的污染物排放总量进行控制，并对污染物排放总量控制指标的完成情况负责。

各级政府应当对特定重点污染物规定强制性减排目标和达标时间表，并向社会公布。

第 30 条 （排污许可）

县级以上地方人民政府环境保护部门应当依据同级人民政府确定的污染物排放总量控制目标，通过发放排污许可证，将排污指标分配到各个污染物排放单位，并监督执行。排污单位必须严格按照排污许可证的规定排放污染物。

排污许可证制度与环境影响评价制度、“三同时”制度进行衔接。建设项目投入试生产，根据环评批复的排污量核发临时排污许可证；建设项目竣工，“三同时”验收达标，换发正式排污许可证。

第 31 条 （排污申报）

国家实行排放污染物申报制度。排放污染物的企业事业单位应当按照国家有关规定向环境保护部门申报登记。

拒报或者谎报有关污染物排放申报登记事项的，由环境保护行政主管部门给予警告或者罚款的行政处罚。

第 32 条 （环境质量状况评价指标体系）

国家建立环境质量状况评价指标体系。环境质量状况评价指标体系由国务院环境保护部门会同国务院行政监察部门制定和发布。环境质量状况评价指标体系是考核地方各级人民政府履行环保职责和环保目标实现情况的依据。

第 33 条（累积污染、复合污染和二次污染管理）

因污染物的长期排放（包括长期达标排放）及其累积效应造成污染的，各级人民政府环境保护部门应根据国家环境基准、国家环境质量标准，为有关的污染源制定比其适用的国家或地方污染物排放标准更为严格的污染物排放标准，确保消除累积污染。

各级人民政府环境保护部门应当采取措施防止复合污染和二次污染。

第 34 条（被污染场地的再利用）

被污染场地再次进行开发利用的，被污染场地的产权所有人应对其进行环境质量评估并公布评估结果。在利用之前，被污染场地的产权所有人应当对被污染场地进行无害化治理。无害化治理费用由造成污染的企业或个人承担。无法查证企业或个人责任人的，无害化治理费用由被污染场地所在地的地方人民政府承担。

第 35 条（土壤污染治理资金保障）

各级人民政府应将土壤环境保护和综合治理纳入本级政府环境保护计划，保障土壤环境保护工作经费。

按照“谁污染、谁治理”的原则，督促企业落实土壤污染治理资金；按照“谁投资、谁受益”的原则，充分利用市场机制，引导和鼓励社会资金投入土壤环境保护和综合治理。

第 36 条 （生态环境保护）

保护生物多样性，保护生态环境，保障生态安全。开发利用水、海洋、土地、矿藏、森林、草原、湿地等环境要素，应依法制定并实施有关生态环境保护、治理和和恢复的方案。

引进外来物种应当遵守国家有关法律、法规的规定。

第 37 条 （温室气体控制）

国家采取措施减缓人为温室气体的排放和适应气候变化。具体方案由国务院发展与改革部门会同有关部门制定，由国务院颁布实施。

地方各级人民政府对本行政区域内控制温室气体排放工作负责，对各种温室气体实行统一控制，合理协调温室气体控制与其他污染物控制目标之间的关系。

大力开展节能降耗，优化能源结构，努力增加碳汇，加快形成以低碳为特征的产业体系和生活方式。

第 38 条 （行政限批）

国务院环境保护部门对超过环境容量总量控制指标、生态破坏严重或者尚未完成生态恢复任务的地区，应当暂停审批新增污染物排放总量或对生态有较大不利影响的建设项目。

对被国务院环境保护部门暂停审批新增污染物排放总量或对生态有较大不利影响的建设项目的区域，该区域所在地的县级以上地方人民政府环境保护部门应当同步暂停审批该区域内相关建设项目的环境影响评价文件。

国务院环境保护部门对超过环境容量控制指标的行业，应当暂停审批该行业的新增污染物排放总量的建设项目。

对被国务院环境保护部门暂停审批新增污染物排放总量建设项目的行业，县级以上地方人民政府环境保护部门应当同步暂停审批该行业建设项目的环境影响评价文件。

环境保护行政限批决定应当抄送相应级别政府的环境咨询委员会并向社会公布。

环境保护行政限批办法，由国务院环境保护部门制订，报国务院批准后施行。

第 39 条 （环保基础设施建设和监管）

县级以上地方人民政府负责规划、投资、建设和扶持本辖区的污水处理厂、污水管网、垃圾收运设施、垃圾填埋场等环境保护公用设施。

县级以上地方人民政府的环境保护部门应当依法监管其管辖范围内的环境保护公用设施的运行。

各级地方人民政府应当加强本行政区环保基础设施能力建设，建立适应城镇发展需要的污水管网、污水处理厂、生活垃圾收运和处置设施、污染物集中处理设施。

国家应当通过转移支付等方式对各级地方人民政府的环保基础设施能力建设提供资助。地方各级人民政府应当引导社会资金参与城乡环境保护基础设施的投入，完善政府、企业、社会多元化环保投融资机制。

第 40 条 （工业开发区环境监管）

县级以上人民政府的环境保护部门对超过污染物总量控制指标、环境污染严重的工业开发区，应当暂停审批新增污染物排放总量的建设项目，并责令其限期整改。

第 41 条 （限期治理）

企事业单位违反法律规定，严重污染环境的，由县级以上人民政府环境保护部门按照国务院规定的权限决定限期治理；逾期未完成治理任务的，由有决定权的人民政府决定停业或者关闭。

环境保护部门应当根据完成限期治理任务的实际需要，合理确定限期治理期限。限期治理期限最长不得超过 1 年。由于不可抗力的原因，导致被限期治理的排污单位不能按期完成治理任务的除外。

对于特殊行业等确需要延长期限才能完成治理任务的，由具有管理权的政府环境保护部门作出评估后决定是否准许延长治理期限。延长期满仍未完成治理任务的，由具有决定权的政府决定停业或关闭。

环境保护部门的限期治理决定，应当抄送相应级别的政府环境咨询委员会并向社会公布。

有关停业、关闭的具体实施办法由国务院环境保护部门会同有关部门另行制定。

第 42 条 （环境应急管理）

各级人民政府应当建立环境应急处理和决策信息通报机制并保证上下级人民政府之间的信息交流渠道的畅通。

各级人民政府环境保护部门应当会同有关部门制定本级政府的环境污染事故和其他环境紧急状态应急方案。

发生环境污染事故或者其他危害环境的紧急状况时，环境保护部门和其他有关部门应当立即启动应急方案，向本级政府和上级政府环境保护部门报告，通报可能受影响的地区的政府环境保护部门，及时向社会公开有关信息，采取应急措施，控制、减轻或者清除污染、减少损失。

控制、减轻或者清除污染所发生的费用由导致环境污染事故或者造成危害环境紧急状况的责任者承担。责任者无力承担或者责任主体暂时不明确、无法落实事故应急处理费用的，由具有管辖权的人民政府先予统筹安排，再依法向责任者追偿。

第 43 条 （企业环境信息公开）

企业按照自愿公开与强制公开相结合的原则，及时、准确公开环境信息。

下列信息应当强制公开：

1．环境影响评价报告书和报告表；

2．污染物排放超过国家或者地方排放标准，或者污染物排放总量超过地方人民政府核定的排放总量控制指标的污染物排放信息；

3．突发性环境污染信息；

4．企业产品供应链的环境资质和污染物排放信息；

5．上市公司的环境信息。

不公布或者未按规定要求公布环境信息的，由县级以上地方人民政府环保部门依据相关法律规定，处以相应罚款，并代为公布。

第 44 条 （公布严重排污者）

县级以上人民政府环境保护部门应当定期在指定媒体上公布其管辖范围内的造成严重环境污染的排污者的名单。

被环境保护部门认定的造成严重环境污染的排污者，应当在环境保护部门公布名单之日起一年内，每季度在所在地主要媒体、相邻社区以及敏感点如实公布其污染物排放情况和所采取的环境保护措施等环境信息，并将向社会公布的情况报环境保护部门备案。

对纠正严重环境污染，达到有关环境标准的排污者，环境保护部门应当及时将其从造成严重污染的排污者名单中去除，并在主要媒体上公布。

第 45 条 （企业环保信用信息管理）

各级人民政府环境保护部门应当与工商部门密切合作，建立信息沟通机制。环境保护部门应当依法向工商部门提供企业环境信用信息。工商部门在审理工商登记申请时，应当参考企业环境信用信息。

企事业单位的环保信用信息应当作为环境监督管理、财政支持、政府采购的参考依据，并可以作为银行信贷、外贸出口、企业信用和企业上市等方面的参考依据。

企事业单位环境信用信息管理办法，由国务院环境保护部门会同有关主管部门另行制定。

第 46 条 （排污者与环保部门会商改正方案）

环境保护部门发现违反本法和其他环境保护法律的行为，除依法应当决定停业、关闭的和紧急情况以外，不论是否应当给予行政处罚，都应当立即向违法行为人发布命令，命令其在一周内来环境保护部门会商改正方案。改正方案应包含关于纠正违法行为的措施、效果、时间表等内容。环境保护部门应当将改正方案抄送相应级别人民政府的环境咨询委员会并向社会公布。环境保护部门违反此项规定的，依法对责任人追究行政责任。

企业依据本法第 41 条公开其超标排污信息和超总量排污信息的，应当公布信息之后一周内与当地环保部门联系，会商改正方案。

第 47 条 （联合执法）

各级人民政府环境保护部门可以在法律授权的范围内，联合有关部门对污染环境和破坏生态等违法行为进行检查和处理。各有关部门应当在职责范围内对违法行为依法做出处理，并将处理结果及时通报环境保护部门。

环境保护部门应当及时向相应级别人民政府的环境咨询委员会和社会公布联合执法的情况。

第 48 条 （跨界环境污染防治和监管）

省、自治区、直辖市人民政府应当预防和治理本行政区内的环境污染，防止跨界环境污染的发生。

国务院环境保护部门应当会同有关国务院有关部门和省、自治区、直辖市人民政府，制定跨界环境质量考核办法。

第 49 条 （环境污染风险与损害评估）

国务院环境保护部门和省、自治区、直辖市人民政府环境保护部门应当会同有关部门，建立环境污染风险与损害评估机构，并制定相关的制度、程序和标准。

环境污染风险与损害评估的结果作为环境损害赔偿、环境污染纠纷和跨行政区环境纠纷的解决、企业市场准入、企业保险和企业申请上市、再融资的参考依据。

环境污染风险与损害评估办法，由国务院环境保护部门会同有关部门另行制定。省、自治区、直辖市的环境污染风险与损害评估办法，参照国务院环境保护部门会同有关部门制定的环境污染风险与损害评估办法制定。

第 50 条 （排污交易）

国家鼓励实行排污交易制度。排污者可以国务院环境保护部门规定的条件下有偿转让污染物排放指标。排污交易的具体办法由国务院环境保护部门会同有关部门另行制定。

第 51 条 （环境保护综合名录）

国务院环境保护部门编制环境保护综合名录，对行业产品的排污特性、工艺、产能、贸易等指标进行分析，为有关经济部门制定政策提供依据，以环境经济政策优化产业结构。

相关部门应采取差别化的经济政策和市场监管政策，将环境保护综合名录作为企业上市、融资的重要依据，遏制“高污染、高环境风险”产品的生产、消费和出口，鼓励企业采用环境友好工艺，减少或淘汰重污染工艺，加大环境保护专用设备投资。

第 52 条 （“绿色信贷”——信贷的环境风险防范）

国务院环境保护部门、中国人民银行和国务院银行业监督管理部门应当加强合作，共同防范建设项目和企业的环境信贷风险。

国务院环境保护部门应当会同中国人民银行，制定可纳入企业和个人信用信息基础数据库的企业和个人环境信用信息标准。

县级以上人民政府环境保护部门应当按照该标准对县级以上人民政府工商管理部门的企业和个人信用信息基础数据库提供关于企业的环境保护审批、环境保护认证、清洁生产审计、环境保护奖励和企业环境违法等信息。

县级以上人民政府环境保护部门应当及时向当地人民银行、银行业监督管理机构和金融机构通报建设项目和企业违反环境保护法律、法规的情况。金融机构应依据国家建设项目环境保护管理规定和环境保护部门的通报，严格贷款审批、发放和监督管理。对未通过环境影响评价审批或者环境保护设施验收的项目，不得新增任何形式的授信支持。

金融机构应当依据国家产业政策，进一步加强信贷风险管理，对鼓励类项目在风险可控的前提下，积极给予信贷支持；对限制和淘汰类新建项目，不得提供信贷支持；对属于限制类的现有生产能力，且国家允许企业在一定期限内采取措施升级的，可按信贷原则继续给予信贷支持；对于淘汰类项目，应停止各类形式的新增授信支持，并采取措施收回已发放的贷款。

金融机构在审查企业流动资金贷款申请时，应根据环境保护部门提供的企业环境信用信息，加强授信管理。对有环境违法行为的企业应采取措施，严格控制贷款，防范信贷风险。

第 53 条 （“绿色证券”——上市公司环保核查）

国家对首次申请上市的重污染企业和申请再融资投资于重污染行业的再融资上市企业实行上市环境保护核查。重污染企业的范围由国家环境保护部门确定。

首次申请上市的重污染企业和申请再融资投资于重污染行业的再融资上市企业申请上市环保核查，应向国务院环境保护部门提出上市环保核查申请。对通过了上市环保核查的企业，国务院环境保护部门出具企业上市环境保护核查意见。未取得企业上市环境保护核查意见的，国家证券监督管理机构不予受理上市申请。

首次申请上市的重污染企业和申请再融资投资于重污染行业的再融资上市企业申请上市环境保护核查的具体办法，由国务院环境保护部门会同国家证券管理部门制订，报国务院批准后施行。

向国务院环境保护部门提交上市环境保护核查申请的企业，应将核查申请及其技术报告同时抄报该企业所在地的省、自治区、直辖市人民政府环境保护部门。省、自治区、直辖市人民政府环境保护部门应向国务院环境保护部门出具关于该企业的环保审查意见。

对于已经通过上市环境保护核查的上市企业，国务院环境保护部门应当要求各级地方人民政府环境保护部门及时进行上市后督查。

第 54 条 （“绿色证券”——上市公司环境信息披露）

国家实行上市公司环境信息披露制度。上市公司的环境信息披露实行强制公开与自愿公开两种形式。强制公开的范围由国务院环境保护部门确定。国家鼓励上市公司定期自愿公开其他环境信息。

国务院环境保护部门应当会同国家证券监督管理机构，制订上市公司环境信息披露办法。

第55条 （“绿色采购”——政府优先采购环保标志产品）

各级国家机关、事业单位和团体组织（以下统称采购人）用财政性资金进行采购的，应当优先采购环境标志产品。

采购人或其委托的采购代理机构未按上述要求采购的，有关部门应当按照相关法律、法规和规章予以处理，财政部门视情况可以拒付采购资金。

政府采购过程中，采购人如发现产品生产者或产品原材料提供者有重大环境违法行为的，采购人有权解除采购合同。

环境标志产品政府采购办法，由国务院环境保护部门会同国务院财政主管部门另行制定。

第56条 （环境税）

国家通过税收加大对污染环境、破坏环境行为的调控力度。

第57条 （生态补偿）

国家通过财政转移支付等方式，建立、健全饮用水水源保护区、其他敏感生态区域和跨省级行政区的生态补偿机制。具体办法国务院另行规定。

省级行政区之内的生态补偿办法，由省级人民政府规定。

第58条 （绿色保险）

国家实行环境污染责任保险制度。对重大环境风险行业、工艺和设施实行环境污染责任险强制投保。其他行业、工艺和设施的环境污染责任险的投保自愿进行。

国务院环境保护部门应当会同有关部门制定重大环境风险行业、工艺和设施目录。

国务院环境保护部门应当会同有关部门制定重大环境风险行业、工艺和设施环境污染责任险强制投保办法。

第四章　政府环保履职监督

第59条 （政府环境信息公开）

各级人民政府环境保护部门应当依法编制政府环境信息公开目录，并向社会公开政府环境信息，为公众获取政府环境信息提供便利。

县级以上人民政府环境保护部门应当建立企业环保诚信档案，记录其环保诚信信息，将企业遵守环保法律、法规，承担环保社会责任等情况载入企业环保诚信档案。

政府环境信息公开办法，由国务院环境保护主管另行规定。

环保部门违反环境信息公开有关规定，由监察机关、上级环保部门责令改正；情节严重的，对行政机关直接负责的主管人员和其他直接责任人员依法给予处分；构成犯罪的，依法追究刑事责任。

第60条 （公开听证会）

除依法需要保密的情形外，编制规划、制定政策和审批建设项目等与公众环境利益密切相关的重大决策，政府主管部门应当通过听证会等形式公开听取公众意见。听证会的结果应当对社会公布。

第61条 （人大监督）

县级以上人民政府应当每年向同级人民代表大会报告环境保护工作。人民代表大会闭会期间，县级以上人民政府应当根据同级人民代表大会常务委员会的要求向其报告环境保护工作，接受同级人民代表大会常委会的监督和检查。报告的内容包括本行政区域环境状况和环境保护目标的实现情况，环境保护规划、计划、预算的执行情况和环境保护法律、法规的执行情况。此报告应抄送相应级别人民政府的环境咨询委员会并向社会公布。

县级以上地方人民政府对本行政区域发生的重大环境污染事件应当向本级人民代表大会常务委员会专项报告，依法接受人大监督。

县级以上人民政府应当根据同级人民代表大会及其常务委员会关于改进政府环境保护工作的决议和建议，采取相应的整改措施。整改情况应当向同级人民代表大会及其常务委员会做出专门报告，并抄送相应级别人民政府的环境咨询委员会和向社会公布。

公民和社会组织有权向其所属选区的人民代表反映当地的环境污染和生态破坏情况。人民代表应当依法及时将此类情况报告其所属的人民代表大会机构。

第 62 条 （约谈和环保履职行政建议）

国务院其他部门和县级以上地方人民政府不依法履行环境保护职责或履行不力的，国务院环境保护部门应当及时了解情况，与有关部门或地方人民政府的负责人约谈，并提出环境保护履职行政建议。环境保护履职行政建议中应当包括适当的改正期限。环境保护履职行政建议应当抄送国务院公务员管理部门、行政监察部门和国务院环境咨询委员会。

国务院其他部门和县级以上地方人民政府在同国务院环境保护部门约谈并收到环境保护履职行政建议后，在改正期限内仍不履行环境保护职能或履行不力的，国务院环境保护部门应当将有关情况报请国务院公务员管理部门和行政监察部门处理。

地方各级人民政府除环境保护部门以外的其他部门不依法履行环境保护职责或履行不力的，同级人民政府的环境保护部门应当及时了解情况，与有关部门的负责人约谈并提出环境保护履职行政建议。环境保护履职行政建议中应当包括适当的改正期限。环境保护履职行政建议应当抄送地方人民政府公务员管理部门、行政监察部门和省、自治区、直辖市人民政府环境咨询委员会。

地方各级人民政府的其他部门在同级环境保护部门约谈并收到环境保护履职行政建议后，在改正期限内仍不履行环境保护职能或履行不力的，同级人民政府的环境保护部门应当将有关情况报请同级人民政府的公务员管理部门和行政监察部门处理，并抄送省、自治区、直辖市人民政府环境咨询委员会。

第 63 条 （上级政府督办和代办）

当出现以下情形之一时，上级人民政府环境保护部门应当单独或联合有关部门对管辖该区域的人民政府环境保护部门的执法工作实行督办：

1．发生重大、特大环境污染事件或生态破坏事件；

2．限期治理没有按期通过验收；

3．经催告后，管辖该区域的环境保护部门仍不依法对环境违法行为进行处理。

督办必须明确办理责任人员、办理期限和方式。被督办的环境保护部门应当及时向督办部门报告办理进度和结果。

督办期满后，被督办的环境保护部门未能完成督办目标的，该部门的执法行为由督办部门代为执行，并依法对被督办的环境保护部门的办理责任人员给予处分。

督办的环境保护部门应当将督办通知和督办结果抄送相应级别人民政府环境咨询委员会并向社会公布。

第 64 条 （行政机关和国有企业领导成员环境保护工作实绩考核）

国家实行行政机关和国有企业领导成员环境保护工作实绩考核制度。考核结果抄送同级环境咨询委员会并向社会公开。

国务院和县级以上地方人民政府公务员管理部门和行政监察部门应当依法对国家行政机关领导成员和国有企业领导成员遵守和执行本法的情况进行监督、检查和考核。

国务院公务员主管部门应当制定行政机关领导成员环境保护工作实绩考核指标，将其纳入各级行政机关领导成员工作实绩考核方案，对国务院各部门和地方各级人民政府及其各部门的领导成员履行环境保护职责的情况进行考核。

国务院中央企业管理部门和地方人民政府国有企业管理部门应当制定国有企业领导成员环境保护工作实绩考核指标，将其纳入国有企业领导成员工作实绩考核方案，对国有企业领导成员履行环境保护职责的情况进行考核。

环境保护工作实绩考核指标包括贯彻执行环境保护法律、法规和标准的情况；环境质量改善情况；主要污染物排放总量控制指标完成情况；环境保护重点任务完成情况和人民群众对环境保护工作的满意度等。

国务院公务员管理部门和行政监察部门应当会同国务院环境保护部门制定行政机关和国有企业领导成员环境保护工作实绩考核办法，报国务院批准后施行。

第 65 条 （环境公民诉讼——督促政府履行环保职能的特殊手段）

公民、法人和其他组织如果有初步证据证明地方人民政府或其部门有疏于履行本法或者其他法律规定的应当由其履行的环境保护职责之嫌，可以对该政府或政府部门发出书面通知，告知其疏于履行职责的情况并要求其依法履行该职责。

如果被告知的政府或政府部门在书面通知送达 60 个工作日内仍未依法履行有关职责，则公民、法人和其他组织可就该事项向人民法院提起行政诉讼，请求人民法院裁决其依法履行有关职责。

对本条规定的行政诉讼，不论原告胜诉与否，人民法院可以判决被告为原告支付适当的律师费用、监测鉴定费用或其他诉讼费用。

本条第 1 款所称“本法规定的”环境保护职责指的是本法规定的有关重大决策的环境影响评估意见抄送环境咨询委员会并征求其意见；在做出可能对环境产生重大影响的决策之前书面征求国务院环境咨询委员会的意见；可能对环境带来重大影响的行政决定和经批准的综合性规划或专项规划的备案和抄送；邀请环境咨询委员会参与主体功能区划的制定；邀请环境咨询委员会参与环境功能区划和生态功能区划的制定，并向社会征求关于环境功能区划和生态功能区划的意见；邀请环境咨询委员会参与重点区域、流域生态保护规划的制订并征求其意见；规划环评、行政限批、工业开发区环境监管、政府信息公开和举行公开听证会的政府职责。

第 66 条 （举报和投诉）

县级以上人民政府的环境保护部门应当依法为有关环境保护问题的投诉、行政复议、信访和举报设立受理设施，规定处理程序，积极办理此类投诉、行政复议、信访和举报。

有关环境保护问题的举报和投诉经人民政府环境保护部门查证属实的，举报人和投诉人可以依照有关规定获得奖励。举报人和投诉人要求保密的，环境保护部门应当予以保密。

第五章　纠纷处理、责任与问责

第 67 条　（环境纠纷处理和跨区污染责任）

因开发、利用、保护环境而发生纠纷的当事人应当通过调解、仲裁、行政机关调处或法庭诉讼等和平方式解决纠纷。

省级以上人民政府应当建立、健全有关环境纠纷的司法鉴定、仲裁、调处机构和制度，为环境纠纷当事人解决纠纷提供便利的服务。

依据本法设立的环境污染风险和损害评估机构应当应环境纠纷当事人的请求，为其提供环境损害评估服务。

跨行政区的环境污染纠纷，由有关地方人民政府协商解决，或者由其共同的上级人民政府协调解决。各级人民政府的环境保护部门和其他有关部门应当在其职权范围内积极协调解决跨界环境污染纠纷。

因环境污染影响相邻行政区域环境质量，造成人身、财产损失和环境损害的，由污染者承担赔偿责任，污染者不确定或逃逸或无力赔偿的，由环境污染发生地人民政府承担赔偿责任。污染发生地人民政府应当依法追究造成跨界环境污染的肇事者的责任。赔偿的具体办法由国务院环境保护部门会同有关部门制定。

第 68 条　（环境公益损害赔偿与评估）

污染或破坏生态环境的，应当赔偿对公共环境和生态系统的损害。对公共环境和生态系统的损害，由依本法设立的环境污染风险与损害评估机构评估。

国务院环境保护部门应当会同有关部门，制定关于设立环境污染风险与损害评估机构的具体办法。

第 69 条　（环境公益损害赔偿金的归向与使用）

国家设立专门基金，将环境公益损害赔偿资金纳入基金，专款专用，并接受由有关各方组成机构的监督。

第 70 条　（支持环境民事诉讼的权利）

环境保护部门和有关社会组织可以依法支持因环境污染受到损害的当

事人向人民法院提起诉讼。

第 71 条 （环境公益诉讼）

对污染或破坏生态环境等损害社会公共利益的行为，县级以上人民政府环境保护部门、其他依照法律规定行使环境监督管理权的部门以及依法登记的环境保护社会组织，可以向人民法院提起诉讼，请求人民法院责令侵害环境公益行为人停止侵害行为、排除危害，并采取措施恢复环境原状，不能恢复原状的，应承担修复环境费用及损害赔偿金。

提起本条规定的环境公益诉讼可以缓交诉讼费。若原告败诉，应免交诉讼费；若被告败诉，则由被告支付诉讼产生的证据费用、律师费用、监测鉴定费用或其他诉讼费用。

第 72 条 （法律援助）

国家鼓励法律服务机构和律师为环境污染损害诉讼中的受害人提供法律援助。

第 73 条 （环境损害赔偿诉讼时效）

因环境污染损害赔偿提起诉讼的时效期间为三年，从当事人知道或者应当知道受到污染损害时起计算。

第 74 条 （行政处分）

国家行政机关及其工作人员违反本法规定的，由上级行政机关、具有管辖权的公务员管理部门和行政监察部门依法给予行政处分。

企业事业单位中由国家机关任命的人员，对其供职的企业事业单位违反本法和其他法律的行为负有责任的，由上级行政机关、具有管辖权的公务员管理部门和行政监察部门依法给予行政处分。

第 75 条 （环境污染责任终身追究制）

企业经营者及产权拥有者的环境污染责任为终身责任。污染者必须承担污染治理全部费用的责任。

污染企业发展中的所有获益者，都必须为企业造成的污染承担共同和连带责任。如果污染责任方无力负担其依法应偿付的污染清理费用和损害赔偿费用，有关控股或参股的组织和个人，向其贷款、借款及销售过保险的组织和个人，均可以成为被追究责任的对象。

第 76 条 （双罚制）

对违反本法规定，造成环境污染的企业事业单位，在环境保护部门处罚违法单位的同时，对其法定代表人（负责人）和其他责任人员处以罚款。

第 77 条 （按日计罚）

对违反有关法律规定排污，受到环境保护部门处罚，并被责令改正或者限期改正，逾期不履行行政处罚决定，经催告仍不改正的，作出处罚决定的环境保护部门，在依法采取行政强制措施的同时，可以自责令改正或者限期改正期限届满之日起，至改正之日止，根据污染物排放总量和污染损害程度，每日处一万元以上十万元以下的罚款；继续超标排污、超总量排污或者继续造成显著不良环境影响的，由作出处罚决定的环境保护部门报请县级以上地方人民政府责令停产整顿。有关法律规定对逾期不改正行为已经加处罚款的，从其规定。

第 78 条 （行政强制措施）

根据《行政强制法》的有关规定和环境执法监管的实际需要，县级以上人民政府环境保护部门或者其他依照法律规定行使环境监督管理权的部门，有权查封、扣押违法生产、销售、使用、进出口的生产设备、设施、原料及产品。

第 79 条 （民事责任）

造成环境污染危害的，有责任停止侵害、排除危害、恢复原状以及进行生态修复、环境功能替代，并对直接受到损害的单位或者个人赔偿损失。

赔偿责任和赔偿金额的纠纷，可以根据当事人的请求，由环境保护行政主管部门或者其他依照法律规定行使环境监督管理权的部门处理；当事人对处理决定不服的，可以向人民法院起诉。当事人也可以直接向人民法院起诉。

完全由于不可抗拒的自然灾害，并经及时采取合理措施，仍然不能避免造成环境污染损害的，免予承担责任。

第 80 条 （举证规则）

环境污染损害赔偿诉讼，依照有关法律规定举证责任倒置。

第 81 条 （治安处罚）

违反本法规定的下列行为，构成违反治安管理行为的，依法给予治安管理处罚：

1. 违规设置排污口或者私设暗管排污；

2. 违法排放有毒有害物质的；

3. 暴力抗法；

4. 擅自涂改污染数据，销毁污染证据；

5. 排污单位故意不正常使用水污染物处理设施，或者未经环境保护部门批准，擅自拆除、闲置水污染物处理设施；

6. 排放污染物超过规定标准，可能造成重大环境污染；

7. 法律规定的其他行为。

第 82 条 （刑事责任）

违反国家规定，严重污染环境的，对有关责任人员可以比照刑法第三百三十八条的规定，追究刑事责任。

第 83 条 （对环境保护监督管理人员的问责）

环境保护监督管理人员滥用职权、玩忽职守、徇私舞弊的，由其所在单位或者上级主管机关给予行政处分；构成犯罪的，依法追究刑事责任。

第六章　附　则

第 84 条 （名词解释）

本法所称“环境”，是指影响人类生存和发展的各种天然的和经过人工改造的自然因素的总体，包括大气、水、海洋、土地、矿藏、森林、草原、湿地、野生生物、自然遗迹、人文遗迹、自然保护区、风景名胜区、城市和乡村等。

本法所称“企事业单位”包括个体工商业者。

本法所称“政策建议”，是指关于拟由县级以上人民政府或县级以上人民政府部门的名义发布的政策或其他决策的建议，不包括《环境影响评价法》中规定的各种规划。

本法所称“可能对环境带来重大影响的行政决定、经批准的综合性规划或专项规划有重大环境影响的行政决定”分别指由各级人民政府及其有关部门在其职权范围内制定、发布的，可能对环境造成重大影响的具有普遍约束力的决定、命令等行政规范性文件；各级人民政府及其有关部门在其职权范围内组织编制的，可能对环境造成重大影响的土地利用规划和区域、流域、海域的建设、开发利用规划；各级人民政府及其有关部门在其职权范围内组织编制的，可能对环境造成重大影响的工业、农业、畜牧业、林业、能源、水利、交通、城市建设、旅游、自然资源开发等专项规划。

本法所称“温室气体”，是指大气中吸收和重新放出红外辐射的自然和人为的气态成分。

本法所称“政府环境信息”，是指环保部门在履行环境保护职责中制作或者获取的，以一定形式记录、保存的信息。

本法所称“企业环境信息”，是指企业以一定形式记录、保存的，与企业经营活动产生的环境影响和企业环境行为有关的信息。

第 85 条　（与原《中华人民共和国环境保护法》的关系）

自本法生效之日起，原《中华人民共和国环境保护法》（1989 年制定）失效。

第 86 条　（生效）

本法自颁布之日起生效。

《环境保护法》修改思路专家研讨会 参会人员

杨朝飞　中国环境科学学会副理事长
李庆瑞　环境保护部政策法规司司长
别　涛　环境保护部政策法规司副司长
韩　敏　环境保护部政策法规司副巡视员
王　曦　上海交通大学教授
汪　劲　北京大学教授
王灿发　中国政法大学教授
孙佑海　中国环境资源法研究会副会长
李艳芳　中国人民大学教授
李启家　武汉大学教授
唐大为　中关村汉德环境观察研究所所长
柯　坚　武汉大学副教授
胡　静　中国政法大学副教授

《环境保护法》修改思路专家研讨会会议记录

主 持 人： 杨朝飞

会议时间： 2012 年 12 月 20 日 13:30—17:30

会议地点： 北京福州会馆会议室

杨朝飞： 这次会议主题是《环境保护法》修改。近 10 年来，社会上有关修改《环境保护法》的呼声越来越高，一方面公众对修改《环境保护法》的要求非常迫切；另一方面修改《环境保护法》多年来没有进展，举步维艰，处境困难重重，这关键是因为对于要不要保留环保法、要不要修改环保法、怎么修改环保法的思想认识差异巨大。第一种观点认为，环境法治建设虽然重要，但可以通过加强其他法律即专项环保法律，来解决环境变化立法不足的问题，《环境保护法》没有特定的调整对象和法律功能了，可以适时取消了；第二个观点认为，当前的主要法治问题是执法不到位的问题，如果各项环境法律法规都落实到位了，环境问题早就解决了，环境立法本身没有问题，现在修改《环境保护法》没有必要；第三种观点认为，大改环保法难度很大，如果小改、快改可以早见成效，对上对下、对领导机关、对社会都可以有一个交代，其本质是要通过简单的立法过程搞出一个工作政绩工程。以上三种观点影响修订《环境保护法》多年了，经过激烈的争论，各个方面对要不要保留环保法、要不要修改环保法的认识基本统一，现在最主要的问题是究竟应该如何改法。这个问题很重要、争论也很大，专家们写了很多很好的论文，但是对改法的思路并没有真正坐下来系统地整理。在这样一个大的社会背景下，汉德环境观察研究所筹划设计召开一个国内最高水准的环境法专家研讨会，专题研讨、统一修改《环境保护法》的思路。汉德环境观察研究所的想法得到了能源基金会的支持。

今天会议可以说是国内环境法界最高层次的专家会议了，在座的专家不仅在环境法理论方面有很深的研究，而且也参加了许多国家和地方环保方面的法律法规、行政规章的调研和起草工作，在立法方面有着非常丰富的经验。所以希望通过今天会议的研讨，能够提出一个较为权威、较为统一的《环境保护法》修改思路。

唐大为：跟大家很长时间没有见面了，今天见面很高兴。我主要讲两点，第一，向大家介绍汉德环境观察研究所。汉德环境观察研究所是在中关村国家自主创新产业园区注册成立的非营利机构，属于国家先行先试（没有主管单位只在民政局注册）的试点，发起人包括在座的汪劲老师和企业家许国栋先生、宣教中心贾峰主任等十几位环境界的老朋友，还有当时参与超级基金项目的老师和同学。国内需要这样的非营利平台，整合产业界、高校、政府、研究机构、媒体各个方面的研究资源，突破体制、机制的界限，供大家通过不同视角的观察与研究，共同解决一些现实问题。第二，希望基于理清《环境保护法》修改思路这样的工作追求，通过本次研讨会能把各位老师、各位专家请到一起，对中国环境法走上正确和有益的道路做一些力所能及的事。在这里，我感谢能源基金会给予的支持，也感谢各位专家的热情响应，预祝这次会议圆满成功！

杨朝飞：这次研讨会得到能源基金会的大力支持，能源基金会对我们国家温室气体减排和节约能源做了大量工作，近年来对环境保护也给予了很大支持，如为修改大气法组织去美国的考察，支持排污许可证研究、环境税研究等一些跟能源、跟环保法治有关的项目。下面请赵立建博士致辞！

赵立建：特别荣幸参加这次会议。能源基金会是在民政部注册的 18 家国际自然基金会之一，主要推动节能减排相关政策研究，有节能项目、推动可再生能源的项目。我本人负责环境管理项目，主要关注能源及其对本土造成的环境影响。要解决环境问题，离不开一些基本的法律制度，像《环境保护法》这样的基本法律也是很重要的方面。

《环境保护法》修订一次的确不容易，如何真正把核心的、大家一直推动的事情纳入修订范围的确需要研讨。我感触比较深的是，大家历来谈的违法成本低问题，有没有可能通过《环境保护法》的修改，加强违法处罚的力度，加强法律的权威性。另外环境权益、环境损害赔偿、信息公开、公众参与、公益诉讼等问题，都需要《环境保护法》来解决。我们与汉德研究所也在商讨，一方面希望专家能够对以上这些内容做一些研讨；另外形式上，能不能形成小的报告把几个核心问题阐述清楚，以适当形式为我们立法决策做出一定的参考；甚至是否可能利用公众媒体，例如微博，来做相关的呼吁。

杨朝飞：环保部政策法规司是我们修改《环境保护法》非常重要的一个部门，一是许多法律法规的草案都是出自他们之手；二是他们这么多年也做了大量的研究工作，积累了丰富的经验。下面请他们谈谈看法。首先请庆瑞司长发言，他非常重视《环境保护法》修改，做了大量的调研和组织工作。欢迎！

李庆瑞：首先向大家对《环境保护法》修改工作给予的高度重视、积极配合表示感谢，也对今天汉德研究所发起活动，以及能源基金会的支持表示感谢，对人大环资委的翟主任听取大家意见和建议，更加表示感谢。我想这个会议非常有意义，能够对《环境保护法》修改以及其他环境保护法律法规发挥作用。

有关《环境保护法》我想提几个观点。第一，修改《环境保护法》时机很好。现在大家都在学习党的十八大会议精神，党的十八大将关于科学发展观上升为指导思想的问题、生态文明纳入“五位一体”总体布局的问题、建设美丽中国问题、迈向生态文明新时代的问题以及第八部分第四个问题专门强调加强生态文明制度建设的问题，对我们修改《环境保护法》工作以及众多环境法律法规都是难得的机遇和契机，是强劲的东风，对于我们工作作用非常之大。最近学习党的十八大，我们根据杨总过去在担任司长和总工时的教诲和指导，司里组织多次学习和研究，包括学习宏观战略研究的成果，我们提出一系列修改《环境保护法》和法治建设的想法。这些想法在前天环保部学习党的十八大司局长交流大会上，我代表法规司做了汇报。大致意思是积极推动法律生态化建设，为生态文明提供法律的制度保障。

第二，还是建议对环保法要做较大的修改、重点的修改。较大的修改与过去一开始所提出的、有限的目标相对应，有限的目标也是通过评估产生的结论，但是一提“有限”，开始就有限制，就和实事求是、和实践的需要有差距。有重点的修改还是建议能够把党的十八大生态文明新理念、人民群众新期盼、社会各界新建议，特别是环境法学专家的科学建议认真地吸取，把《环境保护法》修改好。

第三，是建议修改为环境领域基本法律，或叫基本法也好、基础性法律也好、母法也好或者政策法也好，总之起到基础性、综合性的基本法律的作用，宣示国家在环境领域一些重大的主张，比如说基本的指导思想、原则、方针、政策，还有一些重要的制度，对具体制度多做一些原则性、衔接性的规定，为制定或者修订专项法律法规、规章乃至有关部门制定规范性文件，以及制定地方法规埋下伏笔、奠定基础。《环境保护法》是以调整政府责任为主的法律，而专项法律法规是以调整企事业单位责任为主的操作层面的东西，这样，法律定位相应比较清楚了。当然修改《环保法》当中，我们非常赞成杨总前不久在全国人大常委会所做的环境保护基本情况和法律法规专题讲座，这个讲座上表述大致五个方面的类别，其中一类是科学决策类，比如生态文明的理念、坚持环境保护基本国策、最严格的环境保护制度、经济发展要与环境保护相协调等重大理念，根据理念再延伸到具体的原则和制度。

关于法律生态化问题，我们学习了宏观战略研究成果，当时提的建议是“加强环境法制建设，实现国家法律生态化”。李克强同志曾经指示“把环境宏观战略研究的成果转化好应用好”，在法律生态化问题上，就是在《环境保护法》修改和其他环境法律法规修改都要体现生态文明理念；要使生态文明入宪，党章既然写入了生态文明内容，入宪的条件已经具备，宪法应该把生态文明理念写进去，要把环境权写进去，把环境保护目标任务写进去；除了环境法律法规之外，其他像刑法、民法、民事诉讼法、经济法等法律法规，在原来基础上更多融入环境保护的内容；除了这些宪法和法律法规，还有以《党章》为代表的党内“法规”在修订的时候，也应该注重生态文明建设。这样，在横向上由宪法到党内“法规”、由环境法律法规到其他部门法律法规，然后再到规章、再到规范性文件、再到地方立法，在纵向上从立法、守法、执法、司法，使生态文明建设融入经济、政治、文化、社会全过程。

《环境保护法》已由人大环资委提请人大常委会 8 月份的一审，现在法工委在进一步调查研究、继续广泛征求意见、反复论证，这就为深入反复研究、继续提出意见和建议，让有关方面论证得更充分一点，修改得更好一些，提供了时间和空间上的环境条件。所以大家今天和下一步的活动都会发挥很重要的作用。

杨朝飞：刚才庆瑞司长谈了很好的观点。下面请别涛副司长作主旨发言。别涛也是研究环保法多年的学者，有很多很好的观点和想法，请他来做一个系统的介绍，既代表政法司的观点，也反映他个人的研究成果。

别涛：人大环资委《环境保护法》草案征求意见时，我们提了几点看法，这个意见主要来自专家学者，部分也代表我个人意见。环保部对这个草案基本评议是“赞成修改、充满期待”，这个评议是实事求是的。在草案向社会公开意见时，我们提了四点意见：

第一，在处理经济与环境保护的关系上缺乏有效的保障措施，草案也提出若干口号，里边有原则性的东西，但是缺乏具体的措施、程序、规则的保障。

第二，如李司长所说，处理环境法律领域现状中《环境保护法》与各个专项法、单项法的关系上，基本定位不清楚，我们建议科学合理解决定位的问题，我觉得它应该处于基础性、综合性的地位，基本法的提法有争议，但是基础性的地位我想应该是可以说的。目前的草案和单项法中间存在很多交叉，调整对象有交叉、制度有重叠、条款有冲突。我们认为《环境保护法》主要解决国家在环保领域的基本原则，规定基本体制，在对象上确定政府的责任、公众权益保障、企业基本法律义务，还有通用的环境经济政策市场手段和通用的处罚的法律规则，这是关于基本定位的设想。

第三，关于体制上，从十七大到十八大都提了推进大部制改革，但目前在体制没有大的变化的情况下，我们主张暂维持现行的体制，草案有几项制度措施有大的变动，对于工作可能不利，更主要从法律技术上又会带来新制定的基本法和原有特别法不一致，导致修改无效，比如总量、监测、标准等。

第四，环保实践走在法律前面，过去十年、过去五年甚至过去三年，我们环境方面的实践是丰富多彩的，有很多证明是相对有效的，需进一步上升到法律，为进一步制定法规、规章、规则提供应有的依据，比如市场手段、经济手段、公众参与的程序、权益保护、公益诉讼等应当有所体现。另外分析草案关于几项制度措施，如“三同时”、限期治理等，目前草案跟专项法规定都存在冲突的地方，该写的没有写进去，已写的与实际不一致，建议草案做较大的修改，重新论证，争取更加符合实际并展望未来 5～10 年。

我们对草案的这些具体意见和建议在 2012 年 11 月初回复了全国人大法工委，同时有意识地在网上向社会公布，内部对此有不同的看法，也有人提出不同的意见。我们认为既然这个草案已经向全社会征求意见，我们把公众反馈的意见整理汇报给人大，我们的意见来自各个方面，是公开透明的，我们不认为有什么不妥。我们的意见大家可以在网上看到。

杨朝飞：别涛的发言简明扼要，观点非常鲜明。下面请政法司韩敏副巡视员发言，一方面韩敏也是环境法律专家，另一方面反映政法司对环保法修改非常重视，今天由庆瑞司长带队，三位司长参加今天会议，非常难得。

韩敏：刚才李司长和别司长对环保法修改已经讲了很多意见，我都同意和赞同。下面讲一下个人的观点，我认为《环境保护法》修改，不管是大改还是小改，有几个关键点必须考虑到：第一是明确其基础性和综合性的法律定位，是环保领域的基本法，一定要在这部法律中向世界、向社会宣示国家重大的环境政策方针；第二是党的十八大有关生态文明建设的精神要体现出来，应当全面研究考虑把生态文明理念融入到环境立法中，考虑怎么用生态文明理念重新审视现行环境保护政策制度与措施，如何落实在保护中发展、在发展中保护的要求等；第三是政府责任问题，政府责任细化和可操作性是必须解决的，现行的《环境保护法》规定政府对环境质量负责，但是地方政府怎么对环境质量负责，它有什么权力，承担什么义务，如何保证与监督等，法律应作出具体规定才能落实，要有可操作性；第四是现在修改草案有关法律制度的规定与单项法的规定有重复、矛盾甚至冲突的地方，应尽量避免，《环境保护法》应对主要的、通用的环境保护法律制度措施进行整合和完善，如环评、排污许可等，具有特色的具体的制度措施应留给有关单项法律规定；第五是法律责任，现在存在的违法成本低、守法成本高，资源环境在经济发展中代价过大等问题，既有执法不严、不到位的问题，也跟法律责任设定、相关权利（力）义务规定不合理不科学有关，必须认真研究科学合理设定。要让环境权益真正得到切实有效保护，真正让守法者受益、违法者必受严厉制裁，将环境违法行为的责任追究到位，而且追究到痛处。这方面有很多案例，近期最典型的就是美国墨西哥湾油污案例和我国渤海油污案例在责任追究、损害赔偿等环境权益维护和处理上的天壤之别。这是我粗浅的几点看法，供参考。

杨朝飞：刚才韩敏提了五点意见，也谈了看法。环保部政策法规司已把他们的观点和思路呈现给大家。下面请孙佑海会长。

孙佑海：非常感谢。关于这个法，我在全国人大环资委工作的时候，也在积极推动，这个法定位各方面的确比较难，所以当时没有把它往前放。

既然这一届有可能上不了，我想我们思想可以再打开一点，不要受目前框子的束缚。我主要想讲几点：

第一，环境法应不应该有自己的相对独立的法律体系？我们环境法历来主张建立自己的法律体系，但是全国人大经过多年的讨论，就没有理会我们环境法学界的意见，七大法律部门没有环境法，所以我们以后再提环境法是独立的法律体系，有点不太合法了。但是我个人认为，不能叫完全独立的法律体系，但是可以建立相对独立的法律体系，这个相对独立的法律体系我们曾经设想有一个《环境保护法》（试行），有一大堆条例，但是由于受海洋环保法的各种影响，自然法和水、气、声、渣的法都出来了，的确在法律位阶上出现“乱伦”情况，小法全有了，大法没有什么可弄。历史上 1989 年想搞全国人大通过类似基本法，由于认识不太一致，环保界的力度不够，所以没有搞成。我认为环境法应该有相对独立的体系，理由是：环境法有共性的东西、共同的行为、共同的理念、共同的制度、共同的管理结构，所以还是应该有相对独立的法律体系，这个法律体系在小法专业法上边，应该有一个独立的环境保护法存在，而且它实际上也是起到了母法作用，指导思想、基本原则、基本制度应该可以统领整个环境保护法律的，而且相对独立法律体系并不违背全国人大七大法律部门。七大法律部门也是实践当中不断发展，不是完全不可攻破的。我认为应该有相对独立的法律体系，跟其他法律之间做到不矛盾、相互衔接就可以的。

第二，与相对独立的法律体系相关，母法不应该跟专项法位阶上相同的。宪法规定一些国家基本制度由全国人大常委会制定，只要全国人民代表大会通过的法律就是基本法律，虽然不叫基本法，但是带有基本属性。党的十八大将生态文明上升到五位一体，具有突破性。哪怕跟着政权节奏走，体现十八大特点，法律上应该有一个亮点，由全国人民代表大会通过这部《环境保护法》是完全可以的，体现我们党对环境保护、生态文明高度重视，也有利于处理《环境保护法》和其他专项法的关系。

第三，是虚与实的关系问题，《环境保护法》作为一个具有统帅地位的法律，下边还有专项法的存在，关系怎么处？有三种写法：一种虚写，写虚话，不写责任，就不跟别的法矛盾；第二种处理是搞环境法典，编纂一下就可以；第三就是虚加溜缝儿这也是一种写法。我认为反对虚写，因为我们党的作风都是求真务实，就是解决实际的问题，是要解决具体的问题，你要整序言，《宪法》也行，而且法律位置也高，党的十八大关于生态文明的报告，也不用全国人大专门通过一部法律写，而且“八项作风”都是求真务实、节约资源，我认为不要虚写，虚写没有出路，我的观点就是写实。关于写实的问题也不是学者在书斋坐着想出来的，要到环保一线了解情况，目前在保留几部法律情况下，本着解决实际问题、照着基本法地位来写，如果写到某些专项法律不能存在了，可以再来改它（专项法）。

第四，关于修改或制定新的《环境保护法》的指导原则——环境法治是民主、公平、正义、科学的环境法治。（1）民主的环境法治是什么意思？第一，立法的时候真正做到立法的民主，真正要求社会各界广泛参与，每一个群体、每一个层次充分发表自己的主张，而不是开会训话；第二，是指我们在环境问题上讲环境民主，在环境管理当中、环境行为当中涉及环境问题上充分发挥社会各界的积极性，我们去美国可以看，公众参与非常实，环保局是给居民服务的，上不上工厂项目是由周围老百姓决定，这才是真正的环境民主。（2）公平的环境法治，与中国目前发展阶段性有关，中国环境保护是在发展中保护环境，在保护环境中求得经济和社会发展，这是中国环境保护的特点，完全为了要绿水青山，但是发展比较弱不是公平，但是延续我们过去发展，竭泽而渔、乌烟瘴气也不是公平的发展。公平的环境法治强调几点：地区之间强调环境保护公平，要体现环境生态补偿、区域环境影响评价思想；与地区公平相关的是机会公平，先发达地区和后发达地区环境发展问题上要求公平，不能说有些地区已经富裕了，不掏腰包情况下让别人保护环境，自己维持高水平的生活质量；代际公平，这代人为下一代人考虑。（3）正义的环境法治，既要约束有关主体的行为，更重要的是从生态文明建设的角度，通过调整公民各方面权利义务，促进环境与发展统一。在我们社会治理结构设计上怎么样有利于环境保护、有利于环境与发展的统一，我们不能就环境保护而讲环境保护，就环境污染防治而讲环境污染防治，在制度设计方面都要有利于环境保护。（4）科学的环境法治，主要是讲我们在制度的设计方面、在对公民和有关主体权利义务调整、设置法律责任各个方面做到科学。走到实践当中去，与一线人员在一起，了解实践的有效、真实需求是什么，做出有针对性的规定，而且这种规定经过上上下下反复锤炼，真正做到科学有效。

第五，关于司法保障问题。从我们社会整体来说，在讲到法治问题时，党的十八大报告批评立法不科学、执法不严格、司法不公正、全民不够守法，所以提出“科学立法、严格执法、公正司法、全民守法”，要求各级领导运用法治方式、法律思维理政。总体来说大家认为司法不公，但是司法不公在不同领域有不同表现，传统的民事方面可能大家指责司法不公的比较多，因为案子很多，全国法院一年民事案件 620 万左右，环境领域主要问题不是司法不公，而是真正让老百姓在法庭里解决环境纠纷的事情太少，所以环境法领域特殊性是要把更多环境纠纷引导到法庭解决，运用司法力量干三件事：（1）惩治破坏环境的犯罪行为；（2）解决因开发建设、社会生活各个方面引发的环境矛盾、环境纠纷，特别要强调公益诉讼，这里边涉及诉讼当事人、诉讼主体的问题，过去老的民诉法 108 条规定是有直接利害关系的当事人，新的法律把这一条做了一定调整，法律规定的机关和有关组织有权对环境污染行为提起诉讼，这次修改民事诉讼法是历史性的突破，把公益性写进去，给了环境公益诉讼以合法地位。目前就写到了有关机关和组织，全国人大环资委开会我在场，“法定的机关”是明确的，只有法律规定的机关，在没有法律明确规定情况下也不行，检察院起诉可以作为公益性诉讼，大家对于检察院起诉主体有不同看法，这个问题需要研究，但不是矛盾焦点。矛盾焦点在后半部分，在美国公民可以做公益诉讼主体的，在中国明确不行，但是有关组织可以。至于什么是有关组织？现在需要一步步往前走，目前情况下法律规定的是有关组织，将来有关范围不断扩大，包括律师事务所、汉德观察所行不行？需要积极稳妥往前推。在法律委员会讨论时，原来写的有关社会团体，面太窄，后来改为有关社会组织，社会组织比社会团体大了，后来讨论，沈成耀提出把“社会”二字去掉，而且“法律规定”只管“机关”，不管“和”字后面的“组织”，组织有放宽的表现。目前情况下争取在《环境保护法》把公益诉讼起诉主体尽量往里写，通过“法律规定”扩大公益诉讼主体。（3）关于行政诉讼，行政诉讼包括诉环保部门、水利、矿产等各方面的单位行政不作为、乱作为，发挥行政诉讼对政府监督的作用，这方面的案件比较少，但随着民主法治不断推进，行政诉讼法也在修改，行政诉讼会往前走。

杨朝飞：刚才佑海同志讲话有非常好的建议和观点，他长期在立法部门，经验丰富，了解情况很多，个人研究也多。他的好多建议对我们修改《环境保护法》有重要的参考作用。

下面请王曦教授发言，事先汉德所也跟大家沟通了一下，一人选一个主题，这样研究也比较深一点儿，当然对其他问题有好的观点也不受约束。王曦教授发言的主题是“政府责任和监管体制”。

王曦：非常感谢汉德环境观察研究所和能源基金会主办这次活动，有机会跟老朋友相聚，分享我最近对《环保法》修改的想法。

开始之前我想说一个意思，即我们研究环保法要注意从环境法学基本概念出发，而不是脑袋蹦出什么想法就从那个想法出发。过去我们学韩德培、金瑞林等先生的环境法教科书，书上写得很清楚：环境法是调整环境法律关系主体的行为规范。在研究《环保法》修改的时候，我们不要脱离这个基本概念和基本原理。这里边有很重要的概念。一个是法律关系，一个是法律关系主体，一个是法律关系主体的权利义务及其相互关系。既然调整法律关系，必然调整主体的行为。考虑行为规范必然考虑主体。考虑主体就要考虑我们国家环境保护事业当中究竟有哪几个主体。从学理、逻辑上似乎应该是这样的。

一个主体是企业，企业排放污染物当然要受到管理。第二个主体就是公民和公民的集合即社会。他们或者是环境污染的受害者，或者是虽未直接受害，但主张保护环境者。第三个主体是政府。在我国，这个主体尤其具有中国特色，需要给予特别关注。因为我国政府，特别是地方政府，在环保事业中有双重身份、双重角色。它们既是“裁判员”，又是“运动员”。在管理企业排污行为时，它们是管理者即“裁判员”。在招商引资、产业发展规划时，它们是“运动员”即经济活动的直接规划者、参与者和推动者。这种规划、参与和推动，如果搞得不对，就会带来严重的环境问题。从环保的角度看，很多地方政府在管理污染者和约束自己的招商引资、产业发展规划两个方面都没有做好。这一点，从最近这些年媒体广泛报道的大量环境污染事件、环境群体事件中可以看得很清楚。最近江苏南通、四川什邡的事件中，市民居然把市领导的衣服都扒掉了。可见在环保事业中政府是一个重要的主体。难道我国的环境法可以忽略这种主体的行为吗？问题这么尖锐了，难道可以忽略它们？法学和环境法学的基本原理是从实际出发的原理。坚持这个基本原理，就是坚持实事求是。所以，我们不能忽视政府这个主体。环境法是不是一个独立的或相对独立的法律部门，不是最重要的问题。最重要的问题是我国的环境法对有关环境的各种主体是否均衡覆盖。现在的环境法，对企业覆盖比较完整，但对政府和公民的覆盖空白较大。这个空白是需要立法者给予高度重视的。这是我想先说的一个重要想法。

关于《环保法》修改，简单讲四点，即视角、观点、方法和预期结果。希望我的这点学术认识，对有关的立法机关和行政机关有参考价值。

第一，视角。

这里的视角指的是怎么看待《环保法》修改工作。我的看法是：对《环境保护法》修改应该从战略看待，而不是仅仅从战术上看待。这个想法去年 4 月份在武汉，向人大环资委和环保部领导当面汇报的时候说过，而且写在汇报材料上。当时因时间有限没有展开谈。我的意思是，要看到《环保法》在我国法律体系当中的地位和作用，看到它对保障我国环保事业的不可或缺的基础作用。对《环保法》修改，应该超出人大以及人大有关部门的任期，看得更长远一些。这就是从战略上看。如果只考虑在本届人大剩下不到一年的时间如何完成修改任务，那就是从战术上看，比较短视。

第二，观点。

这里所谓观点，指的是我对《环保法》的基本功能的观点。我认为《环保法》有两个基本功能。一个是为环保事业奠定法律基础。另一个是规范和制约有关环境的政府行为。这两个功能体现了《环保法》特殊性。为什么研究法的功能？这个也很重要。记得文革的时候有一个电影，其中一个情节是一位动物学教授给学生上课。他走上讲台说今天我要讲的是“马尾巴的功能”，引起学生一片哄笑。（笑）殊不知，马尾巴确实有功能。世界上万世万物之所以存在必然有其存在的理由。《环保法》需不需要存在？如果它需要存在就一定有它的功能。如果没有功能的话就取消掉它。如果有功能就应该琢磨清楚，它的功能到底是什么。我认为《环保法》的功能就是屏幕上显示的这两个。

第三，办法。

这里的办法，指的是修改《环保法》如何着手。我建议以下三个步骤。

一、识别《环境保护法》的特殊功能。

我最近写了一些关于《环保法》修改的文章，集中登载在我的博客上（wangxi7701.blog.163.com）。有一篇文章的题目是：“环保事业基础法”：让特殊的《环保法》特殊起来！2011 年发表在由中国环境文化促进会主办的《绿叶》杂志上。这篇文章详细阐述了我识别《环保法》特殊功能的方法和结果。建议大家看看，这里不再赘述。

二、保持和完善《环保法》的特殊功能。

既然承认《环保法》有两个特殊功能，就承认了《环保法》存在的必要性。随之而来的结论就是：要保持和完善《环保法》的特殊功能。下面进一步讲讲我国《环保法》的这两个特殊功能。

功能一：为环保事业奠定法律基础。

如屏幕所示，《环保法》的这个功能体现在三个方面。一是规定环境法制基本要件。例如，《环保法》规定了“环境”的法律定义。“环境”的法律定义决定了中华人民共和国的所有的关于保护资源环境的法律所保护的“环境”的范围，包括对人的范围、对物的范围、对空间的范围和对时间的范围。这是一个国家环境法制的要件，不可缺少。它不适合由关于污染和自然资源保护的专门法律如《大气污染防治法》和《森林法》来规定。又如，《环保法》规定了国家和地方人民政府环境保护行政管理体制。它规定环保部管什么、农业部管什么、地方人民政府管什么，如此等等。这种规定，也是环境法制的要件，只适合由《环保法》规定，不适合由其他的关于污染防治或自然资源保护等事项的法律来规定。再如，《环保法》规定了特殊的环境污染损害赔偿诉讼时效，跟一般民事诉讼时效有所区别。诉讼时效也是属于环境法制要件的东西。现行《环保法》的总则部分有很多这种要件，它们体现了《环保法》的特殊功能。二是规定一般性环境管理制度。一般性环境管理制度指的是适用于环境保护工作各个领域的基本制度，比如环境监测、环境标准、排污收费、基本环境法律责任等。这些制度不适合由关于污染防治和自然资源保护等事项的法律来规定，只适合像《环保法》这样的“环保事业基础法”来规定。三是为环保经济手段的运用提供法律依据。环保经济手段有很多。它们的运用需要法律承认其合法性。只有法律承认其合法性，它们才能名正言顺地推行。《环保法》是适合做出这个“第一推动”的法，应当由它对环保经济手段给予原则性的规定。现行环保法没有这方面的内容，我认为应该有。这个规定，不适合由《大气污染防治法》、《森林法》之类的法律来规定。以上就是《环保法》的第一个功能。这个功能是其他环保类法律所没有的，也不适合由它们来规定。

功能二：规范和制约有关环境的政府行为。

我个人不太倾向用“政府责任”一词，因为“责任”一词歧义较多，容易引起误解。规范和制约有关环境的政府行为，比较明确。这方面我觉得《环保法》可以规定两方面的内容：

一是规范有关环境的政府决策。规范有关环境的政府决策是环境法预防功能的体现。我们一直说预防为主，但不论是现行《环保法》，还是其他的环境资源保护类法律，在决策阶段预防政府失误这一点上，规定的都不完善。我国环境污染和生态破坏的大量事实证明，决策失误造成的经济、社会和环境的代价往往是重大而长期的。我的建议包括以下几条。

建议恢复环境保护部级联席会议制度。这个制度给环保部门和政府其他部门平衡经济与环境两种价值提供一个平台，使政府决策的时候能够充分听取环保部门的正确主张。在很多重大污染或生态破坏事件中，我们往往看到环保部门说的话没用。环保部门在事前的正确意见，特别是后来被严重污染事故证明是正确的意见，当初没有人听。环保部门在政府内部没有很好的平台充分表达其正确意见，无法和负有经济发展职能的部门进行有效的博弈和平衡。所以我们建议建立这么一个平台。

建议在国务院和省级地方政府设立环境咨询委员会。这个环境咨询委员会成员主要由政府以外人士担任，如人大代表、政协委员、专家学者、居民代表、环保团体代表或其他德高望重人士、有公益心之人士。环境咨询委员会有权列席政府有关环境的问题决策过程。比如列席地方政府讨论地方产业发展规划和招商引资的会议。这种组织形式的好处：一是让政府有个能够听到政府以外的意见和建议的固定渠道，从而预防决策失误。二是把矛盾由体制外转到体制内解决。现在很多环境群体事件弄得非常极端。在体制外以极端方式解决，各方面的社会代价太大。何不通过合法组织结构，把体制外的意见和声音引入体制内表达？这种组织形式是符合党的十八大建设社会主义政治民主的精神的。我国经济发展快，粗放型的经济增长方式引起的社会矛盾相当尖锐。解决的办法是把体制外的矛盾引入体制内，而不是留在体制外。体制外的解决，影响政府的公信力和政权的稳固，结果很不好。现在环境问题这么尖锐，为什么立法机构在修改《环保法》时不来一点与时俱进？我们研究过其他国家和地区的经验，包括我国的台湾和香港的经验，发现政府的环境咨询委员会是一个普遍的现象。例如，香港的环境法规就规定设立市民环境咨询委员会，其职责是监督和协助环保署的决策。香港环保署审查的重大建设项目都要送环境咨询委员会征求意见。我有一次从在上海的办公室直接打电话到香港的环境咨询委员会，结果真有一位工作人员接电话。说明有人接待，如果有意见就可以向他反映。

二是建立政府环保履职监督制度。我在《绿叶》杂志上发表另外一篇文章，题目是“建立政府环保履职监督制度：让确保政府环保履职的达摩克利斯之剑挂起来！”粗放型的发展模式造成代价和危害大家都知道。中央也非常明白，一再说发展的代价过大、资源环境约束加剧。这种情况说明我们的政府尤其是地方政府没有很好履行环保职能。在不少地方，政府履行经济发展职能非常充分，但是把环保职能放在一边。全国加在一起就是发展不平衡和不可持续。要想让政府很好履行环保职能，办法有两个。一个是加强政府的内部监督，跟决策连在一起，特别是政府内部由环保部门对非环保部门的制衡，让非环保职能部门尊重政府环保职能，遵守环境保护法律法规。环保职能是人民政府公共职能的有机组成部分。另一个是在政府外部要有对政府的监督。这一点更重要。政府外部如社会、公民、公民全体，还有人大、媒体等，都应该有一定的途径监督我们的政府。《环保法》的修改应该创立和完善这些途径。我建议在《环保法》中规定中国式的环境公民诉讼制度。例如，法律可以允许公民或者公民团体发现地方政府在环保方面应当作为而不作为时，向政府提出依法行政的要求并允许在一定的通知期之后，例如60天，如果政府仍然不依法行政，公民或公民团体可到法院控告该行政机关。这是一种新的督促地方政府遵守环境法和严格执行环境法的手段。

三、消除功能重复，删除现行《环保法》与其他环境资源保护类法律所重复的条文（即所谓“空心化”条文）。

至于《环保法》与其他环境资源保护类法律相重叠的条款，可以删除。例如，《环保法》关于防治各种污染和保护各种自然资源的原则性规定，完全可以删除。删除之后，《环保法》的两大功能就突出了。

第四，预期结果。

按照这个思路来修改《环保法》，预期的结果有两个。一是理顺环境资源保护类法律的内部关系。《环境保护法》管环保事业的法律基础和有关环境的政府行为。其他法律管污染预防、自然资源保护等问题。各管其事，各得其所，关系比较顺。二是总体提高我国环境法对环保事业的保障水平。如此修改《环境保护法》，将弥补现行法律在有关环境的政府行为和监督政府环保履职方面的严重缺陷，使我国的环境法制建设迈上一个新台阶。

杨朝飞：王曦教授强调首先要从学理、逻辑上思考环保法的修改，要研究该法的法律关系、法律关系主体和法律关系主体的权利义务及其相互关系。其次是明确《环境保护法》特殊功能，一是为环保事业奠定法律基础；二是规范和制约有关环境的政府行为；三是删除现行《环保法》与其他环境资源保护类法律的重复功能。这是有关修改环保法的大思路，应当引起大家的注意。下面请灿发教授发言，题目是“社会组织和公众参与”。

王灿发：非常高兴参加这个会，今天让我讲“社会组织与公众参与”议题，可能考虑到我多年来做 NGO 组织提起环境诉讼的因素。

其实公众参与的重要性，今天参会者肯定都很了解，世界各国的环境保护经验，从美国 1970 年“4・22”大游行导致地球日，第二年导致美国国家环境保护局成立，再过一年召开世界环境会议，说明公众有很大的力量。公众不但有力量而且有参与环境保护的热情，目前来讲国内环境 NGO 组织越来越多，汉德研究所就是一个。他们在拼命找突破口，在法律上找给他们参与环境保护提供的根据，我们法律给环保组织、公民参与环境保护没有提供多少途径，顶多能在微博上叫几句，影响都是不够的。能不能提供法律的途径？《环境保护法》在这方面应该发挥作用，但是现在的修改草案在这方面没有太大的进展，仅仅是在环境信息公开提了一下。

但是公众参与并不是信息公开的问题，还涉及很多问题，比如意见表达权：我对哪个项目、我对什么有意见、上哪里去表达，表达以后能够得到什么反馈。比如为什么启东、什邡发生群体性事件，因为没有给他正常的表达渠道，他肯定会通过非正常渠道来表达，弄得环保部门很被动，特别是地方政府、地方党委都很被动，而且影响社会稳定。这种情况下我觉得发展公众参与、给公众意见表达权很重要，要让他充分把意见说出来，把不稳定因素消灭在建设项目或者一个活动举行之前。

公众参与另一个形式就是执法监督权，好多时候法律规定了，但是没有执行，没有执行在哪？肯定是行政机关应当执法而不执法。例如，制定页岩气开发规划，按理讲是专业规划，根据《环境影响评价法》应该搞环评，但是没有搞，谁该去执法？环保部该去管，现在没有规定这个部门对那个部门的监督，越有权力的部门越不按法律办事，就应该让社会公众参与监督，或者监督规划部门没有做环评而要起诉你，或者是监督环保部门不作为，有这样社会环境法律才能发挥作用。

另外一个公众参与形式就是提起诉讼权，包括行政复议权和诉讼权，现在《民事诉讼法》规定的公益诉讼仅限于民事诉讼，行政诉讼提起公益诉讼还是没有什么根据，前一段时间最高法院组织想在 1 月 1 日之前弄一个司法解释，看来弄不出来，最高法院也有办法，以高民智（笔名）的名义在《人民法院报》连续发表民事诉讼法解释与适用，第二篇发的是公益诉讼的法律适用解释，基本把最高法院的意见反映出来，我估计内部还会通知，让下边各级法院按照这个意见执行。这里头有两点应该重视，一个是环境公益诉讼不仅仅局限于污染造成的损失，还可以扩大到对生态破坏的诉讼；还有吸收了我们的意见，“法律规定的机关和有关组织”的“法律规定”不限定“有关”。目前有限定和不限定两种观点，我认为前边不应该限定后边，现在最高法院意见也是可以不限定后边的有关组织，这样就扩大了公益诉讼主体的范围，不限于现在法律规定的组织才能起诉，只要是有关环境保护的组织，就可以起诉。当然它对这个组织还是限定了一下，必须在民政部登记的组织，不愿意放开太大。但是我觉得这个范围太小，里边也说了“以后如果在其他法律规定了就按有关法律办”，正好《环境保护法》规定了，把它扩大了，民事诉讼法就可以沿用。行政诉讼法也在修订，我估计会沿用民事诉讼法的模式，依靠专业法规定，如果《环境保护法》能把公益诉讼的诉讼主体扩大一点，诉讼对象也不限制于污染，公众参与途径就可以拓宽了，在我们《环保法》修改当中，这方面应该有所作为。

在今天会议八个主题外，我觉得应该增加一个主题：环境法原则。现在修这个法，如果我们环境法基本原则不转变的话，在理念上就没有转变，现在中央也在强调，谈到法治要用法治思维，我们环保法应该用环保思维。现在的草案把环境优先放到“环境规划”里面，优先和不优先是解决环境保护与经济发展关系问题所提出的命题、原则，怎么仅仅放在规划里？我认为在《环境保护法》总则必须明确将三个原则突出出来：

第一，环境优先原则。党的十八大明确提出能源节约优先、环境保护优先，这个我们是有根据的，这个优先解决环境保护与经济发展关系，既然党的政策是灵魂，法律应该是党的政策法律化，党既然提出环境优先，那我们环境法律就应该贯彻进去，规定这个原则。现在许多领导干部脑子接受不了这一点，经济发展是硬道理怎么环境优先。现在我国已经到人均GDP 5 000美元的转折点，很多国家是在这个时候取消协调发展，变成环境优先的。我们在经济上已经有这个实力。在国内也有经验积累，比如2005年落实科学发展观加强环境保护决定之后，广东省做出一个决定明确提出环境优先，这几年广东省环境保护有明显的改进，一个表现就是环境纠纷的投诉，在2005年之前广东省历年的环境纠纷投诉占全国第一，但是到2009年广东省纠纷投诉排名退后，变成每年2万多起，他们最高每年5万起。现在投诉最多的是广西，广东进行环境优先，一些污染企业转到了广西，所以他们纠纷超过每年10万起。可以看到一个观念的转变非常重要，所以我们必须大力疾呼，将党的生态文明的要求转化为环境优先落实到法律上。

第二，风险防范原则。延续30多年的“预防为主，防治结合”，其实还是末端治理，需要废除。世界各国通行的风险防范原则，应该吸收进去，不允许有环境风险的项目存在，有环境风险需要预先采取预防措施才能建，不能等到建好造成污染再去治。

第三，不得恶化原则。虽然法律中未规定，但我们目前实行的是达标合法原则。只要企业污染物排放达标就是合法，一个地方政府环境质量达标，这个地方政府过关了。但是实行这个原则，往往让环境变坏，比如像西藏、青海，他们空气质量在许多情况下都是一级，而我们空气质量二级就达标，还可以建很多污染企业，这样我们《环境保护法》有什么用？你立了法还使环境变坏、变得更差，这个不符合《环境保护法》第一条“保护和改善”环境的立法目的，如果规定上不得恶化原则，就可以使现在好的环境变得更好，使已经恶化的环境得到改善。

有了这三个原则，我们环境才能真正来一个转变。任何原则的实行都不可能一朝一夕完成，有一个接受的过程，但是现在必须在法律里贯彻进去，这是最近一两年我一直呼吁的。

杨朝飞：王灿发教授在社会组织和公众参与方面提出三个权：意见表达权、执法监督权和提起诉讼权，另外也提出《环保法》修改的三个原则，这些都是将来改法的时候要进一步研究考虑的。下面请李艳芳教授来发言，她的主题是“信息公开”。

李艳芳：非常高兴能够有机会到这里同各位专家、各位环保部领导就《环境保护法》修改进行研讨，也非常感谢汉德研究所唐老师对我的邀请。指定题目是谈环境信息公开。其实我很多年前对环境信息公开有过涉猎，这么多年对环境信息没有专门的研究，接到开会通知以后，最近进行加班，对环境信息公开制度进行研究。仔细看了《环境保护法修正案（草案）》中有关环境信息的相关内容，也看了环保部网站上对《环境保护法修正案（草案）》的意见，我没有发现环保部意见中有关环境信息公开的建议，也没有搞清楚为什么。我想全面检讨一下这个制度，然后对草案提出问题，最后提一下自己的建议。

环境信息公开制度列为今天会议专题非常好，因为涉及公众参与的问题、知情权问题、公益诉讼问题、公众监督问题等都是与环境信息公开有关，如果没有环境信息公开，我们提知情权、参与权、表述权、监督权都是空话，什么都不知道怎么能很好参与呢？另外我们国家《环境保护法》第六条规定的“一切单位和个人都有保护环境的义务，并有权对污染和破坏环境的单位和个人进行检举和控告”，也依赖于环境信息的公开。这次党的十八大报告特别提到保障人们的知情权、参与权、表述权、监督权，具体到我们《环境保护法》修改也是非常重要的，未来在环境信息公开制度建设上，应当说是一个非常好的机会。大家也谈到环境事件屡次暴发，也反映了环境信息公开的重要性，我觉得选这个议题还是很好的。

现行《环境保护法》对环境信息涉及两条，第 11 条第二款环境公报的规定，第 31 条第二款环境报告的规定，但这两条和现在提到的信息公开制度有非常大的差距。除了《环境保护法》的规定之外，现行其他法律中有关环境信息公开的规定主要涉及《清洁生产促进法》，其中有四条和信息有关：第 17 条规定进入未达到能源消耗控制指标、重点污染物排放指标名单的企业，应公布能耗和重点污染物排放的情况；第 27 条第四款实行强制性清洁生产审核的企业，应当公布审核结果接受公众监督；还有第 28 条，没有达到重点污染物排放指标之外的企业，自愿搞清洁生产的话也可以在本地区主要媒体公布企业名称和防治污染的情况；第 36 条关于违法责任的规定，是我们国家有关环境信息公开承担法律责任的唯一的法律规定，这个责任比较轻。2002 年《环境影响评价法》是应该规定公开环境信息的，涉及公众环境权益的规划和项目应征询公众意见，但是没有规定有关环境影响评价相关的信息公开问题。2006 年环保总局发布的《环境影响评价公众参与暂行办法》对环境影响评价中的信息公开做了比较全面的规定。

除了环境法律之外，涉及信息公开的专门立法，我们现在有国务院 2007 年制定的《政府信息公开条例》，建立了政府信息公开制度；还有环保总局依据《政府信息公开条例》、《清洁生产促进法》制定了《环境信息公开办法（试行）》，规定了既有政府又有企业的信息公开。

除此之外有关上市公司环境信息公开，有环境保护总局《关于对申请上市的企业和申请再融资的上市企业进行环境保护核查的规定》（环发[2003]101 号）、《关于进一步规范重污染行业生产经营公司申请上市或再融资环境保护核查工作的通知》（环办[2007]105 号）、《关于进一步严格上市环保核查管理制度加强上市公司环保核查后督查工作的通知》（环发[2010]78 号），对上市公司环境信息披露机制、上市公司环保核查信息公开等进行特殊规定。这三个规定是递进的关系。

在梳理了现有主要法律和部门规章以后，总结我们现有关于环境信息公开制度法律规定的主要内容，涉及环境信息公开主体（政府和企业）、公开方式、程序、范围、监督与法律责任。

通过反思现在关于环境信息公开的规定，我的感觉是初步形成了环境信息公开的制度，但是现有环境信息公开制度的立法有非常明显的问题：

第一，立法层级比较低。除了《环境保护法》和《清洁生产促进法》对环境信息公开有零星、原则规定之外，其余有关环境信息公开的规定主要规定于环境保护部的多个部门规章中，效力等级明显不足。

第二，立法比较分散，整体性制度建设不足。《环境保护法》第 11 条关于环境质量状况公报、第 31 条关于污染事故通报的规定仅是对政府与企业环境信息公开的很初步的规定，涉及环境信息公开的规定主要散见于《清洁生产法》、《环境影响评价公众参与办法》、《环境信息公开办法（试行）》、《关于进一步严格上市环保核查管理制度加强上市公司环保核查后督查工作的通知》等中。这些规定虽然反映了中国环境信息公开法制建设进步的过程和成果，但是这些规定比较分散，各有侧重，没有形成集中的、全面的制度性规定。

第三，法律责任缺位或者过轻。《环境保护法》的两条规定没有对应的违法法律责任，环评法也没有规定相应的法律责任，《清洁生产促进法》规定了未达到能源消耗控制指标的企业未按规定公布能源消耗情况的责任，但是责任过轻了。因为法律规定的缺位和局限，导致对环境信息公开作出具体规定的部门规章虽然对环境信息公开的主体、程序、范围、方式进行了详细规定，但是对违法的后果无法规定。如《环境影响评价公众参与办法》对建设单位、环境影响评价机构、环境保护行政主管部门公开有关环境影响评价的信息的义务进行专节规定，但是对这些主体不履行有关义务的后果未加规定。《环境信息公开办法》对承担强制环境信息义务的企业不履行信息公开的义务，只遵照《清洁生产促进法》的规定，处十万元以下罚款，并代为公布。

从国外情况来看，像美国有《应急规划与社区知情法》，欧盟、奥地利、德国、英国都建立了环境信息公开制度，跟我们国家相比较，我们也做了很多工作，但是制度不完善。

最后谈谈《环境保护法修正案（草案）》的建议：

草案有关环境信息公开的规定在保留原来的第 11 条和第 31 条规定内容基础上，又增加第 11 条第二款要求公布监测数据，第五章监督检查中第 34 条环境信息公开的三款内容:“国务院环境保护行政主管部门统一发布国家环境综合性报告和重大环境信息。县级以上人民政府及其环境保护等有关行政主管部门，应当依法公开环境质量、突发环境污染事件以及环境行政主管部门的许可、排污费的征收和使用等环境信息。公民、法人或者其他组织，可以依法向县级以上人民政府及其环境保护等有关行政主管部门申请环境信息。县级以上人民政府及其有关行政主管部门应当在国家规定的时间内予以答复。”

但是这些规定的问题是：第一，对环境信息公开制度的定位不准：没有将环境信息公开制度作为一项环境保护管理的基本制度加以规定。把环境信息公开制度置于监督检查部分非常不恰当。第二，对环境信息公开内容未加以整合，分散规定于不同条款，没有形成环境信息公开制度应当形成的整体合力和制度效应。第三，对现行成熟的、急需予以公开的内容没有吸收。如环境影响评价中的信息公开。第四，对企业环境信息公开义务没有规定。第五，对政府不履行环境信息公开义务的法律责任未加规定。

我的建议：

第一，将环境信息公开制度作为一项基本法律制度在《环境保护法》适当的位置加以明确规定以提高制度效力。

第二，整合现有法律、行政法规、部门规章中有关环境信息公开的成熟规定，在《环境保护法》中用一至两条加以整体规定。

第三，增加企业环境信息公开的义务性规定特别是上市公司等企业的环境信息强制公开义务。

第四，对违反政府信息公开和企业强制信息公开义务的法律责任作出明确规定。

第五，公开的内容上特别应当强调对环境影响评价信息的公开；对上市公司环境信息公开义务进行特别规定。

杨朝飞：刚才李艳芳教授对信息公开阐述她的观点，先讲了意义，对现状进行描述，介绍国外信息公开立法的情况，最后对现行《环境保护法》在信息公开方面存在问题梳理，并且提出五条建议，建议都非常好，将来在改法时应当充分考虑五条建议。下面请汪劲教授发言，重点谈一谈公益诉讼。

汪劲：谢谢汉德研究所邀请，我想谈两点，因为公益诉讼实际和公众参与、公众权益保护以及李艳芳老师谈的信息公开都是联系在一起的，它原本也应当是 8+1 议题当中很重要的内容，可惜这次《环境保护法》没有规定。所以我想今天按照安排谈谈公益诉讼问题，谈公益诉讼之前我还有几个想法。

最近一段时间琢磨环境制裁制度创新过程当中有几点想法，我认为是未来环保部组织《环境保护法》修改的时候应该考虑的。当前有两个背景，我觉得是我们很好的契机，第一是十八大报告加强社会主义法治建设的背景，即“科学立法、严格执法、公正司法、全民守法”的背景；第二个背景就是生态文明建设、建设美丽中国的主题，而且专门提到五位一体布局和结构；再加上马上实行大部制契机，我觉得在这样大的背景下，我们应当把环境保护法的修改往上隆重推出，我在国合会上也专门建议了，通过对现有全国人大草案批判过程当中，我发现环境保护法修订矫枉应当过正。从人们理念来讲对环境保护法律怎么规定都不为过，不要像现在草案一样，把所有困难想到、把所有产生的争议都退回来，这个做法要摒弃。《环境保护法》要按照中国《立法法》的规定，上升到国家基本法律位阶上，我们有这个信念。日本环境基本法在法典当中标有一个小圆圈打一个点，表明是重要的法律，我觉得《环境保护法》作为国家基本法律的定位应当确立，作为国家基本法中应当有这样一部法律。

法律责任问题。（1）违法制裁条款在《环境保护法》修改当中应当简化，具体处罚措施留待于单行法。1997 年李新司长带着国务院法制局的同志开会，我提《环境保护法》要么废止、要么升格，因为我们没有政策法和基本法的模式。现在我认为《环境保护法》和单项法很大的区别还是规定基本制度、方针，相当于准则，法律责任设计除了违反基本制度的制裁以外，其他规定留待于单项法去规定。（2）行政制裁要和刑法处罚衔接，建立人身罚中的治安管理处罚、拘役、有期徒刑有机衔接的人身罚制裁制度。我们研究很长时间的双罚法，我们社会主义法律体系学习前苏联，和法治国家的最大不同，其制裁理念是单位，法治国家首先制裁违法行为人，在此基础上如果法人犯罪，单位才受到处罚。我们需要从目前以罚单位为主转变到自然人制裁为主，这样的话个人在特定岗位就不敢污染环境，企业就不会轻易违法。以罚款为主到行政指导和训诫为中心。刚才说顶层设计从规划开始、到标准实施、地方划定、到许可证发放、环评、功能区划分应当考虑企业情况，企业有困难时，有行政指导条款帮助企业排忧解难，在此基础上以责令为中心，如果责令不履行再采用执行罚保障。按日计罚不是行政处罚，这不是英美法的处罚方法，这是大陆法系的执行罚手段，不是处罚，一般适用不了，改变违法行为就不会出现这个问题。

赔偿制度的设计，除了对私益损害侵权条款之外，生态损害、环境损害索赔和相关规则应该确定。民事诉讼法除了引入公益诉讼条款外，第 79 条规定鉴定引入专家证人，对过去司法鉴定制度是突破，证明我们国家民事诉讼法在环境污染、知识产权等技术性比较强的领域，可以请专家到庭，这个进步在未来无论公益诉讼还是私益诉讼设计上都可以引入进来。

最后专门说环境公益诉讼顶层设计问题。最高法院公益诉讼指导意见稿的起草和修改工作还未完成，这个稿有大量的认识实际是错误的，一旦出台，对未来公益诉讼条款写入《环境保护法》有非常不好指引，有一些理解按照民事庭法官的理解，有些我认为是错误或者不利于环境公益诉讼的理念和方法，一旦确立指导思想当中，会带来不好的影响，为未来我国《环境保护法》展开有负面作用。环境公益诉讼顶层设计问题，第一，受案范围，环境污染是结果还是进行当中就可诉讼。预防性的民事责任是发现有问题就可以诉讼，法院发布停止令让你赶快停止，然后再通过行政或其他方法解决。第二，“优位-补充”问题，认为机关是优位，有关组织是补充，公益诉讼人要交诉讼费用，诉讼担保要有费用，而机关诉讼不用的，一共11 条。像这些东西环保部还要重视一点儿，当然我们也会跟他们沟通过程当中，也会提出我们看法。法律没有规定情况下，最高法院意见和全国人大法工委意见基本一致，很有可能2013 年1 月1 日起，中国没有环境公益诉讼了，因为法律规定的有关机关和组织还没有规定，法院受理那就程序违法，这是在会上这样说的，我们要引起重视。

当前立法和相关发展除了最高法院正在起草司法解释以外，前不久《人民法院报》试探性地以高民智署名文章的形式把意见发给大家了，谈公益诉讼指导意见。现在除了刚才说的问题以外，还有行政诉讼法的修改，民事诉讼法已把环境公益诉讼纳入，很有可能环境行政诉讼入法可能性比较大，因为民事诉讼法对行政公益诉讼入法带了好头，或许《环境保护法》修改涉及有关环境行政公益诉讼问题，如何设计呢？我不赞成全国人大环资委提交的法案，也不赞成环保部给法制办和人大法工委的草案第48条“因污染损害公共环境利益的……要求污染者承担侵权责任”，这个条文是错误的：第一，侵权责任法是不是认同，第二，如果没有损害利益，渐进损害怎么办？而从西方国家环境公益诉讼大多数类型来看，停止诉讼、取消诉讼是最多的，可以依照行政机关停止、可以依照向法院申请禁止令停止，也可以通过行政诉讼如取消许可来停止，比如日本虽然没有形式上的环境公益诉讼，但是日本行政诉讼和民事诉讼法可以通过这两类诉讼停止、消除正在进行的危险。

《环境保护法》涉及的公益诉讼条文可能只给一个条文若干款。我觉得第一个必须明确诉讼主体是哪些机关或者组织？我们很清楚，一是代表国家行使环境监督权的部门（行政机关），这个和海洋环境保护法一致，而且这个规定应当被我们人大常委会委员接受；二是除机关以外的人民检察院的地位，我个人看法是人民检察院应当针对行政机关不作为、渎职、失职，不赞成检察机关作为环境民事诉讼的原告/主体，检察机关可以设计为环境行政公益诉讼的主体。前一段时间《法制日报》说有一个典型案例“定扒案件”让我评，我认为只有标志意义没有标本意义，该案在我看来是行政机关失职，法院履行行政机关职能是错误的。因此，主体有关机关分两大类，一个检察机关、一个有监督管理权的行政机关。

第二，提出哪些诉讼？最高法院民事庭的理解总是重视出现漏油、环境损害、生态损害、替代、修复等造成结果的情况，不认为渐进中的环境损害可以提起诉讼，认为污染环境损害公共利益的行为解释为一定要有结果出现。我认为公益诉讼不见得要有结果出现，大量公益诉讼不是损害结果作为诉讼原因之一，有一定的知识、明知这个风险肯定来临，还继续往下走，就可以提起诉讼。

第三，条文当中还应当明确表示你的诉讼请求要达到什么目的，比方说我们以前经常在课堂上讲预防性民事责任，民法通则有十种民事责任承担方式，有很多都是预防性的。恰恰公益诉讼问题上，损害赔偿诉讼如果出现国家财产损失这是广义的公益，这个时候不是公益，是国家机关代表国家向加害人索赔，如果明确有个人、组织财产受到损害也不是公益，所以这两种情况下诉讼请求是什么应当再研究。而且可以请求停止侵害、发出停止令，发生污染事故造成国家财产损失可以采取恢复原状申请，比如替代、修复、期间损失等都是恢复原状的替代方式。最近无锡一个案件，建一个动物园违法规划多侵占了当地的地，于是环保团体提起诉讼，法院受理了判不了。行政机关是否违法省里不表态，法院为难。我给他们建议采取替代的方式：对造成的损失进行评估，如果恢复损害需要 800 万元，再找一个受污染的地，拿 800 万元把地整治好。这是我从美国学来的：佛罗里达州一个公民团体和陆军工程总部的纠纷，陆军工程总部多占了地，法院处罚他，他说愿意拿出钱再修复一块土地行不行？当地居民说行。这个方法据说动物园方面感到满意，愿意拿钱出来修复一块无锡被污染的土地，中华环保联合会马勇他们也赞成。替代性的恢复原状诉讼请求是一个解决环境损害的很重要的方法。超级基金、土壤损害修复等一定要有依据，包括环境保险的确立也是依据。诉讼请求和污染环境损害公众利益行为，我们要进一步解释指引到除了损害结果以外，进行中的损害也应该是公益诉讼的对象。

另外还有几个地方要做出安排：第一诉讼费用，第二如果公益诉讼原告胜诉，这个费用应该怎么使用？像美国、中国台湾的法律有这样规定，公益诉讼原告一旦胜诉，它是社会组织的话，法院应该判决给社会组织一部分费用，目的一个是奖励他，一个是让被告支付由于公益诉讼产生的证据费用、鉴定费、律师费等费用。

总之，我认为矫枉应当过正，前怕狼后怕虎是对的，但应当把狼和虎分析一下，尽可能让狼和虎接受我们观点，不行再慢慢一步步往后退。不是大家容忍程度在什么地方就规定在什么程度，更不能向环资委草案那样规定的比容忍程度还不如，谢谢！

杨朝飞：刚才汪劲教授谈了很好的观点，第一要在公益诉讼部分把十八大精神融入进来；第二提出环保法不仅是环保法制的基本法，还应该上升到国家法制的基本法；第三谈了关于公益诉讼制度顶层设计的看法。另外谈了有关公益诉讼费用等若干问题的具体意见，我觉得这些意见是非常好的。

下面请政法大学胡静教授发言。

胡静：我想《环境保护法》修改首先要有实效，不能为纯粹解决和单行法的矛盾而做这样的工作，第二不应该做成纯粹的总则法，不应该单纯把各个单行法的共性提出来规定在总则当中，做成民法总则、债法总则那样。要注重实效，即缺什么补什么。我很赞成王曦老师观点，应该把政府作为主体对待，在这里有一对关系可能需要理清，就是中央政府和地方政府之间的关系，我们国家是中央集权的国家，这样子必然决定地方政府不仅仅是地方利益的代表，而且一定也是中央利益在地方的代表，这样的话它的角色就是双重的，不可否认它一定是地方经济利益的代表，它实际很为难，我觉得是不是应该正视地方政府是地方经济利益代表的正当性，给机会承认它，因为这个也是正当利益。

当承认地方政府经济利益是正当利益的时候，处理中央和地方关系上，地方不仅仅是要服从，地方因为是地方经济利益代表和环境利益代表，和中央应该有博弈。即便是单一制国家，中央和地方的契约精神是必要的。不仅有“大棒”还要有“胡萝卜”，通过转移支付，《环境保护法》执行得好就多给你项目。现在我感觉可能整个中国，只有一只猫就是环保部，别的都是老鼠，地方环保局也被地方政府变成了老鼠，这种情况下应当正视地方政府利益诉求，变盗猎者为看林人，这是一点，要管地方政府。让地方和中央的博弈台面化、明朗化，这就可以谈判、协商。不要像现在这样，上有政策、下有对策，如果中央不给地方表达诉求的机会和尊重地方权利，地方就通过逃避义务来应对，这是双输的结果。

另外有一点我觉得要管部门，环保部门以外的部门。为什么管部门？环境保护不是一个行业，不仅是环保部的事情，也不是某一个行业的事情，这就决定了环保部和别的部门相比有很大的不同，有一些部只管其中的某些企业，有些部门只管一个点，比如工商登记，登记就完了。而环保部管几乎所有企业，是过程管理不是点的管理，是对所有行业某些行为的过程管理，这样子难度很大，无论如何环保部一家管不住。所以在批项目上，比如环评、立项，我觉得环保部不应该进行分段决策，不应当是报告书到这里批一下。比如现在东西送到发改委，需要发改委给意见，发改委应该把这个东西交给环保部征求意见，发改委在前台，环保部在后台，将这样的方式真正贯彻基本法包括单行法中，通过这样的方式落实统一监管，如果环境保护法律能够把统一监管说清楚就是成功。这是事前的。在批项目之前环保部在幕后，这是“统一监督管理”中的“统一监督”的体现，但是项目建成之后，变成了实实在在的污染源，环保部就走到台前，对企业进行检查，这是“管理”，监督对象是地方政府和其他部门，管理对象是企业。单项法主要规定“管理”制度，基本法主要规定“统一监督”机制。我觉得管部门方面环保部应该这样，这样子必然导致单行法当中有很大幅度的修改，包括环评法。这样动作会比较大，我觉得应该有壮士断腕的决心，既然是基本法就应该有基本法的尊严，不应该迁就现有的单项法。

缺什么补什么，不仅应该做锦上添花的事情，更应该做雪中送炭的事情。这是我的一个不成熟的观点。

杨朝飞：胡静老师讲得不错。地方政府是双重利益的代表，过去我们只是看做单重利益的代表，现在双重利益代表也得承认。中央政府和地方政府关系不是简单地服从，过去老是讲政治服从。中央利益和地方利益在任何国家都会产生矛盾，因此应当承认两者有博弈关系。既然承认有博弈关系，在处理双方关系的时候，该用“大棒”时就用“大棒”、该用“胡萝卜”时就用“胡萝卜”，这个观点在《环境保护法》修改当中应当很好的考虑。下面请李启家教授谈司法保障。

李启家：很高兴参加这个会，也非常感谢唐老师。前面几位教授发言都涉及司法保障问题，他们所谈的意见我持赞同态度，我想给他们做点补充。

第一个补充王灿发教授提到的环保优先，我认为这不仅是原则，应当是理念。以前都是按照功利主义态度，强调利益最大化，现在应该采用以损失最小化设计环保优先。因为经济发展也好、社会发展也好、环境保护也好，这都属于具有正义价值的利益，我们大家知道在发展中的理论阿列克西议题：正当价值不能进行比较，无论你这个利益多么具有正当性，不能否定另一个正当利益。利益最大化恰好是具有利益否定的意思，损失最小化就是对任何正当利益都表示尊重，我们设计的时候应该把思路从利益最大化思路改为损失最小化的思路，这就是相互让步。在相互让步基础上，我们在法律条文设计的时候应该有两个层面的设计：一个层面明确宣布在发展经济、社会和科技的时候，必须兼顾环境保护，应该首先要明确这方面要兼顾环境保护，第二个层面当经济社会科技发展对环境有严重不良影响或者危害的时候，应当是环保优先。这个分成两个层次，经济社会发展、科技发展必须兼顾环境保护，当经济社会发展对环境有严重不良影响或者产生危害的时候，我们才提出来环保优先。环保优先并不是不计条件、任何条件下优先，是经过比较和选择的利益优先，是有限度的优先。这是我个人对环保优先想法，可以说王灿发教授意见的补充。

给我分的命题是司法保障。20世纪90年代中期以后，欧美对法律功能有新的理解，就是法律有效性，当然司法保障是法律有效性很重要的方面，我觉得有几个理念必须考虑：（1）救济穷尽原则，司法保障是所有法律保护的最后屏障，不应当频繁使用，是在其他救济手段不能发挥作用的前提下才采用司法保障，避免讼垒。我们在谈到司法保障的时候，应当充分考虑环境纠纷的行政救济。现在只是说环保部门可以调解纠纷，我想我们还要再考虑。如果纠纷一股脑儿全到法院未必对环保部门有利，要慎用。（2）司法保障发挥双头鹰功能，一个制约企业，再一个制约政府，这种创新功能，因此我们设计和考虑司法保障的时候不要把司法保障变成行政附庸，变成行政机关的补充。（3）要避免环境“利维坦”现象发生，还要避免环境民粹主义的兴起。不要把司法保障变成单方面巩固政府权威或者行政行为延伸或行政机关的附庸。

在司法保障中关于行政处罚问题、犯罪问题，前几位教授都谈了，我是赞成孙佑海教授、汪劲教授，还有翟勇主任的意见，应该把“违反本法”文字去掉，污染和破坏环境构成犯罪应当追究刑事责任。

关于环境污染民事责任，我觉得我们现在草案中不大理想，提几个建议：（1）全面恢复水污染防治法的有关精神。水污染防治法都已经进步了，结果我们《环境保护法》修改没有进步反而退步了，起码应当确认和巩固水污染防治法的立法进步，先守住不能退，这是一个。（2）不仅不能退，还得往前进，进从两个层面：一个明确宣布污染环境、破坏环境或者其他使环境质量下降、使环境质量受损、对环境有严重不良影响的行为，应当承担减轻、消除危害，对损失修复的责任。先从正面上作出规定，你必须承担。前面也不加“违反本法”、“不符合标准”，直接定义这种行为，你有这种行为就应该承担责任。第二个层面，后边才跟着受损害的可以提出减轻损失，有权要求减轻、消除危害、赔偿损失。我们从正反两方面，你有责任，我有权利，就把权利义务关系结合起来，有利于环境公益诉讼。因为你有义务，在行为中我认为你违反义务了，就可以提出诉讼请求，这样反而有利。（3）但这种情况仅适用于损害者比较明确的，如果污染者、破坏者已经不存在或者无法确知，包括中国台湾及日本、印度、奥地利、德国这种情况发生都是政府承担责任。（4）在有些国家立法中不仅是环境污染、生态破坏，还有对环境不良影响，还加上环境风险，对可能造成污染破坏环境严重不良影响和环境风险有责任，根据我们自己实际情况还要再分析、再讨论。如果把环境风险放进去还是有一定意义的，还得进一步论证。

杨朝飞：启家教授讲的几点挺好，一个是我们对法律思想从功利走向包容，过去一些领导总是用一部分人正当权利否定另一部人的正当权利，所以侵害群众利益的事件屡屡发生；将来应该走向包容，既然大家都是正当的利益就应当都保护起来；第二关于司法救济三个原则，救济穷尽原则、双头鹰作用、避免利维坦原则，最后对环境污染、民事责任讲了几个具体的建议，将来可以作为改法的参考。最后请武汉大学柯坚教授发言。

柯坚：前面几位都是我的老师，讲得都很透彻，我做些补充。想结合这两天感受，谈谈对《环境保护法》修改的想法。前两天去韩国参加一个气候变化背景下中国碳排放交易立法问题的会议，韩国立法研究院属于韩国总理府下边 23 个思想库中的法律思想库，通过跟韩国同行交流，我有一个很深的感受，我们环保法修改和其他法修改存在一个很大的误区，就是舍近求远，往往一说立法就考虑美国、欧洲怎么做，事实上中国台湾、日本、韩国环境立法特别是环境基本法的发展远远超出我们想象，他们的经验对我们有非常直接的借鉴意义。比如韩国除 2000 年制定了环境基本政策法之外，又制定了可持续发展法、绿色增长法，都是宏观性、总括性的立法，2000 年的环境基本政策法还是处在引导地位。中国台湾也有环境基本法，台湾叶俊荣教授提出一个观点，全世界范围包括东亚地区都处在环境时刻或环境时代，国家政策应该顺势而为，制定环境保护基本法或综合法是时代的需要。韩国立法研究院有一个制度，外国来的客人都要在留言簿上留一句话，我留的是：绿色增长不仅仅意味着人类健康、可持续增长，还意味着和平的增长。

日本 2000 年国会提出一个概念环境立国，一直筹划中的德国法典，其背后的前提有一个重要的概念：德国试图在宪法上确立环境国。从宪法条款出发，引申到环境基本法、环境单项法，提供了非常广阔的环境立法空间。党的十八大提出生态文明，从中国国情来看，某种意义是一个促进环境基本法《环境保护法》很强的政策契机。2005 年韩敏巡视员和我参加一个《环境保护法》修订的会议，主讲是我还有一个日本环境署官员，我当初提出一个观点，从中国现状出发制定环境基本政策法是最合理的，立法模式选择是一个“筐子”，如果“筐子”太大，空空荡荡，如果“筐子”太小，很多新的环境保护政策法律的要求进不去。从实际情况出发，我觉得某种意义上说，制定环境基本政策法是最合理的选择。

通过今天的专家讨论，我发觉我们已经识别了很多我们国家在目前和未来需要解决的环境保护法律基本政策问题，包括政府责任、环境权益、信息公开、社会组织与公众参与等不同层面的环境保护政策，如环境保护的社会政策、经济和产业政策。很多环境保护的基本方法、理念、价值已经形成了，可以通过基本政策法把这些价值固定下来使之明确化，为以后的环境法治奠定基础。另外，受刚才李启家教授的启发，很多不同价值如经济发展是正当选择、环境保护也是正当选择，很多情况下没有办法事前判断，基本法要规定必要的基本程序权利包括信息公开、表达、监督、控制等，为解决正当利益的纠纷埋下法律伏笔。

最后特别强调草案存在权力和权利的失衡，过分关注环保部门的制度需求，环境保护问题不是部门事业，是渗透社会各个领域、各个层次的全面性国家性的工作，也是社会公共利益的选择。因此在这样情况下，一定要强调国家行政权力和社会环境保护公共事务权利的结合。

杨朝飞：柯坚教授讲了很好的意见。一个是修改《环境保护法》不要舍近求远，在韩国、日本、中国台湾都有很好的做法，将来我们对这些国家和地区环保法要研究；第二如果叫环境基本政策法，不要筐子太大，还是突出政府责任和公众参与等一系列相关问题；最后讲权力和权利失衡问题，实际上我们近几年环境立法更多的是公权力的立法，真正对私权利的考虑太少，对老百姓私权利保护远远不够，不光环保部门，其他部门立个法也是给政府增加一大堆公权力，老百姓私权利却没有引起必要的关注，没有得到法律的足够保护。

按程序的发言都发言完了。大家看还有什么补充建议。

王曦：我想补充三点。我看了党的十八大报告，其中有一个提法对《环境保护法》的修改特别重要，即所谓新的“两个凡是”：“凡是涉及群众切身利益的决策都要充分听取群众意见；凡是损害群众利益的做法都要坚决防止和纠正”。现在环境问题涉及群众利益太多了。党的十八报告讲得这么清楚，给我们修改《环保法》提供了重要的指导，这是第一点。

第二点，刚才几位老师说到“环境基本法”或“环境政策法”。这些法律有一个共同的特点，就是管政府。美国《国家环境政策法》和日本《环境基本法》都对有关环境的政府行为做出规定。

第三点，《环保法》的修改要在事前预防和事后救济两方面下工夫。事前预防很重要，事后救济也很重要。现在相对较弱的是事前预防方面。《环保法》在这两方面的制度设计怎么和基本法律如民事诉讼法、行政诉讼法等衔接，应该是环境法学研究的重点。

汪劲：我觉得我们制度设计一定要学会隐含，不要太直白。有很多制度明着写会遭到反对，隐含可以将制度实施条件创造出来，通过隐含规定延伸出来未来想做的事。比如环境污染责任保险，反对声音很大，可以规定在环评、发放许可证时，针对企业污染的风险大小，要求为排污设备缴纳可能发生危害的担保，这个是西方国家通行的做法，没有财产担保就会去买保险，这样环境污染责任保险就隐含在规定中了。

不笼统写的条文。（1）环境污染犯罪，还有治安管理处罚，不赞成笼统写。现在的写法是“违反本法规定，构成违反治安管理行为的，依法给予治安管理处罚；构成犯罪的，依法追究刑事责任”，全国人大做了解释，但还不够。应当把相应的行为和治安管理处罚法的行为直接挂上钩。我到地方五个省调研了解的情况是，有的环保部门跟公安机关关系好还可以，好多省公安机关说证据你们拿，我直接处罚。这条写得细一点公安机关便于执法，起码有利于配合。（2）污染环境损害公益的行为描述得更确定一些，几个方面都涵盖进来，比民诉法写得更细一点。

污染环境犯罪的写法。治安管理处罚15日最高，拘役一个月到一年，跟治安管理处罚高位有点衔接，有期徒刑六个月到三年，并处或单处罚金，情节特别严重的上升到七年。这里边的界限我们划不清楚，早点让最高法院给划清。给你一个月拘役判你有罪，是对违法犯罪的威慑，一定将我们公权力制裁有机衔接起来，不要将行政处罚和刑罚制裁分离开，前苏联制裁模式应该改变。在当前情况下，应该将这个规定到环保法这一基本法中去，单项法就是纯的，环保法要起法律适用法、准则法、准据法这个作用。

唐大为：我本来是为这个会议做服务的，没有准备发言。各位老师讲了这么多，我也想说几句。我特别赞成王老师讲的，立法过程中应该追踪到立法本质。金老师的教材，开篇就讲什么是环境法，那就是通过调整人与人的关系来调整人与自然的关系，这也是环境法有别于其他法律的不同地方。

基于这一点，我曾给年轻学者提过一个建议，希望他们搞一个关于环境规划法律地位的研究课题，《环境保护法》第四条规定环境规划必须纳入国家发展规划，但是这个规划有没有法律地位？从实际中看，这么多年制定这么多规划，也进行规划环评，但没有太高的法律地位。我们开展很多激励性的制度，比如生态示范区建设、生态工业园区建设、模范城市建设等都要求先编规划，但有多少人认真执行？所以我想说，在《环境保护法》新修编后，如刚才王老师讲的，一定把预防和事后补偿两件事情搞清楚。事先预防主要靠国家政策性引导和法律保证，而环境规划具有相应的法律地位和合适的程序保证则是必要的。

杨朝飞：大家还有很多意见和建议要讲，时间关系我简单对会议进行一个总结。首先这个会议开得非常不错，我们跟庆瑞、别涛、韩敏连续多年研究环保法，今天听了大家的发言收获非常大。一是大家发言思想解放、观点创新，确实涉及很多过去没有人考虑的问题，有些属于禁区、半禁区的，但是今天都讲出了非常精彩的观点。二是大家的发言参考了大量国外的经验和做法，而且又联系了国情，为改法提供了非常有益的借鉴。三是大家的发言对今后改法提出了很有参考价值的意见，拓展了我们改法的思路，其中一些具体建议可以直接采纳入法。所以我们可以对会议给予非常高的评价。

下一步的工作：一是把会议发言记录一定整理好，要原汁原味；二是在元旦之前把发言记录印发给所有专家本人，请他们修改和完善，元旦之后把意见返回；三是在此基础上汉德环境观察所写一个关于《环境保护法》修改思路的总体建议，把专家们的精华观点吸收进去，等这个建议稿完成之后，再印发与会专家征求意见。以上工作争取在 1 月底完成。

“《环境保护法》修改思路的建议”主要有三方面的作用：一是报送环保部政策法规司在改法时参阅；二是择机报送全国人大法工委、人大环资委、国务院法制办参阅；三是创造条件通过内部渠道直接往上报。争取将改法能够纳入明年的国务院立法计划或全国人大五年立法规划之中。这个课题不是简单的会议开完就完成了，一定要把大家的智慧形成一个成果，真正发挥作用。

最后我作为会议的主持人，谢谢所有参会专家，谢谢汉德环境观察研究所大为所长和工作人员，谢谢赵立建先生和能源基金会提供的资助。

《环境保护法》修改思路社会组织建言会参会人员

杨朝飞　中国环境科学学会副理事长
别　涛　环境保护部政策法规司副司长
汪　劲　中华全国律师协会环境资源与能源专业委员会主任
许国栋　全国工商联环境服务业商会监事长
金嘉满　全球环境研究所执行主任
王晶晶　公众与环境研究中心副主任
马　勇　中华环保联合会环境法律中心督查诉讼部部长
张建宇　美国环保协会中国项目负责人
徐　楠　中外对话北京办公室副总编辑
王小颖　阿拉善基金会资助项目官员
胡勘平　中国生态文明研究与促进会研究与交流部主任
高胜达　中国环境修复网主编
孙月新　中国产业发展促进会业务主管
严惠清　环境保护部宣传教育司综合处
赵立建　能源基金会环境管理项目主管
陈德清　中持（北京）环保发展有限公司总经理
唐大为　中关村汉德环境观察研究所所长
李　伟　中关村汉德环境观察研究所特约研究员
王社坤　中关村汉德环境观察研究所环境法研究中心主管

《环境保护法》修改思路社会组织建言会议记录

主 持 人： 杨朝飞

会议时间： 2013 年 1 月 15 日 13:30—17:30

会议地点： 中持环保第一会议室

杨朝飞： 环保法的修改由来已久，1979 年环保法发挥了重要作用，1989 年修改，到现在有 20 多年了。从 2004 年开始，全国人大、全国政协每年的“两会”，每年出现修改《环境保护法》的议案。对环保法的修改有几种争论：第一种是环保法可有可无，因为环保主要领域的专项法都齐全了，如果需要改哪个法，就改哪个法，《环境保护法》与专项法有很多重复，没必要存在；第二种是《环境保护法》还是有必要，但是怎么修改，一直没有找到太好的思路；第三种是小改快出，希望尽快见到实效。在全国人大向社会公开征求意见时，大概收到 11 000 多条网上修改建议，范围非常广泛，32 个省市全有意见。这是环保方面立法中社会反映最多的一个法，多数人都不同意小改，觉得小改不解决大问题，特别是不解决根本性问题。所以，从网民的反应上，还是希望大改，真正改出一部有用的、管用的法。

全国人大原本 2012 年 12 月进行最后一次审议，但是推迟了。推迟并不是不重视，而是认为现行的草案非常不成熟。估计环保法将会纳入新一届全国人大的五年立法计划。但是咱们现在不能等，我们在全国人大换届期间要做好研讨的准备。12 月我们开了一个法学专家的研讨会，这次是有关 NGO 组织的研讨会。下面请课题承担单位汉德环境观察所唐大为所长致辞。

唐大为：各位朋友，下午好，欢迎大家参加这个会。中关村汉德环境观察研究所是2012年5月成立的，是在民政局注册的非营利机构（民办非企业单位）。汉德研究所成立以后，得到了有关的领导、企业、专家、朋友以及很多资深环保人士的支持。修改《环境保护法》研讨会是我们所近期的一项重点工作，研讨会得到了能源基金会的支持。

汉德研究所是作为独立于政府和企业的第三方机构，这个机构创建之初，我们认识到环境问题不是某一个学科的单纯问题，而是一个综合性的社会问题，需要一个能够整合智力资源的平台，携手各行各业的志同道合者，通过多角度的观察、多层次的研究，为不同的环保主体提供高端智力支持。我们期望，汉德应是观察者，致力于通过记录、解读、剖析重大环境事件，来提高公众环保认识；汉德也应是思考者，开展政策性的基础研究，推动制度创新，为政府提供决策支撑；汉德还应是实践者，针对现实环境问题，为地方和企业提出一揽子解决方案，并积极参与实施。

这次研讨会是希望进一步征求大家意见，理清修法思路，提高修法质量，推动修法进程。杨总刚才讲了，之前我们开了专家研讨会，这次开一个相关社会机构的建言会，未来是要形成一个综合报告，争取在“两会”之后提交给决策者。

这次社会组织建言会，邀请到咱们在座的这些专家和朋友，我们将围绕《环保法》的修改展开讨论，希望大家积极发言，预祝这次会议圆满成功。谢谢大家！

杨朝飞：下面请项目资助单位能源基金会的才婧婧发言。

才婧婧：很高兴这次来参加这个研讨会，我主要也是抱着学习的态度，听专家们的意见。能源基金会也希望能够为《环境保护法》的修改提供智力支持。

杨朝飞：下面按议题讨论，每人发言不超过一刻钟。首先请中关村汉德环境观察研究所特约研究员李伟发言。

李伟：最近仔细学习了《环境保护法》修订前和修订后的版本，总体感觉目前的修改版本还有较多欠缺，没有达到我们的预想。主要存在以下问题。

第一，新《环境保护法》和当前国家社会经济发展阶段环境保护特点的关系没有充分体现出来。可以分成两个层面看。一是中国工业化、城镇化进程非常快，通过二三十年的发展，环境污染源已经是生活源和工业生产源的排放并重，目前法律总体上对工业生产的污染防治法则较多，但对于城镇化以后的生活领域的污染排放着墨不多，比如对老百姓机动车排放的污染防治缺乏关注。二是过去30年的我国社会经济发展情况和环境保护立法环境发生了较大变化，新《环境保护法》对于自身定位的重新审视和对环境、经济未来协同发展的促进作用没有体现出来。如果对比国家节能法，节能机制提出的总量控制、倒逼机制对能源与经济的协同发展起到了较好的指导作用，新的《环境保护法》也应该起到这样的倒逼和指导的作用。环境保护不是狭义的保护，而是体现推动发展、立足发展、服务发展的这样一个保护的理念，环境保护和经济发展应当有所融合、衔接，这点没有充分体现出来，从生态文明建设的高度来看，这部法的相关表述和立意都需要再提升调整。

第二，目前的修改版本从责任关系上没有理顺地方政府发展经济冲动和环境保护责任之间的矛盾悖论。政府是我国区域经济发展的重要推手，同时又对环境保护、环境管理具有最大的责任，造成了实践中政府到底怎么样统筹协调二者关系的难题。环保部是国务院落实这种责任的代理部门，是委托代理关系，再往下，又很明确地把地方政府作为区域环境保护的第一责任人，国务院、国务院环境保护行政主管部门、地方政府、地方政府的环境保护行政主管部门四者之间的委托代理关系链条并不通畅，落到地方上，地方政府的环保责任和对粗放经济增长的依赖形成了一个悖论。具体而言，地方政府把发展经济作为第一考量，有牺牲环境质量，保护环境污染企业的冲动，这部法没有在这方面有更深层次的考虑。

第三，政府和市场主体的关系仍没有完全理清，社会主体责任关系没有明确界定。目前的环境法强调政府责任为主，而政府责任和市场关系强调得较弱。企业主体、社会组织、公民个人，每一个排放者，在环境保护的责任落实的原则还不明确、完善。跟上一版比，政府从监督管理变成了环境管理，政府的责任一方面是环境保护和改善，另一方面是环境管理，把政府做成了环境管理全流程的参与者了，而把市场主体放到了很偏的位置。政府是一个主导力量，还是中间的监管力量？全社会的各类主体的责任怎么体现？这需要在下一轮改法中明确。

第四，环境管理体系在构成上还需要在多个维度上进一步完善。关于新增加的环境管理的体系，这个版本列出了六条构成：标准、监测、保护规划，区域协商的机制环评、跨区域的政府协商，但是在我看来，这六个层面不足以构成国家环境管理的体系。如果跟节能领域包括总量控制管理等多个维度的管理体系构架相比，显得滞后了。

第五，关于环境规划的法律效力问题现在还没有明确。新修改版本的第十二条，提出各地方都要加强规划的制定，但这个规划的法律效力足不足？光靠规划能不能保证各方面工作的实施？从现实情况看，规划的法律效力恐怕不足。现在规划框架下，市规委主导城市的空间规划，发改委主导国民经济规划，国土局主导土地开发规划，这是三个基本规划，还有环境保护规划，现在又出来一个主体功能区规划，现在又提出了“三规合一”、“五规合一”，这几个规划之间，能不能形成高度的法律效力，把环境保护规划的法律效力提升。

第六，关于环境保护的区域责任与协同的条款较弱。环保有多个空间层次，从整个国家来看有一个大环境，再聚到一个地区，再聚到三平方公里、二平方公里的局部空间，再落实到一个企业。过去在环境保护中的环境影响评价等，其实是对微观尺度和小格局层面的环境保护强化得多，如果要上升到区域、流域，按生命线、国家层面来看环境保护，这个体系还是相当弱的，这也是恰恰造成了现在很多重大环境问题的根源。例如山西和河北的例子，长治和邯郸协商流域环境用水合作，但是这种合作没有稳定的机制，难以保障环境安全和用水安全，这说明，我国急需要一套机制，从国家层面建立组织体系推进区域协同合作，区域协商这个机制对于大尺度上解决环境问题是完全不够的。另一个例子是生态环境中的候鸟迁徙跨区域的通道缺乏，不是一个微观尺度能解决的问题，这种生态湿地的布局，不是一个区域或流域的概念，而应该有自然生物迁徙生命线的概念，类似此类的考虑，在这个法律和中央部门统筹管理中都比较薄弱。

第七，从源头控制角度看，政策环评难以解决所有问题。一些战略性的政策应该去做评价，而且从产业政策层面已经得到了比较充分的讨论，例如汽车产业政策，已经讨论到中国的环境容量适合不适合每个人拥有一辆车的微观问题。但是在一个地区或园区层面，产业准入政策和环境影响评价怎么结合？和环境保护的理念怎么结合？在这部法里体现不足，应该上升到生态文明这个角度，从经济建设、政治建设、文化建设、社会建设、生态文明建设“五位一体”的角度表达和阐述。

第八，环境信息公报和公众参与相关描述也有不甚明确的地方。第三十四条规定，国家部门依法公布环境信息，公民或法人可以依法去申请环境信息。如何给“环境信息”一个准确定义？从语境上看，应该指的是狭义的环境质量信息。但是环境法应该对广义的环境信息有所反映，还应包括企业主体排放信息等多种类型，因此也就很难限制为“国家部门依法公布环境信息”。关于环境信息的界定和这个市场主体、公众主体，在产生环境信息源和渠道方面，还应该在信息化时代的背景下，进一步明确界定相关信息内容和公开责任。

第九，关于环境问题有一个主要矛盾和次要矛盾的关系悖论，应在本次《环保法》修订中给予界定。比如城市的垃圾处理厂的选址建设就是一个典型问题，如果不处理垃圾，肯定造成很大的环境问题，如果处理，过程中产生的二次污染和环境问题会遭到周边居民的激烈反对，像广东的番禺、北京的阿苏卫等。这部法里提出加强保护环境，既包括一次环境问题，也包括二次污染等问题，其实就是主要矛盾和次要矛盾，或者说矛盾的主要方面、次要方面的问题。如果《环保法》只是泛泛地谈论环境问题，很多的现实问题都没有考虑到。

最后，本次《环保法》修订应该更强化国家层面的统筹管理协调责任。一方面，目前的环境保护工作有大量的需要跨区域、跨领域的协同要求，既有跨区域污染防治，又有各地方试点、各部委试点，都会遇到国家相关的税收、财政等各种各样的政策制约，难以突破。另一方面，现在版本里，环境主管部门跟国务院是一种委托代理关系，这个职责又没有形成在环境这条线上能统筹部门的一个全权代理机制，与其他领域发展管理部门之间成了对立的关系，阻力很大，环保部门的工作要么只能停留在末端治理，被扣上限制发展、制约发展的帽子，现在的《环保法》不能只是站在末端管理的角度。另外，从社会发展阶段上看，改革开放前在城乡格局既定的情况下，环保工作更强调“保护”，如果现在正处在建设发展的阶段，“保护”是不是涵盖了“建设”，现在的环境法体系，对于“环境建设”方面的要求很薄弱，新环境法应该是更能体现生态文明、生态效益、生态质量，兼顾发展和保护的法。

我就抛砖引玉，谈点个人不成熟的想法。

杨朝飞：刚才关于政府责任的意见很重要。关于按区域保护候鸟迁徙生命线的建议很新颖，地区间的分隔保护，的确不可能够实现环境保护目标，在有关法律中应当加以解决。有关河流上下游的关系是一个普遍的问题，刚才谈到邯郸和长治的关系就是属于流域性的环境问题。下游城市要告上游城市，这次污染事故你污染了我，我要提起公益诉讼；上游城市反而却说，你嫌我污染了河水，以后我干脆就不向下游供水了，把所有的水都截流下来，就不会产生污染问题了。如何解决流域性的环境问题，这应该在修改《环保法》中认真研究的。

下面的发言，不一定非要批评现有的这个草案，因为这个草案确实很片面、很不成熟，建议大家可以从建设性的角度提出意见。下面请全球环境研究所执行主任金嘉满发言。

金嘉满：我不是专门研究法律的。前一阵，我们与一群环保志愿者和学者，一块研讨《保护地法》，才更多关注了法律问题。在这个过程中，我们把保护区法，非常仔细地逐条阅读，包括所有的责任、权利界定范围、法律执行的框架、可执行性，有过很多次的碰撞和讨论。为这次会议，我第一次非常仔细地来看环保法。

看完这个法，我自己有一个感觉，觉得有很多界定不是特别清楚，作为一个法律，可以先宏观界定，以后有细则，这是中国习惯的做法。但是，就是宏观界定，我觉得也应该再界定得更清楚一些。有几个界定层面，我觉得应该做。

第一，监督和管理需要界定清楚。我们这个《环境保护法》是什么样的环境需要保护，我觉得这个法要界定其范围，现在的第一、第二条这两条能怎么样协调界定得更清楚一些，让我们知道这部法是要保护什么。

我不是特别同意刚才的意见，就是把建设搁在保护里面来考虑，我们应该从保护大的概念来做，因为它是一部保护法，而不是短期的目标，将来可以完善，但是宏观上还是要立足于环境保护，只是《环境保护法》要界定清管什么。

第二，因为我报的发言主题是监管体制，所以我特意看了一下该法的监管部分，改的地方比前面的要好得多。原来第二章是监督管理在一起的，现在起码把管理和监督分开了，在第二章做了管理，在第五章做的是监督。但是，我觉得作为一部法律，它应该非常清楚地做一些规定，就是环境管理到底管理什么？谁管理？管理的范围？管理的资金？是不是都是一部法律应该能够界定的。这部法律说政府来做管理，后面监督主体又是政府。所以监督和管理成一体了，运动员和裁判员是一个。所以，在法律中对此界定更清楚一些才会好。

在管理的这部分，刚才李伟说管理体系太薄弱了，我觉得比以前还是要好得多。但是，我觉得权利、管理范围和内容，界定得不是特别清楚，而且是不是国家需要有一定的资金给予管理工作一些支持。

在监督的方面，应当有公众参与，我觉得政府做监督，上下级的监督可以，但应该有第三方监督。法律应该规定人人都有享受环境保护的权利。国家应该给予我们保护环境的权利，这样，才有可能在有人损害环境的时候，我们可以利用法律工具进行起诉，要不然这个法律就没有实效性。

再一个，比如说第十一条，都说到国家建立监督网络和监督数据信息系统。这个国家是指谁？是政府部门建立呢，还是谁都可以建立？这个国家应该明确。甚至可以像前面说的，环境保护行政主管部门或者是什么，要不然太笼统了。

还有，我再问一下，哪些数据是应该公开使用的？比如说污染的数据，比如说淮河等河流的污染监控数据，是不是可以公布。如果在法律里界定了人人都有享受保护的权利和可获得环境信息的权利，政府工作受到公众监督，这部法会好很多。

第十一条里说到了，监督数据、监测数据依法公开，依什么法？什么样程度的数据进行公开？

我认为，有关管理权利范围，监督的权利范围，一定分清楚，将来这个法才能执行。因为法律就是要界定什么能做，什么不能做。但是，整个这个法里，界定可能差一点。

另外，在保护区法里，虽然是一个讨论稿，但是它已经添加了处罚内容，但是在这个法里，没有处罚的内容。

杨朝飞：金主任讲了四个界定。界定概念、界定监督和管理，界定监督网络和监督数据信息系统谁来建、管、用，最后界定处罚，很有新意。下面请美国环保协会中国项目负责人张建宇发言。

张建宇：我们一直在从事民间组织工作，从环境保护的角度讲，确实应该加大民间力量的参与，也是符合中央精神的和实际操作的必要。环境是典型的公共产品，应当大家共同保护，如果完全依靠政府，肯定会有疏漏和不足的地方，如果更多让社会力量参与，群策群力，想得会更全面一些，同时拾遗补阙把做得不好的地方共同来做。希望民间组织团结起来形成更大的力量。

我主要谈一点宏观的想法，按照唐所长的要求，我们已提了一个书面意见。

我的一个核心想法，立法的时候肯定得有一个指导思想，从现在的这个法律修订中，它是自己有一个指导思想，但它这个思想不是特别明确，而且由于技术支撑和公众参与得不够，体现得也不是特别好，这是在我国的修订法当中的一个通病。这次修改的草案本身有很多问题，但是修法的过程暴露出来的问题，比如为什么有些部门不同意，为什么这么多意见等，更值得研究。

我觉得有两点体现得特别深刻，第一，对新时代特点，即国家、政府、企业、社会个人在《环保法》当中是一个什么样的关系，没想清楚或没写清楚，这个东西在里面没有体现出来。信息公开、处罚责任、中央地方关系，需要一个指导思想，这是一个前提。如果没考虑清楚，落实到文字上势必有偏差。第二，这部法实际上试图做一个超越部门的立法，试图站在更高的角度来看问题，它试图体现全民参与环保或者各个部门参与环保，试图站在综合部门的角度立法的这样一个指导思想。这个想法我自己觉得是特别好的，试图把各个部门在《环保法》中的作用进行相互制衡的设计或者进行功能的补充或者说吸引调动各部门的积极性。但是因为没有充分的支撑和探讨，这里的表述，有些可能是拍脑袋或者没有经过非常审慎的思考之后把它写出来，自然会引起很多部门的反应。比如，“国务院发展改革部门会同有关部门应当遵循公平、科学、合理原则，研究提出国家重点污染物总量控制约束性指标分配意见”，这个提法需要经过推敲、研究的探讨，说明为什么是由发改委来制定而不是环保部门。总之，一是参与方定位问题，由国家一头独大向国家、社会、企业个人各方面参与过渡，这个精神是好的。二是综合部门的立法，部门间关系处理有些夹生了。

我有一个观点，现在我们确实有一种被捧杀的危险。我们老是在提，比如大家看环境公报里，环境问题恶化的趋势得到扭转，环境质量得到基本改善等，我觉得在这样的过程中，强化环境保护部门的职能是非常重要的环节，我们在整个社会的污染趋势没有得到彻底扭转之前，过多强调综合性的环境治理，包括很多事情都要用生态文明加以统一，弱化环保部门执法权，希望通过软的方式，包括我们提的双赢的方式，不把发展和环境保护两个之间的矛盾暴露的情况下问题就解决了，我觉得还是不行的。还是要有尖锐的矛盾过程，只有通过强化环保部门的处罚权才能解决。

还有一个小点，我们的立法部门缺乏足够的技术支撑，人力和物力的支撑，它可能有一个好的出发点，但是没有足够的技术支撑，不能很好落实到文字上。以后立法中，如果不注意，这个问题还会存在。

具体到《环保法》的修订，我们提交了一个稿子，基本上是处理好四个关系和一个公开，是我们一个基本的态度，供唐所长参考。我们认为，此次修订最为紧迫的是，从“四个关系一个公开”的角度来梳理各种环境管理制度，确立一个清晰的环境管理思路。即，处理好“总量控制与环境质量之间的关系”、“事前审批与全过程管理的关系”、“事后处罚与事前预防的关系”、“碳控制与传统污染物控制之间的关系”，同时积极推动环境信息公开制度。

杨朝飞：建宇谈了改法的指导思想，第一，参与各方要准确定位，政府定位最重要，政府不能包揽所有的环境事务；第二，这部法一定要超越部门利益，当然环境监管也很重要，那种认为淡化环境监管，直接走到生态文明，靠大家自觉保护环境的观点，是不能解决环境问题的；建宇又谈到了四个关系和一个公开，也是有参考价值的。下面请中华环保联合会环境法律中心督查诉讼部部长马勇发言。

马勇：我先专门谈一下公益诉讼，这块在我们新的《环保法》的草案当中是一个空白。在后面的讨论环节再谈我对《环保法》修改的其他建议。

第一大方面，环境公益诉讼的法律依据。

2012年8月，新民事诉讼法里专门加强了公益诉讼的内容：“对污染环境、侵害众多消费者合法权益等损害社会公共利益的行为，法律规定的机关和有关组织可以向人民法院提起诉讼。”这个规定出来之后，对于我们搞环保的人或者搞环境法的人来讲，确实是充满了希望，也充满了期待，但是，也有些困惑。这个实际上也是一个原则性的规定，具体没有可操作性的内容。比如说法律规定的机关，到底是哪些机关，有关组织到底是指哪些组织？怎么去提起这个公益诉讼，这块都没有细化的规定。

我们原本想，在《环境保护法》修改当中，能把公益诉讼加进去，并且得到一个细化的规定，令我们大失所望的是，草案不但没有细化，反而根本没有加进去。在整个《环保法》的修改当中，我们多次向环保部提出一些建议稿，我自己参与起草的文件，向人大法工委至少提了三份报告，最近的报告是以中华环保联合会法律专家委员会的名义提交了意见书，得到高度重视，人大法工委近期将专门做一份简报向委员长报告。

民事诉讼法规定之后，全国人大并没有对环境公益诉讼作出一个立法解释。现在，最高人民法院试图要做一个与司法解释类似的这么一个文件，应该叫一个指导性文件。最初是想做一个环境民事公益诉讼的指导意见，汪劲老师和我也参与了，我们都提了具体的意见。这个建议提出之后，他们估计有所顾虑，后来采取比较稳妥的方法，在 2012 年 12 月 7 日，在人民法院报上面，以论文的形式刊登了这么一篇文章《关于民事公益诉讼的理解与适用》这个作者并不是一个真人，是笔名，实际上是最高法民四庭。

新民事诉讼法的规定比较原则，只是为这项诉讼制度的创立提供了法律依据，而具体的实施规则尚需在司法实践中进一步探索。

一、关于适用范围。新民事诉讼法第 55 条规定民事公益诉讼的适用范围是“污染环境、侵害众多消费者合法权益等损害社会公共利益的行为”。即：污染环境、侵害众多消费者合法权益的行为只有在损害公共利益时，才可基于维护社会公共利益提起公益诉讼。如果针对污染环境、侵害消费者合法权益的行为，直接请求保护个体利益，则不属于本条公益诉讼的范围，而属于一般普通民事诉讼即私益诉讼。公共利益的核心在于公共性，涉及不特定多数人的利益。尽管代表人诉讼涉及众多当事人，但受害人可以确定，诉讼目的是为维护个人利益，故仍然属于私益诉讼。界定了他们所理解的公益诉讼。公共利益的核心在于公共性，涉及不特定多数人的利益。涉及特定多数人利益的可以用集团诉讼的手段，不适用公益诉讼。

二、关于起诉主体的问题，“法律规定的机关和有关组织”。关于其中“法律规定的”限制范围问题，目前有两种不同观点。第一种观点认为“法律规定的”既限制“机关”，又限制“有关组织”；第二种观点认为“法律规定的”仅限制“机关”，而不限制“有关组织”。综合分析有关立法资料和立法工作者的释义可知，立法本意并不强调“有关组织”须由法律规定，而是说明“至于哪些组织适宜提起公益诉讼，可以在制定相关法律时作出进一步明确规定，还可以在司法实践中逐步探索”。他们赞同第二种观点，认为“有关组织”不受“法律规定的”限制，但应当与起诉事项有一定的关联。这对我们社会组织来说是较好的消息。

关于“法律规定的机关”，含义是可以提起公益诉讼的机关，要有明确的法律依据。这个依据不仅要求机关的设立和职能由法律规定，其可以提起公益诉讼的权利也要由法律明确规定。从现行法律看，目前可以提起民事公益诉讼的机关，仅有《中华人民共和国海洋环境保护法》第90条第二款规定的“依照本法规定行使海洋环境监督管理权的部门”。因此，环保部提起公益诉讼是无法可依的。

关于“有关组织”的范围，需要人民法院在司法实践中逐步探索确定。鉴于司法实践经验不足，有关社会组织的技术力量、诉讼能力等情况参差不齐，为保障在维护社会和谐稳定的前提下有序、有效开展公益诉讼，建议人民法院目前原则上先探索受理具备以下条件的有关组织所提起的民事公益诉讼：(1)依法登记成立的非营利性环境保护组织或者消费者协会；(2)按照其章程长期实际专门从事环境保护或者消费者权益保护公益事业；(3)有专职环境保护、消费者权益保护专业技术人员和法律工作人员10人以上；(4)提起的诉讼符合其章程规定的设立宗旨、服务区域、业务范围。如果《中华人民共和国消费者权益保护法》、《中华人民共和国环境保护法》修改后，作出了相关规定，再依照特别的规定受理。应该说他们这些限制条件是很严格的，使很多组织不能提起公益诉讼。

结合我们做过的一个案件来谈谈限制条件。这是我们在2009年的一个案子，是由社会组织提起的第一起公益诉讼，我们与当地的一位居民代表作为共同原告在江苏对一个集装箱公司提起了诉讼。对于中华环保联合会主体资格的认定是这样的："另查明：中华环保联合会，是由国务院批准设立、隶属于环保部管理的一个非营利性社团组织，主要职能是从事全国范围内环境投诉案件调查、代理诉讼、代理投诉人与地方政府协调处理环境案件等。"对我们诉讼资格的认定："中华环保联合会作为非营利性的社团组织，依据国家批准的主要职能，为维护生态环境和周边居民的生活环境有权提起民事公益诉讼。"这个案件是在民诉法修订之前提起的，法院对于中华环保联合会诉讼资格的认定是基于其职能。

高法的这篇文章还提到特别建议，对于以下两类公益诉讼，人民法院不宜受理：一是单纯以诉讼为业的组织提起的民事公益诉讼。因单纯以诉讼为业的组织是接受委托作为诉讼代理人参与诉讼，而不是直接作原告提起诉讼。这是对律师事务所的排除。二是针对破坏海洋生态、海洋水产资源、海洋保护区造成国家重大损失的行为，有关组织提起公益诉讼索赔国家损失的。因为《中华人民共和国海洋环境保护法》第90条第二款已经明确规定："对破坏海洋生态、海洋水产资源、海洋保护区，给国家造成重大损失的，由依照本法规定行使海洋环境监督管理权的部门代表国家对责任者提出损害赔偿要求。"该条款既是赋权条款，也是限定条款，即将海洋生态资源损失索赔主体限定为行使海洋环境监督管理权的部门，排除了有关组织。

第二大方面，环境公益诉讼面临的困难。

一、环境信息公开严重不足。在我们具体做法律援助的过程当中，环境信息公开出现了很多的问题，企业是绝对不会给的，即使我们到环保局要一些环境信息作为我们的起诉依据，也很难很难。结合这个困难，去年，我们尝试着提起了一起信息公开的诉讼："中华环保联合会诉贵州省修文县环保局不履行环境信息公开法定职责案。"背景是我们在当地提起了民事的公益诉讼，为获得关于这个公司的环境信息（这些信息都是由环保局掌握的，它要不给你的，一般情况下你是拿不到的。如果你拿到了这些环境信息，将来在环境诉讼当中，就非常有用），我们申请公开这些环境信息，他们在法定的时间内没有公开，我们请贵阳市环保局督促它公开这个环境信息，结果它在法定的规定时间中，还是没有公开。然后我们提起了环境信息公开诉讼。最终一审中华环保联合会胜诉了，环保局不服，提出上诉。二审开庭前的两天，它承认“环保局向公民、法人及其他组织主动公开政府信息是其义务和责任”自行撤诉。这个案例说明中华环保联合会这么大一个组织，要求环境信息公开都这么困难，普通公民更是难上加难。环境信息公开，对我们开展环境公益诉讼是非常大的一个困难。

二、环境损害鉴定评估问题多。“中华环保联合会诉贵州定扒造纸厂污染南明河案”，在诉讼请求当中，本来想对它排污导致环境损害要求它作出赔偿。但在损害鉴定过程当中，我们就出现了很多的问题。一个是损害鉴定评估，时间比较长，收费又很高；二是评价出来的结论，如果说原告去委托做，将来被告会提出质疑的，说你们提出鉴定的时候我们没在场，我们不同意你们鉴定结果。再做鉴定要法院指定，原被告双方都认可的机构。这个过程漫长，费人费力。后来，我们在这个案件当中，完全没有提损害赔偿，但是我们从中实现了一个突破，就是由法院判定被告承担了我们的诉讼费用包括律师费。

在具体实践过程当中，现在损害评估这块出现的问题非常多，我们有好多老百姓去打官司，并请了损害鉴定评估机构，去对损害因果关系做鉴定，得出的结果是有直接关系。结果企业请的鉴定机构，得出了完全相反的结果，说完全没有关系。到法院这块又推倒重新来，企业就可以做很多的工作。往往，在损害鉴定案件当中，受害当事人确实处于一个非常弱势的地位。

我们现在这个《环保法》草案当中，对这块关注非常不够，应该得到足够的重视。

三、赔偿损失钱款归向不明。最高法的意见是把公益赔偿损失的钱款纳入国库。“目前有争议的问题主要是民事公益诉讼的原告可否请求损害赔偿。从《中华人民共和国海洋环境保护法》第 90 条的规定看，民事公益诉讼的原告是可以请求赔偿损失的。但是，民事公益诉讼的性质决定了原告不能通过诉讼获得私利。原告代表国家提起诉讼，人民法院判决责任人承担赔偿责任的，一并判决原告受领赔款后向国库交纳。原告申请人民法院执行有关生效判决时，人民法院应当要求其提供财政部门指定的收款账户。”现在包括法院系统的很多人不同意这个意见。归国库后资金怎么安排？按照诉讼目的，应当专款专用，但打入当地财政账户可以随意落实，监督成问题。我们提出，能否设立基金，将损害赔偿纳入其中，由多方管理监督。

第三大方面，环境公益诉讼需要更多司法实践。

第一，环保组织应积极开展环境公益诉讼实践；

第二，环保组织应加强自身能力建设；

第三，通过实践形成环境公益诉讼的基本程序。

杨朝飞：刚才马勇结合他们的实践，谈到了公益诉讼的法律依据问题；谈到了公益诉讼的三点困难，即信息公开不足、司法鉴定难、赔偿款项管理不规范的问题；最后提出推动环境公益诉讼，还需要更多的司法实践。下面请中华全国律师协会环境资源与能源专业委员会主任汪劲教授发言。

汪劲：我今天是代表律师的这样一个身份来参加这个会。最近这 10 年，中国的环境律师代理的环境纠纷案件我们做了简单的分析。大概代理政府的不到 1/5，代理被害人的在 2/5～3/5，代理有关企业的大概不到 1/5。也就是说，中国的环境律师在维护被害人的合法环境权益方面的工作做得比代理企业和政府机关的要多一些，问题和困难相对来讲也大一些。所以，从中国的律师角度来看，在《环境保护法》修改的过程当中，如何能够公正、公平地让权利的主体能够实现他们的需求和愿望，这一点或许是一个最重要的方面。

下面，从几个方面说一下。

这部法律要修改，当前有一个很好的动因就是党的十八大报告提出了有关生态文明制度建设的这样一个要求。生态文明制度建设的最高要求就是我们现在说的《环保法》，因为党的十八大报告提出实行最严格的耕地保护和水资源管理制度，还有“五位一体”的布局，要把生态文明融合到其他四个文明当中去，这些如果说把它贯穿到法律当中，应当是《环境保护法》修改的理念和思路，包括制度的构建都应当有所创新。

第一，我个人的看法，从律师的角度来看，《环境保护法》应当在某种程度上是一部法律适用法或者法律适用准据法，我们过去在《环境保护法》历史上，1979 年、1989 年，一直到这次修法，不管是 2011 年 10 月的环保部的修改草案还是后来全国人大的修改草案，我觉得都有一个问题，即我们没有关注它具有法律适用准据法的这样一个意味。法律适用准据法这样一个意味，也就是说这个国家之前颁布的法律和我们这部环保法有冲突的时候，应当适用哪个法？这是一个方面，要明确。刚才，我听到大家都在说不明确，这一点和律师们讨论案件的时候，对于法律的理解也是一致的。

我参加过很多学者的会议，政府的会议，政府似乎对这个问题谈得不多，但是在法院、在组织、在研讨案例的时候，大家都认为我们有很多法律上的专有名词没有给出立法解释，从而导致它的适用不明确或者甚至滥用滥解释。所以，从这个意义上讲，法律适用的准据法中有一个意义，就是要明确这个法律和与这个法律有关的其他法律的关系。

还有一个必须由我们作为一个特别法作出规定的程序规则和实体规则。程序规则和实体规则有很多，包括刚才马勇提到的诉讼上的问题。我个人的看法，民事诉讼方面，民事诉讼法和侵权责任法分别从程序和实体这两个方面规定了一个方向，但是这个方向确实是不明确的。这些不明确，有的是它已经指引到法律上来了，如果我们法律不回应的话，那肯定是法律本身的失职。第二个，没有指引到法律上，但是法律已经面对了这样的问题，比方说环境损害赔偿的问题，比方说如果国家机关代表国家向加害人索赔的程序和方法？2007 年在修改水污染防治法的时候就讨论是否应当引入海洋环保法的规定，现在大家在谈到公益诉讼的时候，不论是哪个方面，都说做得最好的是海洋环保法。即使是这样，我们的环保法实际上也没有把它采纳。所以，有很多特别法应当确立的程序规则和实体规则，从法律适用和准据法的角度来讲，环保法应当有它的定位和意味。

第二，环评等基本制度的问题，是不是都可以放到《环境保护法》里来，把它规定得更加完善一些。至于，未来的其他的单项法，是不是可以不考虑这些制度。每一部法律都在它的总则里，写一堆环保法已经规定的内容，这是法条资源的浪费，这种重复没有意义，它应当放到《环保法》当中去。同时，有几个问题应当解决。比方环评的问题，现在有环评法，还可修改，但是除了环评以外，还有标准制度、规划、许可等，这些重要的制度应当把它写得更细一些。行政机关在执行、适用的时候更明确，同时企业在适用的时候也明确，公众作为第三方也明确。所以，它应作为环境保护基本制度的一个法律。

第三，在公众参与的问题上，应当把公众参与的权利具体化。环评法已经规定了公众环境权益的文字，环保法不光是要规定，要鼓励、支持、创造条件。还应当写明它保护的是公众参与的什么权利，比方说知悉权，政府的信息公开实际上是公众环境权益的对称，我有权利知道，你就应当公布。写明公众的知悉权的范围，建言权的范围和效力（我提出的东西你要有充分考虑）。还有一个救济的权利。当然，《环境保护法》当中不仅仅是公众的权利，包括企业、事业单位、政府管理的权利，以及它们的义务，也应当在这里有一个大的明确。我这里强调的是公众参与的权利，只有把这个权利说清楚了，未来遇到纠纷和争议的时候，这就是我们请求权的依据。

第四，处罚的制度应当创新。最近刚刚完成EDF的一个报告，关于中国的环境违法制裁创新的研究，这个研究做了不到两年的时间，我们也跟环保部政法司官员一起做了调研，去了四个省，拜访了好多部门。昨天看了一篇报道，说中国的反腐不能按照前苏联的模式，我觉得这话说得太好了。现在的公权力制裁制度基本上也是参考了前苏联的制裁模式，这个模式现在都在说要改，但是怎么改，环保法应当率先来实现。我们比较了大陆法系、英美法系国家的环境保护法行政处罚制度，人家都是先罚人，如果说这个行为跟企业有关的话，才实行双罚。我们的做法正好相反，出问题后往往是先罚企业，如果问题很严重的话，才把企业的责任人弄出来，弄出来以后，基本上是要追究刑事责任的。为什么我们国家要罚企业呢？这和前苏联的理念有关，因为以前大家都是公家的人，国家的人，咱们都在为国家做事，出了事以后，应当单位来承担责任。而20世纪80年代改革开放以后，我们的所有制也多元化了，但是我们处罚的理念没有发生改变。

我们老说违法成本低，实际上违法成本高，并不是说要罚企业多少钱，如果我们现在建立一个有机的对人身自由的治安管理处罚和刑法第 338 条的污染环境罪有机衔接的处罚机制的话，我想你不需要提高处罚数额，人家一定会害怕了。比方说我们建企业的环境保护责任制度，它是跟人连在一起了，你这个设施设备的责任人是谁，管理人是谁，如果这个设施设备出了问题的话，首先把这个人拘留多少天，在这个基础上，也不罚你多，罚 1 000 元，这比罚一个企业 10 万元还管用。同时，在这个人身罚的设计基础上。和刑法第 338 条拘役和有期徒刑衔接起来的话，15 天以下的是治安管理处罚，30 天以上的 12 个月以下是拘役，12 个月以上是有期徒刑的方式。这个制度设计是有衔接的。处罚制度创新很重要，有很多群体事件，问题本身是可以解决，由于政府失职、企业肆无忌惮酿成了群体性事件。建议环保部门和最高法、公安部、最高检联合发一个通知，将处罚制度有机组合起来，这样不会使受到刑事处罚的人增加，反而会减少。过去的问题是厉而不严，刑法规定得非常严厉，但是平常对这些行为的制裁并不严格，最后把人家非要推到严重的犯罪的位置上再来抓他。

第五，应该有一个正向的鼓励，采取经济刺激的手段，包括我们现在研究的金融的措施，鼓励的措施，减免税收的措施等方法，我觉得都应当是《环保法》当中要解决的，因为这个法的地位，绝对不是普通的单行法的位置。

最后，未来我们修改法律的时候，多研讨非环保的关联法，我国 200

多部法律当中，有很多部法律有很好的借鉴价值。把有些法律当中好的制度、方法、措施直接引用过来。比方说，当年两罚制度最初见于海关法，比方说《环境保护法》和治安管理处罚的关系，草案写了“违反本法规定，构成违反治安管理行为的，依法给予治安管理处罚”，这条写了等于没写，我们到地方调研了，基本上没用。不如把治安管理处罚法当中的与之相类似的行为摘出来，“下列行为依照治安管理处罚的规定，处罚：1、2、3、4、5……”这里可以采取1984年水污染防治法创立的立法类推的方式方法。

这里面涉及制度创新的问题。既然党的十八大报告提出要建设史上最为严厉的制度，要具有生态文明建设、制度建设，要做顶层设计，那这个顶层设计就应当涵盖这样一些内容，而不是迁就一些过时的理论和方法，和迁就现在触动部门利益或者说单位利益的做法，与此同时，2011年提到社会主义法制体系建设的时候，也提到了立法质量的问题，就是说下一步我们的立法工作是要提高中国法律的立法质量，这些都是和我们高层的声音相一致的。

杨朝飞：刚才，汪教授从环境律师代理案件做了概括性的介绍，结论是律师代理受害人的案件相对多些，当然代理受害人存在很多困难。从律师角度探讨了法律的适用，希望《环保法》要处理好与刑法等法律之间的关系；规定环评等基本制度；公众权利具体化；建议创新处罚制度；发挥法律鼓励正向的激励与鼓励措施。下面有请公众与环境研究中心副主任王晶晶发言。

王晶晶：我个人结合几个环保组织提的一些意见，针对信息公开和公众参与这两个方面做一个简单的阐述。

从长远来看，中国需要一部基本的环保法以明确发展与环境保护之间的关系，同时也能够确定基于公众环境权利这样一个新型的治理体系，在环境的权利当中，最重要的是知情权、参与权和司法救济权，这些是能够保证公众维护自己的权益。

在环境信息公开的方向上，此次的修订当中，提到了环境信息公开，我们觉得是一个亮点。因为在2008年的时候，环保部有环境信息公开办法，为中国环境信息公开奠定了基础，但因为法律位阶较低，在执行的时候也有一些困难。所以，在《环保法》当中，提到环境信息公开办法，我们认为是非常重要的一点。

当然，目前只是简单地提到了环境信息公开，相对而言是没有那么明确。比如说，我们在日常的工作中，在申请一些环境信息的时候，地方环保部门会给我们一个说法，说是商业的机密，涉及企业的一些信息，他们需要保密。但我们所申请的本身又属于行政处罚的信息，属于主动公开的范围。所以，在这个基础上，本应公开又没有公开，以商业机密为借口而不予公开的行为，我们建议应该给予适当的说明或者应该有一个法律的依据。

在公众参与的方向上，我们感到比较失望的是，无论在整个原则的描述还是具体的法律条文的规定上，几乎都没有太多涉及公众参与的部分，尤其是涉及像环评、验收、环境评比、限期治理等都没有提到公众参与的制度规定。所以，在这样的方面上，我们认为这没有体现创新社会的管理和综合开展环境保护的思路。所以，建议在未来修订的时候，能够加上公众参与这方面的一些字样，包括对于发展社会组织的这样一些字样。

刚才汪老师也提到了关于公众参与，权利的具体化，还有具体公众参与是什么样的一种权利，我个人非常认同。

杨朝飞：刚才王晶晶谈到了知情权、参与权和司法救济权三个权；信息公开面临的困难和解决问题的建议；公众参与方面需要制度创新等。下面合影、休息。

杨朝飞：下面请“中外对话”北京办公室副总编辑徐楠发言。

徐楠：我来自媒体，为大家补充一个媒体视角。我觉得刚才汪劲老师提到的几个词也是我本身想跟大家分享的，就是顶层设计和法律位阶的问题。

以前大家对于环保法适用的面以及对这部法律的认知，从行政机关来讲，与环保部门关联度最高，从社会影响来看，是跟污染现象关联性更高。2012 年有变化。从最新的事件来说——严重的灰霾和大范围的空气污染让我们感受到：环境问题不仅仅是某一个部门的问题，不仅仅是某一部分行政职能实现的，也不是可以区分不同地区来分割管理的，一定需要更通盘、更全面的综合机制。

从法律位阶上来讲，我们今天的讨论，更多是把民间组织对这部法律的期待表达出来。《环境保护法》在位阶上、影响层级上是时候应当提升了，昨天，北京市环保局召开新闻通气会，北京市经信委负责人也参与了，说明北京市环保局准备面对媒体时候已经认识到，这个事件已经不是他一家能够应对得了啦，必须有更多的部门、从更全面的角度来看待了。

我们的确有必要、有责任做更多的工作，让社会意识、大众舆论和我们的行政意识，各个方面都能提升对这个问题重要性的理解，从意识上提升它的位阶，从而有助于影响这部法律在法律体系里的位阶。

从奥运会以来，北京还是在净化空气方面采取了很多举措。2008 年的限行政策已经取得了一些成效，北京市还一直在进行天然气替代燃煤，目前比四五年前的情况要好得多，北京几乎把燃煤电厂淘汰出去了，重工业基本上都转移到河北。可是这次重大的灰霾事件里，最大的教训是没有地方能独善其身，原来法规里设计的机制，责任主体大多是“各地的环境主管部门”或“各地的人民政府”，但哪一个地方的人民政府能阻碍空气流通呢？这是现实上已经不能自圆其说的一个问题了。从最近的这些环境事件来看，无论应急功能的加强，还是落实日常主体责任，都需要建立更高层级的会商机制，即便短期内还不能建立类似能源委或者食品安全国家办公室这样层级的协调部门，但是客观上也已经需要成立一个更高层级的会商机制。

另外，从信息公开和公众参与的角度，环境影响评价曾经很大程度上提升了整个城市化和工业化里面的环境管理，但现在的情况是重大项目和经济发展的社会综合环境成本越来越高，这里既包括突发群体事件带来的社会成本，也包括变更对项目本身带来的投资风险成本等，对政府和投资主体来说真金白银的成本在提升。在这个情况下，在环境影响评价基础上，加入更多社会影响评价的因素，是客观需求。我认为将社会影响评价纳入立法视野，非常有必要。

还有一点，在立法修法的过程中，民间确实可以发挥更大的作用。今天的会是特别好的范例，方方面面更多加强对话与沟通，更多让民间在立法中发挥作用，这也是我个人希望呼吁和跟大家探讨的。

杨朝飞：北京市的天然气替代取得了很大的进展，落后的工业转到别的地方了，现在是更大范围的污染又出来了。这次，灰霾污染范围远远超过了伦敦事件，伦敦只是一个城市，而在我国几乎波及半个中国，所以只是单个城市去治理污染是不行的。前段时间，我参加了一个专家会，专家不太同意搞天然气替代，觉得现在工业的热源很多，要把现有的电厂、热电厂、水泥厂、钢铁厂、焦化厂的余热都用起来，就不用再新开发天然气了，天然气应当更多地满足民用和农村。现在各地大量的低温余热没有利用起来，如果把这部分热用起来之后，不需要增加新的热力源，供热是足够的。上次跟赵立建讲，想找一个地方专门研究低温能源。现在天然气供热也有好多问题，锅炉越大，供热范围越广，管网损失也越大；天然气的成本也很高，老百姓又承担不起，国家要为使用天然气给予补贴。实际上把余热、低温都利用起来能解决好多问题。这不是个技术问题，而是一个认识问题和政策问题。

另外，徐楠提到环评的风险管理，这个也是非常重要的。

下面请阿拉善基金会资助项目官员王小颖发言。

王小颖：先介绍一下我们的机构。我们是北京市企业家环保基金会，即阿拉善基金会，这是由中国大概 200 个企业家共同出资成立的非公募基金会，主要是服务、支持民间的环保事业。通过资助的方式，支持他们从污染治理、生态保护、应对气候变化等角度做一些民间参与的事情。我们在环境法律里的参与和实践，时间不太长，而且主要是支持草根机构去做一些事情。

第一部分，先跟大家介绍一下我们所支持过的、看到的这些民间的机构，到底在环境法律里做什么事情，到底是如何利用环境法律的手段促进环境保护的。我们看到几个层面：

一，民间机构在参与促进环境保护的执法，包括促进一些执法的监督，从看到的污染事件，发现的污染点，来做举报，促进环境保护相关执法机构的执法，这个是一个层面的工作。

二，在做一些程序的监督，包括环评、环评监审，发现在已有法律之内有规定要求的，但是有一些相关政府机构或者说相关企业没有按照这些规定来做的，从民间参与的角度提出一些整改的意见和建议。

这两部分，现在有一个整体思路，从某种程度上来促进提升违法成本。现在违法成本从责罚的角度，正如刚才汪劲老师谈到的，罚款额度非常小，导致很多企业肆无忌惮，包括一些政府可能也觉得不作为也不太有所谓，民间参与的对于企业的曝光、举报，一定程度上可以提高社会的违法成本。对政府也有促进作用。

三，民间参与在促进一些司法救济，如针对上面的行为，如果政府没有响应的，提起行政诉讼；服务一些地方受到环境污染伤害的个体的民间私益诉讼；发起一些公益诉讼，例如 2012 年我们支持了自然之友所做的云南铬渣污染公益诉讼。

在 2013 年民诉法的修正之后，我们即有计划支持一批民间的公益诉讼的出现。某种程度上也在为民间机构来撑空间。刚才马勇老师提到几条标准，我们自己很难达到，但是有空间尝试。之前很多人觉得民间的草根机构没有能力提起公益诉讼，没有法律的专业知识，我们现在也在尝试对他们做一些能力上的培养，包括在一些机构里请一些公益律师作为与这个机构挂钩的律师，提高他们的专业能力，还有为整个民间公益机构，我们进行环境专业方面以及法律方面提供一些支持，尝试着在民间机构做公益诉讼的时候，从行业自身的角度提供一些支持。

第二部分，提一些诉求。

一个是赋权，包括公益诉讼里，民间机构的诉讼主体资格的赋权，这是能够让民间机构通过法律手段促进环境保护的基本要素；对于公民的赋权，在环境法律里应该有所体现。像刚才大家所提到的知情权、建言权、救济权之类的。能够给到公民参与促进环境法律有一些空间，希望不出现像刘福堂那样做了一些正面促进政府和企业环境改善的事情，反过来却无法受法律保护的现象。

整个的思路，我们认为对于民间机构也好、个人也好，法律应该给它们一些空间，少一些打压。尤其在地方政府执行的层面，而不在于中央政府的政策制定的层面。但是，这些如何监督，如何管控，在法律里要有所体现。

另外，应该在法律里促进对于政府的监督和责罚。例如，新的空气质量标准出来以后，$PM_{2.5}$是有标准，但是现在，至少这几天是没有达到标准的，一年没有多少天达到标准，但没有相应的惩罚，只有一个标准有什么用呢，这两天讨论空气的时候，觉得是一个值得继续完善的地方。

同时，也要有一个态度，不管是民间机构的参与还是公民的参与，出发点都是对于环境问题的整改或者改善。甚至，如果说民间早参与，民间能够利用法律手段规范参与的话，它就可以减少社会群体性事件，在过去的一年里，基于环境的群体性事件非常突出，如果给民间一些赋权，它可以在法律框架之内利用好它的权利做一些事情的话，这些群体性事件都是有可能减少的。

杨朝飞：过去一谈到阿拉善就会想到沙尘暴的，以为你们只是从事防治荒漠化方面的工作。今天听了发言，才知道你们在环保执法监督，司法救济，能力建设等方面做了大量的工作，刚才提的建议也很好。下面请全国工商联环境服务业商会监事长许国栋发言。

许国栋：先提建言。第一，清晰规定环境的内容和目标。我希望新的法律对现在环境的内容能有科学、清晰的分类和定义。同时，目前在这个法里，提到整个环境目标的时候，用词都是国务院环保主管部门，包括国务院环保主管部门要让这个标准达到环境目标，国务院环境主管部门制定规划，包括国务院相关批准，我觉得这对于党的十八大的政策，还是中华民族的生存需要，是远远不对的。我认为我们的环境目标和环境的大规划，应该在这个法里明确指出，到什么时候去做中长期的规划，比如要具体到2020年要做中国的百年环境规划、环境目标，中长期规划，并且要经人大批准，由人大确定。

第二个建言，这个法里应该非常清楚地规定，在环境保护方面中央政府的责任。而且我认为基本上在这个法里，不应该再用国务院环保主管部门这个词，就是中央政府的责任，这个责任可能包括，比如说，环境具体依照这个法要求的相关法规的制定、仲裁的责任、环境的目标区域划分的责任、按照资源禀赋来做环境区域划分的责任（一些只能够按照环境要素去划分环境，不是按照行政要素划分环境的这种责任）、对地方政府的督导的责任，还有资金平衡上的责任。而且就几条，不可能弄个十几条，核心的就这么五六条，这个职责再由我们中央政府具体说，比如说这条环保部来做，那条发改委来做等。

第三个建言，是应该清楚规定地方政府的责任。我国的行政划分是清晰的，不能含糊地说地方各级政府，直接说这个责任一共分几级，哪一级应该负担什么责任，包括它的环境责任、管理责任，应该负担的生态补偿的责任，而且这种补偿的东西应该跟当地政府的财政联系起来，逐步摆脱跟首长挂钩，要跟地方的生存和发展根本性地挂起钩来，谁去都这样，挣10亿，就得把3亿给别人，自然会形成经济和社会的良性生态。

第四个建言，是关于污染者责任和生产者责任。应该对我们传统说的污染者，它的污染性质和处罚以及处罚方式有完全重新的界定。这方面汪老师说得已经非常好了。因为我们对污染的性质和处罚的颠倒，造成了大量的赤裸裸的掠夺和肆无忌惮的伤害，人身伤害有责任，倒一桶硫酸没责任，怎么能这样呢？对于相关联责任，现在环境问题不是简单的污染者的三个字能说清楚的，得有定义，企业的问题、个人的问题、家庭生活的问题，包括垃圾有些东西，从性质上要说清楚。对于产品生产的责任，在《环保法》里，应该给出我们国家准备上这个责任的时间，比如我就告诉大家2020年开始，我要上这个产品责任了，得提前告诉大家。

第五个建言，就中国的情况，对于环境保护的资金运用和资金筹措上，要有专门的原则，不能哪里出事往哪里砸，全国得有一个说法，现在发改委已经在这么做，但却是人治。这个资金应该有个原则性说法，比如说青海，为国家承担了生态责任，就要给它钱，比如说新疆，我们拿了人家的资源，应该给钱，我们从法律上把原则说清楚，让全国人民都清楚。

最后，我还是想评价一下这个法（草案）。

看到这个法（草案）我觉得相当失望，我认为这个法做得相当糟糕，充斥了部门意识、短期意识，含糊不清的新词都在上面，如果立法是这样的水平，这个国家怎么治理？总的认为很糟糕，我认为不是修法的问题，应该完全重新起草，应该换人、换视野，应该给足够的技术支持，重新起草。草案还不如原来的法，原来的法很浅，但站在国家和长远、大局立场看问题，草案则体现了这20年来部门分割的加剧。

杨朝飞：刚才许总谈了一下对环保的概念要有一个明确的界定；目标、规划应该由全国人大来定；规定中央政府的责任、地方政府的责任，对污染者的责任，对企业、个人、生产者、消费者（垃圾）的责任；对资金的运用和筹措，要有一定的规定。这些建言都不错。下面请环境保护部政策法规司别涛副司长发言。

别涛：对于凝聚社会共识，提高立法质量，改善公众参与的方式，这是一个探索。环保部把对草案的工作意见公开之后，法制报有一个评论，说这本身是公众参与立法的积极探索。所以，我觉得我们这个会是正当参与国家立法，高度赞赏。我谈两点：

第一，为什么需要修改《环境保护法》？需要什么样的《环境保护法》？

环保法，到今天已经接近30年，应该说我们已经形成了一个法律体系，不要否认。我想在环保领域，它自成一个体系，大一点说，环保法里，包括污染、自然、生态、资源保护，今天即使在污染控制的领域里，我认为也相对形成了相对完整的框架，虽然缺土壤、化学品，但主要污染要素是有的。在这个法律体系形成的前提下，今天再来分析环保法，1979年《环境保护法（试行）》出来，当时把这个作为环保法领域的基本法，专项法逐步到位，从水法、大气法，经过两三次修改，这些专项法不断修改，并且逐步在趋于完善，特别是2004年的固体法修改，2007年、2008年水法的修改，这些专项法的修订，应该说在逐步完善，放射性污染法的出台，作为单项法制定新法又是比较好的。所以，今天我们回过头来看《环境保护法》，它是空心化，被搁置，基本上可用、可不用。到了今天，讨论环保法修改又有了新的意义。

汪光焘主任做的那个草案，可以说已经成为过去式，他帮助我们统一了一个认识，就是那个稿子是不行的。要重新审议、审视这个《环保法》。2010年初人大环资委委托修订的时候是环保部推动的，中间经过2011年、2012年，环保部报了一个稿子，环资委形成了一个稿子，人大审议，公开之后大家都说不行。隔了两年之后，今天再看为什么修改，我觉得有助于我们进一步统一认识。

基本判断是，专项法方面，现存的我们可以逐步修改，缺位的我们可以有重点的来修正。党的十八大报告也说要抓紧重点领域的立法，我们看准了几个重点领域，土壤、化学品还有核安全的问题。在污染控制的领域里，这些主要的环境要素都有法律了。我们有大气法还再改，我们有些思路，因为一些工作重点的安排，推进的进度比较慢，我相信这一场大雾，一定会推动，这次在全国人大、法制办等一定都会有新的安排。然而，环保法这个基本法，基础性的法律，总觉得挺受约束的，它的内容实在是太过时了，现在我们真正缺的是通过单项法解决不了的问题。

分析现在《环保法》的现状及其改进的方向。基本结论是，《环保法》

应该是解决专项法解决不了的问题、不应该在单项法解决的问题、如果在单项法写会带来单项法之间冲突、不一致的问题。比如，海洋环保法有公益诉讼，大气、水、固体、放射性污染等为什么没有？这说明在单项法做单项突破时，会带来平等领域里面的不平衡的问题，因为这些问题是带有共性的问题，应该在综合性的法律来解决。杨总带我们做的一个措施就是要把环保法定位在环保领域里的基础性、综合性的法律。

为什么修改？怎么样改？通过单项法我们制定、修订，都不能解决的公共性的问题，这就是留给《环保法》要解决的问题。这次会议说的九个议题，我认为都是综合性的问题。

第二，就环保法修改的五个重点问题谈个人想法。

一是政府的责任，现在党的十八大报告提出来，最近有两三个问题值得我们借鉴。党的十八大报告提到国家实行最严格的耕地保护制度和水资源管理制度。最严格的耕地保护制度，1997 年中共中央国务院发了关于耕地保护的规定，2004 年国务院再次发了耕地保护制度，里面提了一些措施，刚才检索了一下，大部分没有落实，只有一条“完善国家土地督察制度，设立土地总督察”做到了，但是滥占耕地仍然没有得到控制。2011 年初中央的水利工作会议，2013 年初发了国务院的水利保护决定，最近国务院批准国办发的最严格的水资源保护制度的考核办法，我也查了一下有一些考核的措施。发现，政府的责任还是缺机制的设计。

我们查了宪法，地方组织法，查了人大常委会的监督法，也查了安全生产法底下考核的一些机制。当时设计了一些东西，觉得政府要定规划，规划要公开讨论，要经过人大批准，这些考核要有五年为期，要有年度计划，中期评估，公众参与，对地方政府的环境质量的改善要有规划的目标。政府责任大家来帮着共同来设计，从宪法组织法上设计，人大跟政府的关系，还有我们可以设计审计、监察这两个机制，国家审计署对环保的审计是很严的，不仅仅是审计资金的使用，还要考虑绩效，规划是不是执行了，再包括监察，像山西一出事，省监察厅，最高检察院，人大的监督、审计的专项监督和监察的监督，这些机制对于监督政府方面，大家可以帮着我们设计。包括人大常委会和人大对政府的监督，例子太少了，如地方的环境问题很突出，人大把这个问题交给政府办，要求政府办了以后给我报告，政府报告的时候，人大不同意，不批准，不通过，对政府具有很有力的约束。这是体制之内宪法规定的政府监督机制，应当更多地引入。我觉得在这个过程中，人大执行的时候应当更多地让一些公众、专业组织、专业人士参与。

二是关于公众参与。不要让体制内的人感到挑战和威胁。汪主任对信息的公开是不反对的，但是对公益诉讼，他是反对的。怕威胁到党的执政地位，担心产生连锁反应。所以，我们设计的这一类问题的时候，也要换位思考。法工委的工作人员也是比较开明的，但是在其位，设计的制度威胁政府统治，就会被问责。我们在设计的时候，要可行，又要不给体制带来威胁和不安全。我们希望维持大体制，改革是渐进的。

公众参与中，大家谈到了信息公开。我认为信息公开可以提，但是还可以设计一些机制，仅仅满足于信息公开的话，会有局限性。大家知道国务院有一个信息公开的条例，国办也有实施的意见，各部委都有信息公开的目录范围程序，这方面更多是执行和完善的问题，大家还可以在公众监督的机制方面更多设计一些，不要仅盯住信息的一个方面。

党的十八大报告里说要民主、要法制，包括社会多元化、多渠道的参与，引导公众有序地参与的机制，绝不仅仅是在信息公开，包括像环评这些决策，甚至我说的规划，对于计划环境质量绩效的评估等，都呼吁公众有建言权、参与权，还应该有一些超越信息之外的机制设计。

三是企业的责任，这一点大家也是有共识的。我们水、大气、固体、放射性物质的具体要求，大多数都是针对企业的。环保法要设计的企业的责任也应该是超越专项法的。例如，生产责任延伸、供应链的问题、社会责任的问题、企业要开放环境信息以及接受公众的考察等，它是要超越那些专项法的具体要求，规定一些最基本的、共性的义务，责任的延伸，后续的工作等。

四是法律衔接的问题，比较专业，法律专家可以更多地思考一些。衔接的问题主要是法律的定位问题，也就是《环保法》为什么要改的问题。汪主任认为这个法应该说专项法不适合他说的，而且规定为专项法今后进一步的改进和修改，提供一定的空间，解决法律衔接的问题。

五是我个人更感兴趣的法律责任部分的问题。行政责任，刚才汪劲老师说了，罚企业罚得再多不如拘留责任人一个星期、十天、半个月震慑大，行政责任包括两罚制、按日计罚等；民事赔偿范围扩大的问题，还有公益诉讼的基本问题，没有哪一个法比环保法更适合规定公益诉讼的了；刑事处罚和治安处罚的问题，可以在这个法律里列举它的主要情形，把它可能适用于那个刑罚和治安处罚的情形列举出来，指明适用刑罚或治安处罚。

杨朝飞：别涛司长回顾了环保法修改的历程，对《环保法》给予了恰当的评价，在这个基础上，提出了两个问题，一是改法以来，一直在问为什么要改这个法；二是如何改和改什么的问题。在改什么的问题上，讲了很多非常不错的意见，一个是政府的责任，第二个是公众的参与，第三个是企业的责任，第四个是法律衔接，最后是法律责任，当然，也还涉及其他很多问题。别涛司长具体分管改法工作，他的好多思想在下一步改法中是要体现出来的，大家的建议他也听取了，将来我们把两个会议的材料整理完之后，专门送法规司参考。他的发言表达了环保部政策法律司对修改环保法的一些重要看法。

下面请汉德环境观察研究所环境法研究中心主管王社坤发言。

王社坤：关于《环保法》修改里的环境权益的问题，我想谈三个层次。

第一层，理念上，环境权应该是人的与生俱来的自然的天赋的权益，这种权利我们过去一直在享有，由于环境污染的加剧，生态环境的破坏严重之后，现在好像变得没有了，于是产生了一种权利的意识，认为环境权是人类生存的一种应有的权利。

第二层，在法治社会，必须把应有的权利变成法定的权利。如何实现这种法定的权利，这次《环保法》的修改提供了很好的契机。环境权入宪、入法，非常必要，而且时机非常好。原因有三：第一，从现在的环境保护实践来看，像汪劲、王曦、蔡守秋老师等都谈过一个观点，其实环境方面的法律关系是一个三角关系：政府、企业、公众。政府代表公共利益维护者，要行使环保的监管职能，企业在经济生产过程里，获得经济收益的同时，有副产品——污染、生态破坏，作为应有权利的享有者，在这样的三角关系里，公众这一环是最弱的。我们想象的平衡理想状态，实际是不平衡的。如何加强这种平衡呢？重新打造平衡的法律关系，赋予公众环境权是非常好的方法。第二，从环境权自身的研究来看，我们会看到以前的理论研究上有很多的争论，就我个人的理解，什么是环境权？它是共享的，而不是独占的，是通过个人权利的行使去维护公共利益的一种途径。我们以前老是觉得公共利益只能有公共权，不能有个人权，这可能有误区，通过个人权利的行使同样可以实现对公共利益的保护。因此，环境权入法是非常必要的。第三，环境权入宪入法也是有例可循的，现在有 60 多个国家已通过宪法或环保法明确规定公民享有良好环境的权利；就中国而言，这种条款也有，在法律层面，环评法中有公众环境权益，但是并没有进行解释，在相应的行政法规和地方性的环保条例里，大概有 14 部左右，里面明确说了，公民享有在良好环境中生活的权利。所以，这是有先例可循的。当然这种必要性还有很好的历史机遇。我们现在的生态文明建设、社会管理创新，这两大政府管理的执政方针、策略，其实都和环境权利是相互呼应的，赋予公民环境权是促进生态文明建设、践行社会管理创新的一种非常好的措施。

第三层，由法定权利变成实有的权利，在生活中可以享受到。如何把法定权利变成实有的权利？结合《环保法》的修改，有两点非常重要：一是公益诉讼。（1）和民事诉讼法的修改相结合，通过建立环境权的救济的途径，尤其是司法的救济途径。在公益诉讼方面，我更倾向于把公益诉讼解释为环境权诉讼，为了维护环境权，以环境权受到侵害为由去提起诉讼，民事诉讼法解决了一方面的问题，即针对从事环境污染或者破坏行为的企业、个人。（2）另外一个非常重要的问题，应该是针对行政机关的。刚才讲的三角关系，政府、企业、公众，公众对企业、政府都是有某种权利存在的，对企业来说不得从事污染、破坏环境的行为，对政府来说要依法履行职责，没有履行职责的话，作为环境权的所有者，可以提起行政诉讼，通过行政公益诉讼的方式来实现环境权保障。二是在环境权实现的过程里，要发挥民间环保组织的作用。刚才谈到政府、企业、公众的三角关系里，公众属于比较弱的一环，一方面公众在采取维权行为的过程中，没有明确的权利依据，另一方面就是公众的力量也比较弱小。但是无论是在经济实力和专业技术方面，社会组织相对于散在的公众来说，都是非常强大的。

跟《环保法》相关的，我有一点不成熟的想法。关于环境权我有两个具体的法条的建议：

第一，能不能在总则的部分，将《环保法》第六条“任何单位和个人都有保护环境的义务，并有权对污染和破坏环境的单位和个人进行检举和控告”，修改成第一款公民享有在良好环境中生活的权利，这是赋权条法，第二、第三款是政府和企业相对于环境权的义务，第二款可以说各级人民政府对本辖区的环境质量负责，依法采取措施维护环境权，第三款任何单位和个人，不得违反国家环境保护规定，从事污染或者破坏环境的行为。

第二，在法律责任部分，法彦云“无救济即无权利”，应该给予侵害环境权的行为，赋予救济途径。比如，可以这样规定：对于污染或者破坏环境的行为，公民或者环保组织有权向行政机关举报，接到举报后，应该在特定时间，如60天之内反馈处理结果，如果行政机关接到举报之后特定时期内，没有采取措施，公民可以委托或者授权环保组织，向人民法院提起诉讼，请求停止这种污染或者破坏环境的行为。最后是针对行政机关的。规定在负有环境保护管理职权的行政机关，没有依法履行环保职责的时候，公民或者环保组织可以向法院提起诉讼，请求行政机关依法履行职责。

杨朝飞：环境权利是人与生俱来的一种权利。我最近看了一篇文章，跟你讲的差不多，认为农耕社会强调人的权利更多的是土地权；工业社会强调人的权利更多的是产权，产权包括对实物财富的产权和对知识财富的产权；生态文明社会强调人的权利更多的是环境权。长期以来的经济发展，已经解决了人们的土地权和产权问题，但是由于人们忽视了工业化、城市化和农业现代化带来的环境退化的后果，使人与生俱来的环境权在不知不觉之中丢失了。而生态文明社会就是要维护和回归人们合情、合理、合法的环境权益。

王社坤发言提出了回归人们环境权的步骤，第一要入宪入法，使之成为一种受法律保护的法定权利。第二要把法定的权利变成一种实体的权利，即权利的实现。第三要在实现实体权利的时候，充分发挥 NGO 的作用，因为 NGO 组织比个人要有更多的力量或能力。最后还对在总则、法律责任中如何写入环境权，提了一些具体的修改建议。

会议规定发言已经结束，下面是自由讨论。

别涛：建议王社坤，可不可以把公民的环境领域的结社权研究一下，参考《消费者权益保护法》。公益组织是怎么出来的？因为公民个人的能力是有限的，所以一定要有结社，要能有合法的组织，然后依法维护自己的权益，这个是有延伸的，建议你参考一下公众有结社的、有法律地位的几部法律，看看可不可以借鉴。

胡勘平：刚才提到了从农耕文明、工业文明到生态文明的权利意识，给了我很大的启发。我们生态文明研促会也在思考如何在生态文明入宪的问题上发挥一些作用。有一个问题，关于环境权入宪入法，在法学界有没有争议？有没有人持有不同意见？

王社坤：肯定是有，从研究层面来看，环境权本身一直是有争议的。比如环境权主体、内容都有争议。但核心的内容没有争议，拥有了环境权之后，都有免于环境污染和破坏的权利，即防御的权利，这点是形成共识的。

高胜达：我结合自己的想法，提一提，我看了之后和大家有一些共通的感知。

第一个要在时代性上面有所体现。我们可以从国外的或者其他的理解上，我们传统意义上的环境保护，一个是指前端的，比如清洁生产，要保证大家要有这种意识，包括垃圾分类等；进入到中间的阶段，就是叫保护或者直接处理的过程，到最后不要到大气，包括我们的水体、土壤，进行危害，改革开放几十年来，我们的大量努力基本上做的是这项工作；现在，中国的环境经过这30年高速发展，已经进入到环境遭受了极大的破坏，就是说环境的负债率非常高。这里面我的理解，大家提起灰霾事件都很痛苦，尽管我们之前做了大量的预防工作，包括排放过程中的监测、治理，一旦形成灰霾了，我们想修复它，非常难。这个说明什么？以前我们比较关注保护，但是实际上保护我们也没有做好，做到完全很好，但是现在已经发现，在没有做好保护的基础上，修复的问题已经接踵而至，修复的问题已经摆在我们政府的面前，而且像大气这样的修复是非常难的，包括水体的修复，涉及控源的问题，很难。还有，刚才提到的土壤、地下水，这些问题都进入到我们的视野。包括现在国务院、中央提出来生态文明建设，新型城镇化，我们看国外高速城镇化的过程中，美国从百分之五十几到七十几，完成城镇化的过程中，它的污染问题、环境问题、突发事件是高发期。像日本，也是这样的，城镇化率跟中国的指标对比，你会发现很有意思，包括它的立法的跟进状态。所以我想提，在这个问题上，以前比较关注的是第一、第二段，现在这个环保法里，至少我没有看到太多的对修复的问题提出来，给予说法。虽然，我们要考虑我们的政治、经济、文化，包括人文理解，对于修复的认知。但是至少，要把修复这个问题有所关注，甚至要解决它，至少把它提到保护、治理、修复，在这三个阶段当中，提到比较高的位置。

第二，政策的连续性和关联性也是非常重要的。以前制定的法要修订，还有我们修改的法律之间的衔接，特别是现在我们还有些规划，重金属的规划，地下水的使用规划，还有现在正在起草的土壤环境的保护法，作为环境法来说，有些事是交给专项法去做，但是《环境保护法》当中，应该就这个问题提出来，包括怎么保护这些内容，同时要给它指明一个方向，这个是应该有所涉猎的。

第三，责任问题，实际上在大气、水体方面的责任确实很难界定，包括大尺度的责任，包括最后修复的状态，包括它的责任是多少。但是土壤和地下水是非常清晰的，国外经验可以看到，是跑不了的。实际上这里应该建立一个责任机制，谁污染谁治理。特别像在国外，像美国发展之后，它的土壤、地下水，包括对环境这块的修复，实际上占了整个环境工作当中非常大的份额。所以，从未来看，我国的经济转型，包括第三产业转型，可能有些中西部，甚至有些产业向东南亚转移，这个里面对责任的追溯，特别是对土壤、地下水，应该有所重点地涉猎。

责任的问题实际上是调节经济的一种手段，让谁来负责，这个责要负到什么程度，这是一个经济手段。另外，实际上责任本身来说，也分很多种，我们要明确，不仅仅是污染者，可能我们的一些连带责任，包括运输者、储存者、贷款人等，一系列相关人都要请他来沟通一下责任的问题。特别在土壤、地下水，如果针对责任的问题加以强制性，在法里有所强制，将来专项法可依做专项的清理，清洁生产的环节不能用胡萝卜，更重要的是用大棒敲它，让它知道清洁生产不是用来奖励你的，而是对你违规造成生态危害进行追究，这是我们整个社会大家的一个意识或者经济调整的一种手段。从国外的经验来看，实际上这种立法大力的出台，除了消除污染的问题，实际上是改变了这个人，包括公众，包括政府，也包括污染企业的行为方式和思考的方式。

还包括规划当中，我们在做地区规划的时候，大区域的尺度，还是应该先要结合现有的环境污染的状况，这个应该有所考虑。

马勇：首先，对环境的概念，只有在《环境保护法》当中明确，大气污染防治法等都是单项的法律，不可能囊括所有的因素。

第二，对环境权的规定，水污染防治法或者大气污染防治法只能对单项的作出规定。

第三，环境保护的基本制度的规定还是要在《环境保护法》当中体现。

咱们修正的《环境保护法》要能够实现和司法的结合，1979 年、1989 年的《环境保护法》绝大部分是行政的内容。一方面通过行政处罚，或者咱们现在做得比较好的企业违法处罚的制度，这也是非常有效的。另外，司法保护这块，在《环境保护法》里要有很好的加强，最好的就是民事诉讼和公益诉讼、私益诉讼。为什么现在企业产生了污染之后，对它影响不是很大，因为它可以对你直接损害的公众进行赔偿，那么这个赔偿如果是作为调解的话，比如你提 100 万元的损失请求，最终就是十几万元，如果去做诉讼的话，你的举证责任是非常沉重的，打赢这个官司是很难的。像我们现有的草案当中，公益诉讼没有加进来，企业对环境造成了损害是完全没有任何代价的。所以，它这个违法成本是相当低的，公益诉讼如果引入到《环境保护法》当中，是非常好的。

《环境保护法》不光能实现行政方面的内容，更多的是，要在司法方面的内容加强。

《环境保护法》的修改，从政府这块来讲，要让政府真正履行它的责任。现在绝大部分环保的责任，都是地方政府失职。一方面你要对自己产生的污染进行治理，由于你造成了损害，你要承担修复的责任。对社会组织和公众来讲，一定要让公众和社会组织活跃起来，因为环保确实是一个全民参与的事。

杨朝飞：先谈一下我个人的看法，然后对会议做一下简单的小结。

近年来的污染事件发生后，民众和媒体的反应越来越认真、越来越强烈了，他们一是质问不负责任的污染企业，二是质问崇尚 GDP 的政府官员，三是要求严格追究责任。我在思考一个问题？关于严厉追究责任的问题，我们喊了那么多年，又处理了那么多的人，但是污染事故和环境事件并没有减少，反而与日俱增。所有的污染事故和环境事件的发生过程、原因、形式、结果都大体相同，实际上我们每时每刻都在复制一个相同的污染事件。山西有事故，广西有事故，黑龙江、吉林有事故，无数个事故、事件的损失越来越大，影响越来越负面。但是所有这些事故、事件其实都很简单。事故发生之前企业肆意偷排、漏排，事故发生之后不惜花大钱消灾，这些钱要比事前预防要多得多；各级政府也是如此，事故发生之前，都在大力招商引资，都是要快速发展经济，都是在走一个牺牲环境发展经济的道路，事故发生之后又不惜血本大把大把地拿着财政资金去清除污染。其目的非常简单，前期就是要通过发展 GDP 为自己升官铺垫；事故出来之后，拿老百姓、纳税人的钱，不惜财力地清污，是为个人消灾保官。无论是群体性事件还是污染事故，都在不停地重复着过去的往事，复制几乎相同的事情。近年来，每一次事故都要处理一大批的人，被处理的人是前赴后继，一个接一个，几年下来，各行各业被行政处分和法律处罚的干部职工人数要比战争时期牺牲的人数也不少了，而受到感情冲击的家人数量更多。我们每一次处理的都是在前线工作的一个一个的个人，但是有谁去追究在事件产生背后的机制、体制问题呢？如果我们不下决心改变产生这些问题的机制和体制问题，老是满足于处理个别人，我们就会陷入一个没完没了的恶性循环，其结果只会越来越严重。因此我们必须要找到切实可行的办法，从根本上改变产生问题的机制和体制，这就是《环保法》最应该解决的问题。

如何处理经济发展和环境保护的关系非常重要。发达国家在处理经济和环保关系的时候，就是规范政府行为。只有把政府行为规范了，环保和经济发展的关系才能真正走向和谐。在此基础上再采取其他的措施，才能使现行的恶性循环恢复到环境保护的良性循环，恢复社会的正常秩序。如果这个问题不解决好，法律越严厉，被处罚的人就越多，到那时财政就越要拿出更多的钱去兴建劳改所、监狱。这就是我现在思考的问题。

我们的法虽然不严，但是这些年处理的人已经不少了。我们靠处理这些人，能不能改善环境质量呢？显然是不能的。核心的问题、根本的问题，就是要通过规范政府行为，来解决环保和经济的协调发展问题。只有这样才能使被处理的人越来越少，环境问题也才能得到改善。如果在修改《环保法》时解决好这个问题，就是一个很大的进步。当然我并不是说《环保法》对违法行为的处罚太严厉了。

这次的会开得挺好。下一步工作：一是整理录音记录；二是印发与会者对发言内容进行修改和认可；三是在此基础上，写一个建议。建议的目的，是送给环保部政法司参考。如果有可能，我们也会向全国人大或是国务院报一些建议，争取纳入国务院的年度立法计划，纳入全国人大的五年立法规划。这次《环保法》的立法，是一次公开的立法，是社会广泛参与的立法，不是过去的那种闭门立法，只是专家参加立法、部门参加立法，公务员参加立法。这是立法方式的创新，是环境信息公开的具体体现。总体来讲今天的会议开得非常好，对与会者，对会议工作人员，对会议的主办方表示感谢。

谢谢大家！

《环境保护法》修改思路相关论文

我国环境法律制度和环境保护若干问题[①]

杨朝飞[②]

20 世纪 80 年代，国家提出环境保护是基本国策，90 年代大力实施可持续发展战略。进入 21 世纪，党和国家提出树立和落实科学发展观，加快转变经济发展方式，建设生态文明，推动我国环境保护从认识到实践发生了重要变化。

一、我国环境立法进展

1. 环境立法起步较早。我国早在改革开放之初，就将环境立法纳入议事议程。1979 年，全国人大常委会通过了《环境保护法（试行）》。1982 年宪法作出“国家保护和改善生活环境和生态环境，防治污染和其他公害”的规定。有关水污染防治、大气污染防治、海洋环保等法律也于 20 世纪 80 年代初相继问世。同国内其他部门立法相比，环境立法起步较早。

2. 环境法律框架基本形成。截至目前，全国人大常委会制定了环境保护法律 10 件、资源保护法律 20 件。此外，刑法、侵权责任法设立专门章节，分别规定了“破坏环境资源保护罪”和“环境污染责任”。国务院颁布了环保行政法规 25 件。地方人大和政府制定了地方性环保法规和规章 700 余件，国务院有关部门制定环保规章数百件，其中环保部的部门规章 69 件。国家还制定了 1 000 余项环境标准。全国人大常委会和国务院批准和签署了《生物

① 本文原刊于《中国环境报》第 3 版，2012 年 11 月 5 日。本文为作者于 2012 年 10 月 26 日在第十一届全国人民代表大会常务委员会第二十九次会议闭幕式后举办的专题讲座的讲稿，吴邦国同志主持了专题讲座。
② 杨朝飞，时任环境保护部核安全总工程师。

多样性公约》等多边国际环境条约50余件。最高人民法院和最高人民检察院还分别作出了关于惩治环境犯罪法律适用的司法解释。

3．环境保护主要领域基本有法可依。我国环境法律制度框架已经基本形成，各环境要素监管主要领域已得到基本覆盖。在综合立法方面，制定了环境保护法、环境影响评价法、清洁生产促进法、循环经济促进法等；在污染防治领域，制定了海洋环境保护法、水污染防治法、大气污染防治法、固体废物污染防治法、噪声污染防治法等；在生态保护领域，制定了防沙治沙法、野生动物保护法、水土保持法、自然保护区条例等；在核与辐射安全领域，制定了放射性污染防治法等。

4．环境保护主要法律制度基本建立。环境法律制度按其性质，可以分为事前预防、行为管制和事后救济三大类。一是事前预防类，主要是指为避免经济发展产生环境危害而设置的制度，是预防原则在环境立法中的具体体现和适用，主要有环境规划制度、环境标准制度、环境影响评价制度、“三同时”制度等；二是行为管制类，主要是指监督排污单位和个人环境行为的制度，其目的在于为环境监管提供可操作的执法手段和依据，包括排污申报登记制度、排污收费制度、排污许可制度、总量控制制度等；三是事后救济类，主要是指对污染行为及其后果进行处理处置的制度，其目的是防止损害扩大、分清责任和迅速救济被害方，包括限期治理制度、污染事故应急制度、违法企业挂牌督办制度、法律救济制度等。同时，在生态保护方面，还建立了生态功能区划制度、自然保护区评审与监管制度、自然资源有偿使用制度、自然资源许可制度等。

5．环境保护行政许可门类较为齐全。根据国家法律、法规和国务院决定，各级环保部门实施了37项行政许可，涉及对项目建设环境管理，放射性同位素和射线装置监管，民用核设施、民用核安全设备监管等的审批，以及排放污染物许可、处置危险废物资质许可及其他特殊环保业务资质许可等，覆盖了环保行政管理的主要领域。

6．环境法律制度与环境行政许可发挥了重要作用。在实施环境影响评价制度方面，“十一五”期间环保部对涉及“两高一资”的822个项目环评作出不予受理、不予审批或暂缓审批等决定，涉及投资近3.2万亿元；在实施“三同时”制度方面，2010年我国建设项目“三同时”执行率达到98%，完成有关验收项目环保投资2 000多亿元，带动了我国环保治理水平的整体提升。在实施排污收费制度方面，2011年全国排污收费突破200亿元，从1978年至今累计收费达2 042.3亿元，为环保事业发展提供了专项资金。在实施核安全监管制度方面，批准了12个核电项目、26台核电机组，装机容量2 655兆瓦，为核电健康发展提供了安全保障。

多年来，全国人大及其常委会高度重视环境立法工作，每年办理大量的环保议案，并组织指导有关部门办理人大代表建议，听取政府的环保工作汇报，开展多次立法调研和执法检查，推进环境立法，督促落实各项环境法律法规，有力地推动了我国的环境法制建设。

二、我国环境问题及成因分析

（一）我国当前面临的主要环境问题

我国环保事业起步于20世纪70年代。近40年来，围绕水体、大气、噪声、土壤与固体废物、生态、核与辐射等领域，开展了持续深入的环境保护和生态建设，环保工作取得积极进展。“十一五”期间，在能源消费和国民经济年均分别增长6.6%和11.2%的情况下，二氧化硫、化学需氧量排放量分别下降14.29%和12.45%，超额完成减排任务。全国地表水国控断面水质优于Ⅲ类的比重提高了14.6%，全国城市空气二氧化硫平均浓度下降26.3%。尽管我国环保事业取得了长足进步，但是环境恶化的趋势尚未根本遏制。当前我国主要面临八大突出的环境问题。

1．水体污染依然严重。

全国部分地表水水质污染较重，湖泊（水库）富营养化问题十分突出。2011年，在国家水系监测的469个国控断面中，劣Ⅴ类水质占比达13.7%，基本丧失水体功能，50%以上的湖泊（水库）出现了富营养化。水体纳污大大超过环境承载力。2011 年，我国废水中化学需氧量（COD）排放总量为 2 499.9 万吨，仍然是影响水环境质量的重点污染物。地下水超采和污染问题凸显。近年来，全国地下水年均超采 215 亿立方米，超采区面积达到 19 万平方公里，55%的地下水监测点位水质较差甚至极差。部分地区饮用水水源地水质安全受到威胁。2011 年，环保重点城市集中式饮用水水源地水质有 9.4%不达标。海洋污染风险增大。部分海湾河口生态破坏严重，溢油、赤潮、绿潮等重大海洋污染事故时有发生。

2. 空气污染日趋复杂。

目前，我国城市群出现了煤烟型与机动车尾气污染共存的复合型污染，具有明显的局地污染和区域污染相互交融、多种污染物相互耦合的特征。区域整体环境质量呈恶化趋势，光化学烟雾、大气灰霾和酸沉降污染频繁发生，大气环境形势进入了大范围的退化阶段。

城市灰霾天气严重。2011 年，在 325 个地级以上城市中，空气质量超标城市比例为 11%。2012 年国家颁布了更加严格的《环境空气质量标准》。照此评价，全国将有五分之四的城市不能达标，有近 6 亿人口生活在不达标的大气环境当中。按欧盟标准评价，我国约 95%城市空气质量超标。长三角、珠三角、京津冀等地区城市大气灰霾和光化学烟雾日渐突出，灰霾天数占全年总天数的 30%～50%。室内空气污染显现。我国公共场所室内空气质量达标率不足 50%。一些城市民居和办公建筑中的甲醛、苯、颗粒物、霉菌、人造纳米材料等室内空气污染令人担忧。酸雨问题依然突出。2011 年，在监测的 468 个市（县）中，有 227 个市（县）出现酸雨，占 48.5%，酸雨区约占国土面积的 12.9%，其中重酸雨区占有很大比重。我国酸雨中硫酸根的沉降量远高于其他国家，是日本的 3 倍，美国的 10 倍以上。空气污染严重影响居民身体健康。2011 年，世界卫生组织发布世界城市空气质量报告，在 91 个国家中我国排名倒数第 15 位；在 1 082 个城市排名中，北京列 1 035 位，我国城市空气质量最好的海口市排名也在 800 位之后。科学数据证明，$PM_{2.5}$ 与肺癌、哮喘等疾病密切相关。世界银行报告认为，2009 年中国因 PM_{10} 污染引发公众发病和过早死亡造成的健康损失占国民总收入的

2.8%。$PM_{2.5}$和臭氧等二次大气污染来源广泛，成因复杂，治理难度大，治理周期长。专家预测按现有污染治理水平测算，我国至少需要20～30年的时间，才能达到新的空气质量标准。

3. 噪声污染成为群众的投诉热点。

我国噪声污染日益突出，已成为仅次于水污染和大气污染的第三大城市公害。2011年，全国仍有22.1%和23.9%的城市区域、重点城市区域噪声超标，城市道路交通噪声群众反映强烈。与2010年相比，全国城市声环境的达标率出现下降态势。夜间噪声扰民问题较为严重。2011年，全国城市各类功能区声环境质量夜间达标率为66.4%，低于昼间达标率23个百分点。噪声污染纠纷频发，扰民投诉居高不下。

4. 土壤污染影响深远。

有关研究报告显示，全国受重金属污染耕地达3亿亩，污水灌溉污染耕地3 250万亩，固体废弃物堆存和毁田200万亩，合计约占总耕地面积的1/5，由土壤污染派生的食品、蔬菜安全问题日益严重。湖南、江西、四川、湖北等省耕地污染严重，长三角、珠三角、京津冀、辽中南和西南、中南等地区土壤污染面积较大。环保部组织的全国土壤污染调查表明，土壤超标率为16.1%，其中轻微、轻度、中度和重度污染的比例分别为11.2%、2.3%、1.5%和1.1%。长期被忽视的"毒地"问题日益突出，许多城市污染场地再开发的环境风险加大，急性中毒伤亡事件时有发生。

5. 重金属、危险废物、危险化学品和持久性有机污染物污染问题凸显。

当前，我国逐步积累的重金属污染、危险废物、危险化学品和持久性有机物污染进入突发性、连锁性、区域性的高发阶段，成为损害群众身体健康的重要因素。重金属污染问题严重。2011年，27个地表水国控断面出现重金属超标现象。全国274个污染企业监测结果表明，土壤重金属点位超标率最高的为镉；9类重金属重点行业中，金属与非金属采矿、冶炼与加工业的土壤重金属超标率高达53.8%。全国有198.2万吨铬渣亟待处置。危险化学品及持久性有机污染物问题凸显。在全国排查的4.46万家化学品企业中，72%分布在长江、黄河、珠江、太湖等重点流域沿岸，距离饮用水水源保护区、重要生态功能区等环境敏感区不足1公里的占12.2%，距离人口集中居住区不足1公里的占10.1%。我国电子废弃物、工业固体废物、医疗废物和危险废物产生量持续增加。非法利用处置现象突出，环境污染严重。如广东贵屿地区长期非法拆解电子废物，当地空气、水体和土壤受到二噁英、重金属等严重污染。我国持久性有机污染物污染危害严重。

6. 环境风险呈上升态势。

因环境污染损害群众财产和健康而引发的群体性事件越来越成为影响社会稳定的突出问题。1996年以来，环境群体性事件数量以年均29%的速度递增。2009年陕西宝鸡凤翔县因数百名儿童血铅超标，引发了群体性事件，数百名村民围堵、打砸运输车辆，冲击肇事企业。2011年浙江德清血铅超标事件中，300多人血铅超标，200多名群众围堵公路并冲击肇事企业。2012年的广西龙江河镉污染事件，发生了柳州市民抢水事件。同时也出现了什邡百亿钼铜项目、启东达标水排海工程等引发的大规模群体性事件。重特大环境事件高发频发。2005年以来，环保部直接接报处置的事件共927起，重特大事件72起，其中2011年重大事件比上年同期增长120%。特别是重金属和危险化学品突发环境事件呈高发态势。2009年至今，我国发生了安徽怀宁、浙江台州、广东韶关“血铅超标”以及紫金矿业、广西龙江河镉污染事件等30多起重特大重金属污染突发环境事件。

2011年国务院七部委组织的防范污染风险大检查发现，我国沿海石油勘探开采、炼制、储运和销售项目达13 048家，局部地区高度密集，超过环境风险承载能力。浙江省2 200公里海岸线共建有111个油码头和361座油库。大连市大孤山石化产品储罐区，油库和危化品仓库密集混建，数量大、种类多，一旦发生事故，极易引发连锁反应，后果不堪设想。

7. 生态系统退化令人担忧。

我国区域生态系统破坏严重，生物多样性减少，生态服务功能整体下降，生态灾害加重，生态系统呈现出由结构性破坏向功能性退化演变的态势。我国是世界上人均生态资源稀缺的国家之一。《中国生态足迹报告》显示，我国生态足迹增加的速度远高于生物承载力的增长速度，是生物承载力的 2 倍以上。1985—2008 年，除西藏、内蒙古、新疆与青海四个省区生态盈余外，其余大部分省份长期生态赤字。生物资源濒危问题日益突出。据《中国物种红色名录》（2004）评估：中国无脊椎动物受威胁的比例为 34.74%，脊椎动物受威胁比例为 35.92%，植物为 70%～86%，越来越多的物种受到灭绝的威胁。普氏野马、高鼻羚羊等物种在 20 世纪已经灭绝，近年来，分布于长江中、下游的白鳍豚基本灭绝，江豚也濒于灭绝。外来物种入侵现象日益增多，严重危害了我国陆地和海洋生态系统。

8．农村污染问题更加突出。

第一次全国污染源普查结果显示，农业源排放的化学需氧量达到 1 324.09 万吨，占全国排放总量的 43.7%。总氮、总磷的排放量分别为 270.46 万吨和 28.47 万吨，占全国排放总量的 57.2%和 67.4%。化肥、农药不合理使用问题突出，农药的有效利用率为 30%～35%，化肥的有效利用率为 40% 左右。农村畜禽养殖污染凸显，化学需氧量、总氮和总磷排放总量分别为 1 268.26 万吨、102.48 万吨和 16.04 万吨。农村环境污染严重。城市和工业污染向农村转移趋势加剧，一些城郊接合部成为城市生活垃圾及工业废渣的堆放地。农村饮用水不安全现象突出，有 2.98 亿农村人口饮水不安全。农村环保基础设施薄弱。全国 4 万个乡镇、60 多万个行政村大部分没有环保基础设施，每年产生生活污水 90 多亿吨，生活垃圾 2.8 亿吨，不少地区还处于“垃圾靠风刮，污水靠蒸发”的状态。

（二）环境问题的成因分析

资源相对不足、环境容量有限，已成为我国国情的基本特征，资源与环境问题成为发展的最大制约瓶颈。伴随着我国追赶型经济发展模式与 30 多年来快速发展，结构型、压缩型、累积型、耦合型的环境污染相交织，环境问题集中显现，环境损害呈上升态势。《中国环境经济核算研究报告 2009》显示，2004—2009 年，我国经济发展造成的环境污染代价持续上升，6 年间增长了 89.5%；2009 年环境污染和生态破坏损失合计 13 916.2 亿元，较上年增加 9.2%，约占当年 GDP 的 3.8%。我国面临的资源问题比世界上任何国家都突出，面临的环境压力比任何国家都大，解决起来也比任何国家都困难。

我国环境问题的成因是复杂的、综合的、多方面的，包括经济增长方式粗放、体制机制尚不顺畅、公民环境意识不高、科技水平整体落后、经济水平尚处于国际产业分工的低端等重要方面，这是众所周知的。下面我仅就干部政绩观、法制建设、市场运作和公众参与等问题汇报如下看法：

1. GDP 唯上的政绩观尚未根本扭转是牺牲环境换取经济增长的内生性原因。

长期以来，一些地方仍是重经济发展，重速度、重规模、重眼前；轻资源环保，轻效益、轻创新、轻长远，以 GDP 论英雄，急功近利，导致环境与经济综合决策失误、行政不作为和行政干预环境执法等现象长期存在。环保部门面对地方保护主义的干扰，在执法中“顶得住的站不住，站得住的顶不住”的问题尚未得到解决。

一些地方片面强调营造“宽松”的发展氛围，有的对工业园区、重点企业实行“封闭式管理”、“挂牌保护”，出台“企业宁静日”等土政策，不准执法部门进园区、厂区检查，甚至禁止或打击正常执法；有的在进行决策时，未严格依法行政，环境信息不透明、忽视公民的环境知情权、参与权，引发一系列群体性事件；有的对环境违法行为睁一只眼、闭一只眼，遇到问题相互推诿，避重就轻，行政不作为或者乱作为。一些地方以牺牲环境换取经济发展，片面追求 GDP，不履行环境责任或履责不到位，已经成为严重制约资源环境保护的重要原因。

2.“违法成本低、守法成本高”是环境违法行为屡禁不止的制度性原因。

我国环境法制建设取得了长足进展，但随着环境保护与经济发展矛盾日益突出，环保监管压力不断增加，环境法制建设存在的矛盾和问题十分突出：一是不断完善的市场经济体制与缺乏有效法制手段、经济手段管理环境的矛盾日益显现；二是建设法治政府、法治社会的要求与环境法制建设粗放发展的矛盾日益突出；三是群众环境维权意识增强、跨界损害事件增多与民事赔偿、调处能力滞后的矛盾日益凸现；四是环境违法现象普遍、环境纠纷群体性事件增多与环保法律法规操作性不强、执法不力的矛盾日益加剧；五是群众环境信访案件走向复议、复议案件走向诉讼的快速变化趋势与有关部门对行政复议工作的认识不高、司法诉讼渠道不畅通的矛盾日益明显；六是国家对环境法制的更高要求与相关的基础性研究、机构设置以及执法能力不强、执法不到位等问题不相适应的矛盾日益加大。

环境法制最突出的问题，就是违法成本低的问题长期没有得到解决。这既有立法不足的问题，也有行政执法、司法不到位的问题。

一是行政处罚普遍偏轻。《环境影响评价法》规定，违反环评规定擅自开工建设的，要求限期补办环评手续，逾期不办的才能给予 20 万元以下的罚款。由于处罚太轻，一些企业为了抢进度，采取边开工建设、边做环评报告，甚至一些企业以交罚款代替环评。《大气污染防治法》对超标排污的罚款上限是 10 万元，造成重大污染事故的罚款是 50 万元；《水污染防治法》对超标排污的罚款为其应缴纳排污费数额 2 倍以上 5 倍以下，造成重大污染事故的罚款仅是污染直接损失的 30%以下。2011 年 6 月，哈药集团被披露多种环境违法问题：恶臭气体排放大大超过国家标准，硫化氢气体超标近千倍，氨气超标 20 倍；污水排放超过国家标准，氨氮超标 2 倍多，COD 超标近 10 倍。哈药集团 2010 年营业收入达 125.35 亿元，利润 13.14 亿元，虽然被依法罚款 123 万元，也仅为企业年收入的万分之一。2010 年 7 月紫金矿业造成汀江重大水污染事故，被法院判处罚金 3 000 万元，其中还包括了行政罚款 956.313 万元。尽管这是我国几十年来开出的最大一笔环保罚款，但却不足企业净利润的千分之三。环保罚单开出后，资本市场看到“紫金污染门”责任追究收尾，利空出尽，紫金矿业的股票立即涨停，当日成交额高达 14.52 亿元之多。

二是行政执行缺乏强制手段。现行法律规定的行政强制手段主要有“停止建设”、“停止生产使用”、“责令限期恢复使用治污设施”、“责令停业关闭”等，但在基层却难以有效执行。当前，环境案件的执行绝大部分都要申请法院执行，法院执行除受司法体制、地方保护主义影响外，还存在着执行期限较长、力度不大等问题。案件处理后要等待复议诉讼期满，还要通过法院的立案、审查、听证、裁定等程序，时间跨度长，而法院系统也很少为环境案件运用先予执行等强硬手段，致使违法污染行为得不到及时纠正。

三是环境民事赔偿法律制度不健全。追究环境民事赔偿责任对于制裁环境违法行为，保护国家和公众的环境权益具有重要作用。然而，由于我国环境民事赔偿相关法律及配套制度不健全，环境民事案件立案难、举证难、审判难、执行难的问题日益凸显。重大环境事件的责任追究，多以行政处罚和行政调解结案，通过司法途径追究法律责任的很少。

四是环保官司难打。我国的环境资源案件数量较多，而且呈逐年上升趋势，但环境民事案件数量却很少，许多重大环境污染纠纷未能进入诉讼程序。据调查，真正通过司法诉讼渠道解决的环境纠纷不足 1%。一方面群众遇到环境纠纷，宁愿选择信访或举报投诉等途径解决，而不选择司法途径；另一方面司法部门也不愿意受理环境纠纷案件。“十一五”期间，我国环保系统受理环境信访 30 多万件，行政复议 2 614 件，而相比之下，行政诉讼只有 980 件，刑事诉讼只有 30 件。2003—2008 年，全国各级法院审结环境资源案件中民事案件 12 278 件，仅占同期审结民事案件总数的 0.04%。在环境污染损害纠纷的处理中，由于缺乏具体可操作的环境污染损害鉴定评估技术规范和管理机制，致使经济损失和人身伤害难以量化、污染损害因果关系难以判断、环境损害赔偿标准难以认定。许多污染案件久拖不决，历时数年，当事人的诉讼成本高昂，污染受害人也往往得不到损害赔偿。

五是生态环境损害难获赔偿。环境公共利益损失的索赔缺乏明确法律支撑，生态环境服务功能损失以及应急和修复等相关费用尚未纳入赔偿范围。2010 年英国石油公司（BP）在墨西哥湾发生漏油污染事件，由于担心受到法律的严厉制裁，主动设立了 200 亿美元的赔偿基金用于赔偿污染受害者和海洋生态环境损失。而我国近年来发生了一系列重大环境污染事故，2005—2012 年先后发生的松花江污染事故、大连海岸油污染事故、福建汀江污染事件、广西龙江镉污染事件等，至今均未被追究环境公共利益的损失赔偿。

3．“资源低价、环境廉价”是导致环境持续退化的基础性原因。

“资源低价”就会过多使用和消耗资源，造成资源的浪费；“环境廉价”就会出现毫无节制的排放污染物，加剧环境污染趋势。我国社会主义市场机制发育还不完善，计划经济时期在资源与环境方面的政策影响依然长期大量存在。由于资源低价、环境廉价甚至无价，企业缺乏节约资源、保护环境的内生动力和外在压力，其资源利用成本和环境污染成本往往被“社会化”或“外部化”，不仅引发了资源环境的危机，客观上也助长了粗放型的开发方式、生产方式和消费方式。以稀土资源丰富的赣州为例，该市因稀土开采造成了触目惊心的环境污染和生态破坏，所需的污染治理和生态修复费用高达 380 亿元，而 2011 年江西省 51 家主要稀土企业全年利润仅 64 亿元，这已经是稀土价格上涨 4 倍后的结果。也就是说，该地稀土资源开发的经济收益很难弥补环境污染治理和生态修复的成本，有关企业的环境资源成本都被转移出去，最终只能由全社会和后代人来承担。

导致资源低价、环境廉价的主要原因有：一是长期以来，人们对资源环境的价值认识不足，认为资源环境取之不尽、用之不竭；二是在各项经济发展战略、发展计划和经济政策之中，未体现资源环境价值，污染治理、生态恢复成本与市场价格相背离，市场机制难以发挥合理配置资源环境要素的基础性作用；三是在政府部门之间缺乏协调合作机制，自然生态系统的整体性与行政管理系统的分割性存在矛盾，地区利益、部门利益之争又限制了适应市场经济的政策出台；四是许多政府官员长期习惯依赖于计划经济条件下的行政手段，而不愿使用也不会使用市场手段、经济手段；五是资源环境经济政策研究能力普遍不足。

4．公众环境诉求表达不畅是环境群体性事件高发的社会性原因。

环境信息公开是公众环境诉求表达的前提条件。目前我国环境信息公开制度尚不健全，相关法律规范不明确，有关规定过于原则抽象，操作性不强，公开内容有限，难以满足公众需求。一些企业环境责任意识较低，不愿公开环境信息，甚至隐瞒环境污染信息，企业违法排污行为得不到公众有效监督。2012 年四川什邡市百亿元钼铜项目是国家地震灾后重建的重点项目，各项审批手续齐全，治污措施有保障。但由于前期对公众宣传解释工作不到位，造成了部分群众的强烈反对，最后该市以“群众不了解、不理解、不支持”为由，宣布永远放弃该项目建设。

三、对策建议

基于对环境问题成因的上述分析，特提出如下建议。

（一）强化政府责任，健全约束和规范政府环境行为的法律制度

环境问题是随着经济发展而产生，又随着经济发展而逐步解决，但环境问题不会自行解决。发达国家的经验表明，通过环境立法来明确政府的环保责任，规范政府行为，是协调经济建设与环境保护关系、根治环境问题的关键措施。很多发达国家都是在经济快速发展与环境保护矛盾最尖锐、最突出的时期，制定了专门约束政府行为的环保法律法规，以协调经济发展和环境保护的关系。比如美国和欧盟的《国家环境政策法》、日本的《环境基本法》、加拿大的《环境保护法》、韩国的《环境政策法》、英国的《环境法》等，都为协调经济发展与环境保护的关系，发挥了非常重要的作用。

为此，建议以修改《环境保护法》为契机，紧紧围绕落实“政府对环境质量负总责”的要求，重点解决一些地方政府环境保护不作为、乱作为、干扰环境执法等的突出问题，创建或强化一批制度与机制，主要包括五大类和若干个具体的制度与机制：一是科学决策类，如战略与规划环境影响评价、环保规划、主体功能及环境功能区划、环境标准、区域限批与行业限批等。二是实施执行类，如环保目标责任制、强制淘汰重污染企业补偿机制、环保基础设施建设制度、跨界环境问题协调解决机制、区域生态补偿制度、环境应急管理及信息通报制度等。三是保障措施类，如环境经济政策、跨行政区的环境监督制度、环境法律救济制度、多部门联合执法机制、环保能力建设、环境教育等。四是监督机制类，如人大监督政府、政

协民主监督政府、政府内部的层级监督与同级监督、信息公开和公众参与、司法监督、媒体监督等。五是责任追究类。通过一批法律制度的建立与实施，将政府的环境保护责任真正落到实处。

（二）严格追究污染者的环境责任，切实解决长期困扰环境保护的违法成本低的问题

“违法成本低，守法成本高”是影响环保法制建设健康发展的重大障碍。“违法成本低”必然降低法律的威严和效率，导致违法排污屡禁不绝；“守法成本高”势必淡薄人们的法律意识，视法律为可有可无。提高违法成本和守法自觉性是完善环境法制建设的首要问题。强化环境损害赔偿，健全环境民事责任，既是保护公民环境权益、维护社会公平和正义的重要措施，又是解决“违法成本低”问题的根本出路。

首先，以制定环境损害赔偿法为重点，完善环境损害救济的法律制度。应在现行侵权责任法规定的基础上，通过制定单行的环境损害赔偿法，明确环境损害责任承担主体、赔偿责任范围、责任承担方式、救济途径等基本制度。将环境和生态系统的公益损害与公民的私益损害，列入赔偿范围。建立环境损害鉴定评估机制，为落实环境责任提供强有力的技术支撑。

其次，建立环境责任终身追究制度，让污染者为其违法行为付出高昂代价。1980 年，美国国会针对历史遗留的大量的污染土地的严重问题，专门通过了超级基金法。该法：一是严格明确了污染者必须承担污染治理全部费用的责任；二是企业经营者及产权拥有者的环境责任将是一种终身责任；三是要求在污染企业发展中的所有曾经获益者，都必须承担共同的连带责任。事实上，这是一种无限责任，即如果污染责任方无力负担其依法应偿付的污染清理费用和损害赔偿费用时，有关控股或参股的组织和个人，向其贷款、借款及销售过保险的组织和个人，均有可能成为被追究责任的对象。美国超级基金法实施后，不仅有一大批污染企业倒闭破产，而且还有一大批银行、保险公司因环境损害赔偿而倒闭破产，从而大大强化了法律制度的权威，提高了人们的环境责任意识。

我国应借鉴发达国家的经验，加大对污染企业的行政处罚、行政强制、民事赔偿和刑事处罚力度，建立健全行政裁决、公益诉讼等环境损害救济途径，切实落实企业环境责任。

（三）强化环境执法，充分发挥司法体系的保障作用

司法作为社会秩序与稳定的基石，是解决社会纠纷的重要防线，也是解决环境问题的重要手段。发达国家解决环境问题的成功经验，就是建立了严格和完善的环境法律体系以及完整、有效的司法模式，采用以行政调解和司法裁决相结合的法律手段，惩处环境违法行为，解决环境纠纷。

强化司法救济途径，倡导更多使用司法途径解决环境纠纷，是环境法制建设的重要任务。司法部门应当以更加积极的姿态推动司法力量介入环境保护，逐步改变目前在环境纠纷处理中司法救济不力和比例偏低的问题。一是及时妥善处理环境损害赔偿纠纷，正确适用环境侵权案件举证责任分配规则，准确认定环境污染与损害后果之间的因果关系，确保环境侵权受害人得到及时全面的赔偿；二是加大对环境刑事责任的追究力度，确保构成犯罪的违法行为得到应有的制裁；三是通过行政诉讼等渠道，监督政府依法履责，规范政府行为，推动法治政府建设；四是建立健全环境公益诉讼制度，及时受理法律规定的机关和社会团体提起的环境公益诉讼；五是在总结贵阳、昆明、无锡等地环境法庭实践的基础上，完善环境审判体制机制，提高环境案件专业化审判水平，从根本上解决环境案件立案难、举证难、审判难、执行难等问题。

同时要从建设社会主义法治国家和法治政府出发，规范行政执法，改变过度依赖长官意志和行政手段的执法方式，改变以罚代管、以罚代过的工作方法，改变“运动式”的行政执法模式。

（四）发挥市场配置资源环境要素的基础性作用，改变资源低价、环境廉价的局面

资源低价、环境廉价是资源浪费与环境污染的基础性原因。只有纠正

在资源环境价格方面的错误市场信号，建立充分反映市场供求、资源稀缺程度以及环境损害成本的价格形成机制，才能将资源环境成本真正内部化，避免排污者将污染成本转嫁给社会，才能使节约资源、保护环境真正成为人们的自觉行为。

为此，建议应当继续完善以下环境经济政策：

一是推动财政政策的生态化调整。建立财政支持绿色发展稳定增长的资金机制；创新财政手段，设立基金补贴、免贷奖励、贴息、担保等市场手段，弱化以专项资金管理为代表的行政手段管理色彩；发挥财政投入的效益，建立中央和地方事权明晰的多级投入机制。

二是完善有利于资源节约、环境保护的税收体制。包括取消不符合节能环保的产品、技术、工艺等出口退税政策，配合节能环保调整消费税，对环保节能产业、现代服务业给予所得税方面优惠等。特别要结合国家的结构性减税工作，改革资源税、开征环境税，逐步提高税率，强化税收的行为调控功能。

三是改革环保收费与环境价格政策。完善城镇污水和垃圾收费政策、脱硫脱硝电价的价格政策、处理处置污染物的收费制度；深化推进水资源、电价、煤炭、石油、天然气等关键性资源产品的定价机制改革，按照市场化定价的原则，逐步改变政府直接控制价格的做法，在重要资源价格形成机制的改革上取得实质性突破。

同时完善绿色金融、绿色贸易政策，建立健全生态补偿机制，深化农村环保“以奖促治”和“以奖代补”政策等。

（五）实行谨慎原则，建立严格的环境风险评估制度

发达国家普遍将谨慎原则作为环境立法的基本准则，这是因为环境损害具有很大的滞后性和不确定性。环境损害主要包括两大类，一类是可以被科学证实的环境损害，如水体、空气、土壤等的环境污染损害；另一类是尚未被科学充分证明的潜在环境损害。由于生态系统高度复杂，人类对于科学知识的掌握仍具有相当程度的局限性，许多环境损害目前还难以被

科学地证明，但不排除将来发生的重大可能。如大量排放温室气体、引进外来物种、转基因技术、纳米技术、新化学品的应用等带来的环境损害，目前还没有完全被科学证实，但如果不谨慎应对，不对潜在的风险进行评估，一旦损害真正发生，再去考虑应对措施，一是代价将会相当高昂，二是可能为时已晚。为防止潜在的、不确定的环境风险或者对人体健康的损害，许多国际环境公约、条约和议定书和发达国家的法律法规都采用了谨慎原则，并且为此普遍建立环境风险评估制度，即在没有充分的科学依据证实其对环境和人体健康无害的情况下，需要谨慎地采取预防性措施，避免潜在的环境风险和健康风险。这些理念和原则已成为国际社会在环境保护领域的共识。如《气候变化框架公约》等国际环境公约、条约多次重申或者援引了这一原则。

为此建议我国也应当将谨慎原则作为环境立法的基本理念，渗透贯穿于环境法律法规，建立健全环境风险评估制度，确保谨慎原则的充分体现。

（六）推动信息公开与公众参与，完善多元化的环境监督体制

公众参与是解决环境问题不可替代的力量。除了政府“自上而下”的推动和引导外，发达国家实践表明，环境保护还要依赖公众“自下而上”的参与。在一定意义上，公众监督是政府监督的补充和延续，公众监督不仅可以强化对污染企业的环境监督，弥补政府监管力量的不足；同时还可以监督政府工作，使其认真履责。我国应当从现行的政府主导型的环境管理模式向包括政府、企业、公众和社会组织在内的主体多元化合作的监管模式转变。

一是加快环境信息公开的步伐。信息公开是国家政治体制改革的一个大趋势。一方面要进一步扩大政府环境信息主动公开的范围，规范和畅通依申请公开的渠道；另一方面要强化企业环境信息公开的责任，要求企业全面、真实、客观、及时地公开环境信息，确保公众的知情权、参与权、监督权及寻求法律救济等权利的行使。

二是建立和完善公众参与机制。进一步完善环境立法、规划、重大政

策和重点建设项目环评等的听证制度，扩大听证范围，规范听证程序；探索实行社区环境圆桌对话机制，建立政府、企业、公众定期沟通、平等对话、协商解决的机制和平台。真正实现公众参与环境保护的真实性、科学性、广泛性、代表性，畅通公众环境权益诉求的表达机制。

三是充分发挥社会组织参与环境保护的作用。社会组织参与环境保护是打破政府包办社会管理格局的重要措施，是社会文明进步的具体表现。因此，在行政管理体制改革中，应将社会公共事务管理的权限和责任从传统的政府职责中适度分离出来，鼓励社会组织承担环境责任，参与环境保护。

推进生态文明建设，是涉及生产方式和生活方式根本性变革的战略任务，应当把生态文明建设的理念、原则、目标等深刻融入和全面贯穿到经济、政治、文化、社会建设的各方面和全过程。为此，我们要积极探索代价小、效益好、排放低、可持续的环境保护新道路，进一步提高我国生态文明建设的整体水平。

科学发展观视角下的《环境保护法》
——兼论修改《环保法》[①]

杨朝飞[②]

随着科学发展观的深入人心，修改现行《中华人民共和国环境保护法》（以下简称《环保法》）的呼声日益升高。十届人大以来，全国人大代表、全国政协委员关于《环境保护法》修改的议案和提案不断增加。2004 年以来的五年中，“两会”共接到关于修改《环境保护法》的议案建议和提案 65 件，占环保立法建议和提案总数的近一半；多达 1 000 余名全国人大代表参与议案、建议的提出，反映出社会各界对修改《环境保护法》普遍而强烈的愿望。国家对 1989 年《环保法》的修改也逐渐提上日程。2005 年 1 月，中共中央印发的《建立健全教育、制度、监督并重的惩治和预防腐败体系实施纲要》第十一条要求“修改《环境保护法》”。2005 年 12 月，国务院《关于落实科学发展观加强环境保护的决定》第十八条要求“配合做好《环境保护法》的修改工作。”2007 年 10 月 27 日，十届人大环资委向全国人大常委会第三十次会议所作代表议案审议结果的报告明确提出：“启动《环境保护法》修改工作的条件已经具备”；“建议将《环境保护法》的修改，列入十一届全国人大常委会立法规划”。2007 年 6 月，在人大环资委召开的《环境保护法》修改专题论证会上，最高法院、最高检察院的代表都表示，现行《环境保护法》的有关规定（如超标排污收费制度）不仅明显过时，而且和有关单项法律法规存在矛盾和冲突，给环境司法过程中的法律适用造成困难，建议对该法予以修改。2008 年，经中央批准的《十一届全国人大

---

① 本文原刊于《绿叶》，2010 年第 9 期。
② 杨朝飞，时任环境保护部政策法规司司长。

常委会立法规划》提出，环境保护法等立法项目“由有关方面继续开展研究论证，视情况作出相应安排”。多年来，各级环保部门，特别是基层环保部门一直强烈呼吁国家有关机关修改《环保法》。《环保法》的修改受到社会越来越多的关注，法学界也普遍支持修改《环保法》。因此，1989 年《环保法》的修改已是势在必行。

一、《环保法》的历史性贡献功不可没

《环保法》于 1989 年颁布实施。《环保法》为我国环境法制建设的发展作出了不可磨灭的历史性贡献。从历史作用上看，《环保法》承前启后，一方面继承了 1979 年《中华人民共和国环境保护法（试行）》（以下简称《环保法（试行）》）所规定的行之有效的制度和措施，另一方面根据当时的现实做出了很多创造性的规定，为政府实施环境管理和环境管理相对人的守法和自律规定了一些重要的基础性制度，使我国的环境保护事业进入了一个新阶段。《环保法》有力地促进了我国环境保护部门法的发展和完善。它为防治大气、水、固体废弃物、噪声、放射性物质等方面的污染的法律的制定奠定了基础并提供了重要经验。在《环保法》之后，关于大气污染、水污染等问题的法律相继颁布并实施，我国法律逐渐覆盖了几乎所有的重要环境因子和重大环境问题。环境保护领域无法可依的局面从此一去不复返。

《环保法》的实施效果是显著而无可替代的。《环保法》为我国环境保护事业提供了基本的法律保障。主要表现在以下几个方面：第一，《环保法》落实我国《宪法》关于国家环境保护公共职能的原则性规定，为我国政府履行这项重要职能做出基本的体制和制度安排。第二，它从法律上界定了“环境”的定义，明确了环境保护法律的保护客体及其范围。第三，《环保法》为政府履行环境保护公共职能规定了组织保障，对环境保护职能在政府部门中的分配做出了规定，保证了政府各相关部门分工履行环境保护职能的有序性。根据《环保法》的规定，我国政府从中央到地方都设立了环境保护行政主管部门，同时政府其他部门也为履行法律规定的环境保护职

能设立了相应的部门或机构。第四，《环保法》为公民、企事业单位、社会团体和政府等各类法律主体规定了在开发、利用和保护环境方面的基本行为规则和制度，使得各种法律主体在环境事务中有规可循。尤其是通过对环境影响评价、“三同时”、排污申报登记、排污费征收、现场检查、限期治理、行政处罚等措施，初步建立了对排污者和开发者影响环境行为的管制。第五，《环保法》规定了对违法者的责任追究和处罚制度和对环境污染和生态破坏受害者的法律救济手段。第六，《环保法》有力地推动了其他针对特定环境因子和环境事务的专门法律的制定。第七，《环保法》有力地推动了地方环境立法工作。

《环境保护法》实施的 20 余年是我国工业化、城市化规模最大、进程最快的 20 余年，环境保护压力前所未有，经济发展与环境保护之间的矛盾十分突出。由于有了《环境保护法》等环境保护法律，我国环境管理队伍不断壮大，环境保护执法日益规范和加强，使我国的环境污染、生态破坏处在可控范围之内，经济发展与环境保护之间的矛盾得到了一定程度的缓解，在一定程度上保护了经济社会可持续发展的物质基础。

二、科学发展观对修订《环保法》提出了新的更高的要求

2003 年中央提出科学发展观。2007 年，在党的十七大上，胡锦涛总书记在《高举中国特色社会主义伟大旗帜为夺取全面建设小康社会新胜利而奋斗》的报告中提出，科学发展观第一要义是发展，核心是以人为本，基本要求是全面协调可持续性，根本方法是统筹兼顾，指明了我们进一步推动中国经济改革与发展的思路和战略，明确了科学发展观是指导经济社会发展的根本指导思想，标志着中国共产党对于社会主义建设规律、社会发展规律、共产党执政规律的认识达到了新的高度，标志着马克思主义的中国化，标志着马克思主义和新的中国国情相结合达到了新的高度和阶段。

科学发展观的提出对 1989 年《环境保护法》的实施提出了新的、更高的要求。

第一，《环保法》应当成为环境保护工作践行科学发展观的制度平台。

2003 年科学发展观将人与自然和谐发展放到战略地位的同时，也对各级人民政府的环境保护工作提出了更为严格的要求。根据“有法可依，有法必依，执法必严，违法必究”的行政法治理念，科学发展观对各级政府环境保护工作的要求最终要以法律的形式确定下来并执行下去。因此，《环保法》及其后一系列环境保护专项法律都是科学发展观在环境保护工作中的贯彻落实的制度平台。

第二，《环保法》应当为规范和加强政府环境管理，改善政府涉及环境问题的重要决策提供法律制度保障。

胡锦涛同志在党的十七大报告中明确指出：“要抓紧制定行政管理体制改革总体方案，着力转变职能、理顺关系、优化结构、提高效能，形成权责一致、分工合理、决策科学、执行顺畅、监督有力的行政管理体制。”①《中共中央关于制定国民经济和社会发展第十一个五年规划的建议》指出：“加快行政管理体制改革，是全面深化改革和提高对外开放水平的关键。”②胡锦涛总书记在中央政治局会议上强调：“推进行政管理体制改革是贯彻落实科学发展观、完善社会主义市场经济体制、建设社会主义法治国家的必然要求。”③当前我国树立和落实科学发展观，需要政府进一步转变发展观念，进一步转变政府职能。“要完善有利于节约能源资源和保护生态环境的法律和政策，加快形成可持续发展体制机制。”④要通过推进行政管理体制改革，加快转变政府职能，改进行政管理方式，加强行政法制建设，形成有利于转变经济增长方式、促进全面协调可持续发展的机制，推动经济社会发展转入以人为本、全面协调可持续发展的轨道。

---

① 胡锦涛在党的十七大上的报告，新华网十七大专题，http://news.xinhuanet.com/newscenter/2007-10/24/content_6938568_5.htm，最后访问 2007-10-24。

②中共中央关于制定“十一五”规划的建议(全文)，新华网，http://news.xinhuanet.com/politics/2005-10/18/content_3640318_2.htm，最后访问 2005-10-18。

③ 坚定不移地加快推进改革，新华网，http://news3.xinhuanet.com/theory/2006-07/12/content_4821476_1.htm，最后访问 2006-07-12。

④ 新华网，胡锦涛在党的十七大上的报告，http://news.xinhuanet.com/newscenter/2007-10/24/content_6938568_4.htm，最后访问 2007-10-24。

科学发展观需要通过立法，从制度上加以落实。在环境保护领域，《环保法》就是一部当之无愧地承担此项重大任务的法律。但是由于历史的局限性，加之法律本身所具有的滞后性和延时性，《环保法》已不能为我国政府践行科学发展观提供应有的制度保障。这个问题既是现行《环保法》亟待修改的原因，也是它的修改亟须解决的中心问题。

第三，在修改《环保法》时应根据科学发展观的要求进行制度创新。

2009 年，胡锦涛总书记又进一步提出："把贯彻落实科学发展观提高到新的水平"、"……着力构建有利于科学发展的体制机制，提高领导科学发展、促进社会和谐的能力……努力实现提高思想认识、解决突出问题、创新体制机制、促进科学发展的目标。……"①根据胡锦涛总书记关于构建有利于科学发展的体制机制的要求。《环保法》的修改工作的重点应当是通过制度创新，为落实科学发展观提出的转变政府发展观念和政府职能的要求提供法律保障。这就需要按照科学发展观的要求进行立法上的制度创新。

三、科学发展观视角之下《环保法》之不足

如上所述，作为国家发展战略，科学发展观对我国政府的环境保护工作提出了非常高的要求。对照这些要求，现行《环保法》主要暴露出以下问题和不足。

第一，立法理念落后。

《环保法》制定于 1989 年。当时，国内正在探索改革开放和新的发展道路，关于环境与发展的新理念尚未成熟。当时，从国际看，联合国 1992 年里约环境与发展大会尚未举行，大会一致认可的可持续发展战略尚未对我国的立法产生影响。

《环保法》在制度安排上缺乏以环保优化经济发展的制度保障、缺乏保障政府科学民主决策和防止政府有关环境的决策失误的制度安排。例如，

---

①中国共产党新闻网，胡锦涛强调：把贯彻落实科学发展观提高到新的水平，http://cpc.people.com.cn/GB/64093/64094/8079393.html，最后访问时间 2008-9-20。

关于环境与发展综合决策，政府内外的监督和制约制度、环境信息公开、公众有序参与环境管理等制度，在《环保法》中要么是空白，要么十分薄弱。此外，该法关于政府官员履行环保职能的激励和问责制度的规定也很薄弱。这些都是时代的局限造成的法律上的缺陷。

第二，《环保法》的“空心化”问题日益凸显。

由于环境保护类法律的发展，《环保法》出现了“空心化”的问题。这里的“空心化”，指的是在《环保法》中仅做了原则性规定的事项，后来逐渐被其他法律做了详细的制度性规定，因而《环保法》中关于这些事项的原则性规定处于“有名无实”的状态。这主要是由于《环保法》公布后，全国人大常委会先后制定或者修订了水、大气、噪声、固体废物、放射性污染、海洋环境保护、环境影响评价等专门法律。《环境保护法》在环境质量标准、污染物排放标准、环境监测、环境影响评价、现场检查、跨界污染、限期治理、“三同时”、排污申报登记、排污收费等方面的原则性规定，绝大部分在上述各项法律中得到展开并做了详细规定。有些还被作了修改。因此，《环保法》的这些“空心化”了的条款，实际上已经失去了存在的意义。在法律上废止这些“空心化”条款，无碍于环境法制和环境管理的大局。我们应当看到，一方面，《环保法》的这个“空心化”问题是时代的进步和我国环境立法的发展带来的结果；另一方面，从优化法律体系，突出《环保法》主要功能的角度看，这些“空心化”条款可以予以删除。

第三，许多制度和措施明显过时。

《环境保护法》是在我国的计划经济体制尚未完全改变的历史条件下制定的。因此它的许多规定不可避免地带有浓重的计划经济色彩。现在看来，这些规定与当前我国社会主义市场经济体制不相适应。例如：《环境保护法》第 13 条针对新扩改建设项目的环境管理规定：项目的环境影响报告书应当由“项目主管部门”预审，同时规定“计划部门批准建设项目设计任务书”。经过六次政府机构改革之后，建设项目的行业性“主管部门”大多已经不复存在，“计划部门”对具体项目“设计任务书”的审批职能也已发生重大转变。《环境保护法》第 29 条和第 30 条规定，对污染严重的企业，由“直接管辖”该企业的人民政府决定限期治理。自 20 世纪 80 年代初，经济体制改革以来，政企关系发生了根本性的变化，绝大多数企业实行自主经营，政府基本上不再直接管辖企业。

第四，《环保法》没有对规范和制约政府环保履职做出有效的制度保障。

从总体上看，《环保法》偏重于对企业等排污者、开发者的规制，忽略对政府环保履职的规范和制约。这个缺陷对于政府依法履行环保公共职能而言，是一个关键性的缺陷。

从法律条文上看，《环保法》共有 47 条，但其中直接用于保障政府决策的科学性和勤勉履行环保职责的条款只有 3 条，即第 6 条（一切单位和个人都有保护环境的义务，并有权对污染和破坏环境的单位和个人进行检举和控告）、第 16 条（地方各级人民政府，应当对本辖区的环境质量负责，采取措施改善环境质量）和第 45 条（环境保护监督管理人员滥用职权、玩忽职守、徇私舞弊的，由其所在单位或者上级主管机关给予行政处分；构成犯罪的，依法追究刑事责任）。相关的条款数量少只是问题的一个方面。问题的另一方面是这些相关的条款都比较笼统，没有形成可操作的制度。

从制度安排上看，《环保法》中规定的各项可操作的制度，都是针对企业等排污者、开发者的，缺乏规范和制约政府有关环境的行政行为的制度安排。例如，《环保法》中规定的环境影响评价制度、“三同时”制度、排污申报登记制度等，都偏重于规制管制企业等排污者或开发者的行为，而忽略了规范和制约管制者即政府的行为。

从环境法律关系主体的覆盖面来看，《环保法》对环境法律关系主体覆盖是不平衡的。《环保法》这类维护社会公共利益的法律，应当对企业等排污者或开发者、公民和政府这三大类环境法律关系的主体的权利（或权力）和义务有同等分量的规定。这是因为环保事业的成功需要这三类法律主体发挥好自己独特的作用，缺一不可。但是，如上所述，《环保法》不是这样。它对企业等排污者或开发者的权利和义务规定得比较翔实，对政府、公民和公民团体的权利/权力和义务规定得比较苍白。

《环保法》未对政府环保履职的规范和制约做出充分的制度安排，是现实中以牺牲资源环境换取短期经济增长的做法屡禁不止的一个重要原因。近 20 多年来，尤其是近 10 年来在新闻媒体上屡屡曝光的很多重大环境污染和生态破坏事件，从 1992 年云南省石林水泥厂空气污染案（当年全国人大环资委曾对该案进行过专项检查和监督），到近年来数次“环保风暴”中环保部的行政限批决定所涉及的违法案件，再到近期在湖南、甘肃、陕西、河南、吉林等地爆发的重金属污染危害人民生命和健康的严重事件，无不与有关的政府或政府部门没有积极、规范地履行环境保护职责有关。一些地方政府在单纯追求经济利益的错误政绩观指导下，大搞地方保护主义，出台各式各样的“土政策”，成为环境违法企业的保护伞、挡箭牌，严重干扰了正常的环境执法。一些地方政府行政不作为，对违法企业下不了决心、动不了手，甚至视而不见、放任自流。一些政府在进行决策时，忽视环境规律、无视环保法律，不进行深入细致的科学评估和论证，致使生态环境遭受严重损害。

政府存在的一个基本理由是管制市场主体，防止市场主体在追逐私利的过程中滥用公共环境资源，出现环境污染和生态破坏这样的“市场失灵”后果。上述情况表明，有关的政府或政府部门在做出有关经济发展但同时又涉及环境公共利益的行为时，在法律上没有受到应有的制约和监督，因而每每行政不规范，导致环境管理无效，甚至放弃了市场监管者和社会公共环境利益维护者的职责，本身成了环境污染和生态破坏问题的深层次原因。在我国，政府是经济发展的主导者。如果政府在推动经济发展的同时忽视了环保职能的履行，企业等排污者或开发者的滥用公共环境资源的行为必然畅行无阻，从而导致一个地方或区域的环境和生态受到严重的破坏。如果这种情况在全国普遍存在，则全国环境状况整体向好的拐点将难以出现。

由于有以上种种缺陷和问题，《环保法》的实施效果不够好，未能充分发挥它所应有的对我国环境保护事业的保障作用。

四、科学发展观指导下《环保法》之修改：加强规范和制约政府有关环境的行政行为的制度建设

从《环保法》的实施效果和历史地位可见，它是我国环境保护部门法中一部比较特殊的法律。对它的修订要做好以下工作：

第一，查明、保留并发展《环保法》的特殊功能。

修订《环保法》首先要求查明《环保法》的特殊功能。如果《环保法》没有其独特的功能，那它就失去了存在的意义。

《环保法》的有些功能是其他法律可以替代的。例如，《环保法》的一项重要功能是在相关的专门法律制定之前，对有关的环境保护事项作出原则性的规定，使各类法律主体先在这些事项上初步有所遵循。《环保法》的那些“空心化”条款，例如《环保法》第四章中关于防治各种环境污染和生态破坏的原则性规定，都承担了这种功能。应当承认，在制定《环保法》的那个历史条件下，这些条款是新生的环境法制所不可缺少的组成部分，具有巨大的创新意义。但是随着我国环境立法的发展，《环保法》的这类条款，已经逐步被详细的专门法律所替代并发展。它们已经完成了其历史使命，没有继续存在的必要了。相应地，《环保法》的这个功能在这些事项上可以并且已经被其他法律所替代。

值得注意的是，《环保法》的另一些功能是其他法律所不能替代的。查明、保留并根据时代的进步和现实的需要发展和加强这些功能，十分重要。《环保法》中关于国家环境行政管理体制；政府、企事业单位等排污者或开发者、公民在环境保护事务中的基本权利（或权力）和义务；对现实中出现的新的需要法律保护的环境客体和需要法律调整的事务做出的规定等，都是体现这种特殊功能的法律规范。这些规范的特殊功能，表现为三方面。其一是贯彻落实我国《宪法》关于政府环保公共职能的原则性规定。《环保法》通过关于国家环境保护行政管理体制的规定，使政府切实、有序地担负并履行环保公共职能。这个从总体上规定国家环境保护行政管理体制的

功能，是其他的针对特定环境因子和环境事务的法律所不能承担的。其二是从总体上组织国家环境保护事业。《环保法》从原则上明确环境法律关系的各类主体在环境法律关系中的地位和作用，使各类社会主体依法有序投入环境保护事业。其三是在环境保护事业初创时期为政府环境管理和我国环境保护事业提供法律依据，并为我国环境保护部门法的发展提供了基本框架。《环保法》这三个功能是其他的环境保护类法律所没有的。正是由于《环保法》的这种特殊功能，它被人们称为我国环境保护领域里的“基本法”。当然，这里所谓“基本法”是带引号的，不应将它与我国由全国人大通过的基本法律相混淆。在这里，称我国《环保法》为“基本法”，只是因为它具有上述特殊功能而已。在国外，不少国家如美国、日本等也都制定了这类环境保护领域里的“基本法”。

从另一方面看，正是由于《环保法》在功能上的特殊性和重要性，如果《环保法》有关这些特殊功能的规定存在缺陷和问题，它必将对国家环境保护事业带来不利影响。因此，在修订《环保法》时，首要的任务应当是查明《环保法》的特殊功能，并健全和完善之。

第二，突出《环保法》的特殊功能，加强对各级政府履行环保职能的规范和制约的制度建设。

修改《环保法》的重点，应当放在加强规范和制约政府有关环境的行政行为的制度建设上。一般而言，不受制约和监督的政府，轻则倾向于懈怠其行政职能，重则出现腐败和滥用职权。对保证政府的制约和监督，是政府正确决策和依法积极履行职能的不可缺少的条件。根据依法治国基本方略和依法行政的基本要求，政府环保履职的强化必须具有法律依据。如果法律在政府环境保护履职方面的规定存在缺陷，则只有通过立法才能弥补该缺陷，从而为政府履职的强化提供法律依据。鉴于《环保法》和其他环境法律中缺乏对政府环保履职的规范、制约和监督制度，当前的当务之急应当是以修订《环保法》为契机，弥补这个关键问题上的缺陷。

如上所述，对政府履行环保公共职能做出制度安排，正是《环保法》

的特殊功能。因此，《环保法》的修订应当抓住这个重点进行制度创新。修改《环保法》的目的，一是规范和保障政府环保职能得到切实的履行，二是规范和保障行政部门以外的各种法律主体对政府有关环境的行政行为进行有效的制约和监督，防止关于环境问题的不当行政。这两个目的相辅相成，互相紧密联系，缺一不可，也不可偏废。为了达到这两个目的，新的《环保法》应根据我国国情和 20 多年来《环保法》的实践经验进行制度创新。其中应包括：关于政府各部门对照科学发展理念检查和调整其行政职责的规定；关于环境与发展综合决策制度的规定；关于环境公共咨询制度的规定；关于行政约谈和环保履职行政建议的规定；关于上级督办和代办、财政激励、行政监察和公务员管理、人大法律监督、信息公开等制度的规定。

第三，填补现行法律的空白。

新的《环保法》应当根据我国社会主义市场经济快速发展的现实，对需要立法但其他环境法律没有做出规定的一些制度和措施及时做出规定。这类制度和措施有环境功能区划和生态功能区划、行政限批、重污染企业退出、环境风险与损害评估等，“绿色信贷”、“绿色证券”、“绿色保险”、“绿色采购”等制度的规定等。

五、结论

现行《环保法》具有独特功能，是一部不可取消也不可替代的法律。它对我国环境保护事业的发展起到了不可磨灭的保障作用。在新的时代条件下，《环保法》暴露出许多不适应时代要求和环境管理现实需要的缺陷和问题，亟须修改和更新。

现实中存在的“发展的资源环境代价过大”的问题加重了修改《环保法》的紧迫性。科学发展观的提出和加快转变发展方式的新要求，为《环保法》的修改提供了新的指导思想和更高的要求。我国环境保护工作的实践表明，缺乏规范和制约政府有关环境的行政行为的制度是我国环境保护法律中的一个较大缺陷。这个缺陷是许多地方政府和政府有些部门中“唯GDP”发展观屡禁不止的一个重要原因。因此，《环保法》的修改应抓住这个问题，弥补这个缺陷。新的《环保法》将填补我国环境保护部门法在法律关系主体覆盖面上的缺陷，建立规范和制约政府环境保护公共职能的履行的制度，使政府在环境保护领域里更好地发挥它应当发挥的作用。

《环境保护法》修改思路[①]

杨朝飞[②]

我国《环境保护法》自 1989 年颁布实施，至今已达 17 年之久。近年来，《环境保护法》修改已引起社会越来越多的关注。自 2002 年以来，全国人大代表、全国政协委员关于《环境保护法》修改的建议和提案不断增加，呼声强烈。2004 年以来的 3 年中，“两会”共接到关于修改《环境保护法》的建议和提案 35 件，占环保立法建议和提案总数的近一半；多达 400 余名全国人大代表参与建议。盛世修法，正当其时。《环境保护法》修改工作影响深远、意义重大，需要进行深入研究和论证。现基于初步研究，就《环境保护法》修改提出以下思路。

《环境保护法》的历史功绩

《环境保护法》是我国环境保护事业进入法律化阶段的重要标志，在我国环境保护工作中发挥了重大作用。主要表现在：（1）界定了“环境”的定义、范围，明确了法律的调整对象；（2）为我国环境和资源保护法律体系确立了基本框架，推动了我国环境和资源保护各单行法律法规的全面创建；（3）把国家环境保护的方针、原则和基本制度以法律的形式确定下来，其中许多法律制度成为我国环境管理中行之有效的重要手段；（4）指导和推动了地方环境保护立法工作。

① 本文原刊于《环境保护》2007 年第 4 期。
② 杨朝飞，时任国家环境保护总局政策法规司司长。

《环境保护法》修改的争论

《环境保护法》颁布实施以来，国内外经济社会以及环境保护的形势发生了巨大变化，我国社会主义市场经济体制逐步完善，人民生活水平日渐提高，国民的环境意识和法律意识日益增强，现行《环境保护法》从理念到内容已显露出诸多缺陷和不足，无法满足时代变化的新要求。目前，社会各界关于《环境保护法》修改的关注程度不断提高，对有关修改的争论日益激烈。

修改论 认为《环境保护法》的基本内容已远远落后于时代，许多规定早已过时，无法适应新时期环境保护工作的要求，应当进行修改。

废止论 认为《环境保护法》的许多规定已在各单行法律中得到体现，其作用已基本被各单行法律架空，《环境保护法》中存在的问题完全可以通过修改单行法律来解决，《环境保护法》已失去存在的必要，可以废止。

搁置论 认为《环境保护法》应当进行修改，但由于目前人们对环境保护规律性的认识以及对重要法律关系调整的认识尚不够成熟，担心修改不好反而会加速这部法律的“死亡”，因此建议应当暂时搁置。

改造论 认为目前政府有法不依是我国环境管理面临的最突出、最棘手的问题之一，究其根源主要是我国环境法律法规中对规范政府环境保护行为存在严重缺陷，因此建议将《环境保护法》改造成一部重点调整和约束政府行为的法律。

《环境保护法》修改的必要性

问题的提出

（1）政府在环境保护方面不作为、干预执法及决策失误是造成环境顽疾久治不愈的主要原因。

政府是环境保护的主要责任主体，政府履行环境责任情况的优劣直接关系到当地环境质量的好坏。近年来所发生的一系列重大环境违法事件，使我们不得不探究政府是否真正履行了其对辖区环境保护质量负责的责任。从 2004 年造成近百万群众饮用水中断 26 天、直接经济损失达 3 亿多元的那起震惊全国的“沱江重大水污染事件”，到 2005 年国家环保总局紧急叫停总投资达 1 179 亿元“未环评先上马”的 30 个大型违规建设项目，再到 2006 年由于政府行政不作为导致的甘肃徽县数百群众血铅超标和湖南岳阳饮用水水源砷超标两起重大环境事件，一件件触目惊心的环境违法事件使我们看到，许多环境违法事件背后都与政府有着千丝万缕的联系。

一些政府在单纯追求经济利益的错误政绩观指导下，大搞地方保护主义，成为环境违法行为的保护伞、挡箭牌。一些政府出台各式各样的“土政策”，严重干扰了正常的环境执法。在 2004 年的环保专项行动中，发现有 18 个地方制定了 200 多项各类违反环保法律法规的“土政策”。一些政府行政不作为或者乱作为，对环境违法行为睁一只眼、闭一只眼，遇到问题相互推诿、避重就轻，致使人民群众健康和财产受到重大损失。一些政府在进行决策时，忽视环境规律，不进行深入细致的科学评估和论证，草率行事，独断专行，一些错误或不恰当的决策致使生态环境遭受严重损害。政府不履行环境责任以及履行环境责任不到位，已成为制约我国环境保护事业发展的严重障碍，必须狠下决心彻底解决。

（2）法律缺失，政府环境责任成为一纸空文。

造成上述种种问题有多方面原因，但主要原因在于：一是目前我国现行各单项环境资源法律多以公民、法人或者其他组织作为主要调整对象，而规范和约束政府行为的法律规定非常有限；二是《环境保护法》中只是原则性地规定了地方政府对辖区环境质量负责，没有明确规定政府部门如何履行责任以及如何保证其履行责任，无法发挥规范和约束政府的作用；三是《环境保护法》对环境监管主体的职能划分不清，责任不明，统管部门与分管部门之间、分管部门相互之间职能交叉，缺位、错位现象大量存在，其结果是，环保部门统一监督管理的职责难以落实到位，有些基层环保部门在上级督办、政府干预、群众上访三重压力中工作，举步维艰，有的地方甚至出现环保局长自己充当举报人写匿名信向上级反映应该授权由他来解决问题的尴尬局面；四是现行法律对中央政府环境保护责任的规定非常有限，且缺乏中央政府与地方政府的协调与配合机制。其结果是，中央政令不畅通，国家环境保护的强烈政治意愿在地方被打折扣，中央与地方政府管辖权限可能出现真空地带。

修改《环境保护法》须以强化政府环保责任为重点

环境保护的关键在政府。通过修改《环境保护法》，突出强化政府的环境保护责任十分必要。

（1）强化政府环境保护责任，是落实科学发展观的政治需要。

“明者因时而变，智者随事而制。”党的十六大以来，党中央提出了科学发展观和构建社会主义和谐社会等一系列重要战略思想和立党为公、执政为民的先进理念，制定了全面建设小康社会的发展目标。这些思想和理念为摆正环境与发展的关系以及在法律中强化政府环境保护责任提供了坚实的政治理论基础和有力的思想武器，成为修法之源、立法之本。

政府是科学发展观的重要践行者。在《环境保护法》修改中强化政府环境保护责任，是落实科学发展观的政治需要和具体体现；政府必须以法律为准绳，规范和约束自己的行为，确保各项政府决策体现科学发展观的思想，落实科学发展观的要求。

（2）强化政府环境保护责任，是贯彻国务院《决定》和第六次全国环保大会精神的具体体现。

国务院《决定》明确指出要加强对环境保护工作的领导，落实环境保护领导责任制，强调政府要将思想统一到落实科学发展观上来，政府主要领导和有关部门主要负责人应是所辖区和本系统的第一责任人，确保认识到位、责任到位、措施到位。在第六次全国环保大会上，温家宝总理提出保护环境是政府义不容辞的责任，要建立环保目标管理责任制，并将环保目标纳入经济社会发展评价范围和干部政绩考核，要建立环保工作问责制。党中央和国务院对落实政府环境保护责任的决心已定，方向已明。

为了贯彻落实国务院《决定》和第六次全国环保大会精神，有必要通过修改《环境保护法》，强化政府环境保护责任，通过一系列法律明确规定把党中央和国务院强化政府环境保护责任的决心和意愿转化为有约束力的具体管理制度和法律责任，从而保证政府在履行环境保护责任时有法可依、违法必究。

（3）强化政府环境保护责任，是实现历史性转变的必然要求。

党中央、国务院明确了今后一个时期我国环境保护的方向和任务，环境保护进入了实现历史性转变的关键时期。在这个关键时期，我国环境形势严峻，环境问题凸显，环境与经济社会发展的关系比过去任何时期都要复杂，矛盾与冲突更加激烈，协调环境保护与经济社会关系的难度更大，任务更艰巨，对政府履行环境保护责任提出了更高的要求。各级政府是中央政令的传达者和执行者，是各地经济建设和社会发展的主导者和公共服务提供者，是各地经济发展与环境保护高速路上的总调度。政府应当站在落实科学发展观和执政为民的高度，对当地经济、社会、环境因素统筹兼顾，全盘考虑，从思想和行动上摆正环境与经济的关系，将实现历史性转变所要求的“同步”、“并重”和“综合”落实在行动中；应当通过实施战略环境影响评价制度，对重大决策实施风险评价制度，建立补救和恢复措施，减少和避免政府的决策失误，并将可能的损失降至最低。

随着社会发展，环境质量已成为群众最为关注的热点之一。对百姓而言，政府不仅要保证人民生活更加殷实、富足，更要为人民提供舒适、优美的生活环境。政府对待环境问题的态度、政府履行其环境责任的行动和效果，已成为党和政府执政形象的体现，这一切应当通过法律来规范化和制度化。

（4）强化政府环境保护责任，是根除环境顽疾的关键点和突破口。

在现实中有两种不遵守法律的现象：一是政府部门有法不依；二是开发者或生产者有法不依。两者相比，前者更具根本意义，更需要法律的规范和制约。长期以来，我国环境污染严重，环境违法现象屡禁不止，已成为环境管理工作中久治不愈的一块“顽疾”，看起来许多违法现象出自企业，但究其根源，责任还是在政府。企业之所以在法律面前肆无忌惮，正是地方政府一味追求经济发展忽视环境保护的后果。

尽管《环境保护法》中规定地方人民政府对辖区环境质量负责，但并未规定如果不履行其责任的后果。在这样软弱无力的法律面前，一些地方领导人选择了“先发展、后环保”的道路，在经济利益的驱使下，不顾当地的资源禀赋、环境容量，贪图眼前和局部利益，“先上车后买票”，个别政府甚至提出“宁可呛死，不要饿死”的荒谬观点，把人民健康、群众利益置于脑后。在一些错误思想的指导下，环境保护工作难上加难，一些环保局长往往要在“乌纱”和“污染”、“位子”和“帽子”中做出选择，“站得住的顶不住，顶得住的站不住”，有时不得不代人受过，甚至成为牺牲者。

历史的经验和教训告诉我们，要从根本上解决我国的环境问题，关键点和突破口在于强化政府责任，在于规范和约束政府行为。必须改变目前《环境保护法》关于政府环境责任规定过于原则化，缺乏责任追究制度的现状。应当通过这部法律修改，强化各级政府作为环境保护第一责任人的责任和义务，使各级政府领导将落实科学发展观和履行环境保护责任真正“入脑入心”，使各级党委、政府对环境保护真正从思想上重视、在行动中落实。

（5）强化政府环境保护责任，是建立规范和约束政府行为长效机制的经验总结。

党中央、国务院领导一直高度重视环境保护工作，先后对一些具体环保工作给予了极大关注，多次作出重要批示，仅晋、陕、蒙、宁 4 省（区）交界地区电石、铁合金、焦炭行业的污染问题，中央领导同志的批示就有 15 次之多，有力地推动了中央和地方的环保工作。

近年来，针对一些重点环境问题，国家也开展了各类环保专项行动，不断加大对违法行为的查处力度和对责任人的追究力度。2005 年，监察部、国家环保总局对九大环境违法案件进行挂牌督办，17 名责任人受到撤职、记过、警告等处分。有 12 个省、区、市在查处环境违法案件时，处分了责任人 163 人，其中政府领导 7 人，职能部门领导 20 人。2006 年国务院七部门开展了“整治违法排污企业保障群众健康”环保专项行动，并已取得阶段成果，极大地震慑了环境违法行为，给一些地方政府敲响了警钟。

我们应当认识到，环境保护是一项长期而艰巨的任务，要从根本上规范和约束政府行为，绝不能仅靠领导批示和专项行动，必须以立法的形式建立起一套规范和约束政府行为的长效管理机制，使各种政策和措施法律化、制度化、规范化。

《环境保护法》修改中强化政府责任就是要不断摸索规律、总结经验、吸取教训，使长效机制的各项制度不断建立和健全，不断成熟和完善，使各种问题能够在法律框架内按照法律所要求的程序、步骤和措施迅速、高效地得到解决。否则，凡事只有靠领导批示处理、遇问题就得靠专项行动解决的就事论事的做法必将使环境保护工作陷入盲目和被动的困境。

（6）强化政府环境保护责任，是依法行政历史趋势的必然要求。

随着依法治国，建设社会主义法制国家进程的不断加快，我国在建立和完善适应社会主义市场经济体制的法律体系方面取得了显著成绩。《行政许可法》、《行政监察法》、《行政诉讼法》、《各级人大常委会监督法》、《最高人民检察院关于渎职侵权犯罪案件立案标准的规定》等一批规范政府行政行为、强化政府依法行政责任的法律法规相继颁布实施，我国司法体制改革进程不断加快。这一系列重要成果对从根本上对解决政府不作为、乱作为具有重要意义。

《环境保护法》修改中强化政府环境保护责任，是我国推进政府部门依法行政历史进程的必然要求，是行政体制改革在环境保护领域的体现和进一步深化。通过法律强化政府环境保护责任，就是要用法律武器给政府环境违法行为以震慑，对敢于公然违法，在环境保护方面徇私枉法、失职、渎职的政府部门，坚决追究其法律责任。

（7）强化政府环境保护责任，是环境保护法律体系的丰富和完善。

经过近 30 年的发展，我国已初步建立了环境保护法律体系，但我国现行环境保护法律中规范和约束政府行为的法律规定非常有限。2006 年初，监察部与国家环保总局共同发布了《环境保护违法违纪行为处分暂行规定》，对政府及其部门的环境责任追究作出了相关规定，但这一部门规章从立法层次和执行效率上都相对较低。

《环境保护法》修改中强化政府环境保护责任，将法律调整对象扩展至政府，并且建立和完善一批规范和约束政府行为的管理制度，是对我国环境保护法律体系的丰富和完善，是建设有中国特色环境保护法律体系的有益探索。

在法律修改中，应当最大限度地吸纳和借鉴现有的立法成果，对一些经实践证明在规范和约束政府行为方面行之有效的管理政策和制度，例如战略环境影响评价制度、生态区划与环境功能区划制度、环境目标责任制、环境质量公告和信息发布制度、生态补偿制度、责任追究制度等，应当通过修改《环境保护法》予以确立，使我国环境法律体系更加健全和完善。

未来10～15年正是我国环境保护的关键时期，规范政府行为需要法律强有力的保障。现有的单行法主要针对企事业单位，不足以解决政府的问题，只能通过基本法来解决。因此，在各方条件基本成熟的情况下应当尽早启动修法计划，从而保证修法过程时间充分、有条不紊、层层深入，避免贻误良机或者草率行事。

国际经验及其借鉴

国外许多环境法律中都有针对政府环境保护职责的规定，尽管法律名称不同，但对政府职责的规定大多见诸于专门法律或综合性法律，如美国《国家环境政策法》、日本《环境基本法》、加拿大《环境保护法》以及英国《环境法》等，极少见于单行法。国外法律对我国《环境保护法》修改中强化政府环境保护责任具有重要借鉴意义。美国《国家环境政策法》作为一部从宏观层面调整国家基本政策的专门法律，其经验尤其重要。

（1）法律调整对象是政府行为，立法目的是使政府各部门的职责与国家环境政策目标相一致。

美国《国家环境政策法》于1969年出台，当时法律对美国政府各部门的授权或多或少存在同国家环境政策不一致的情况。这种不一致，妨碍政府完整统一地行使公共环保职能。该法出台就是要明确政府的环境职责，将政府各部门的职能与国家环境政策统一起来。为此，这部法律确立了环境影响评价和环境报告两项重要制度，从程序上来规范政府行为。其主要做法是：（1）总统每年要向国会提交环境质量报告；（2）任命总统府设立环境质量委员会，对提交环境质量报告提供支持；（3）对人类环境质量具有重大影响的各项提案或法律草案、建议报告以及其他重大联邦行为，应由相关人员提供一份有关环境影响的详细说明；（4）联邦政府各部门要对照《国家环境政策法》检查现行法律对本部门的授权，使其与国家环境政策相一致。

我国目前面临的问题与美国当年有类似之处，我国《环境保护法》修改应当充分借鉴美国《国家环境政策法》的经验，通过确立相关程序和具体管理制度，规范和约束政府行为，使政府决策统一到落实科学发展观、加强环境保护、实现历史性转变的总体目标下。

（2）对政府的环境责任较多采用义务性、原则性、鼓励性规范，较少采用禁止性、强制性、惩罚性规范。

美国《国家环境政策法》对政府行为的规定主要为一些原则性、鼓励性规定。就我国《环境保护法》修改而言，应当借鉴国外经验，在法律中规定政府环境责任时，应充分考虑到规范和约束政府行为与规范和约束企事业机构法人行为的区别；采用刚性规定与原则性规定相结合，义务性、原则性与鼓励性规定为主，禁止性、强制性与惩罚性规定为辅，且少而精的形式。既要避免法律刚性过强难以实施，也要防止法律过于原则性，缺乏威慑力。

通过借鉴国际经验，我国《环境保护法》修改中应突出强化政府环境保护责任，将政府行为作为法律主要调整对象，在法律修改中，建议将该法更名为《中华人民共和国环境法》。

应确立或完善的主要法律制度

《环境保护法》修改应当紧紧围绕落实“地方政府对环境质量负总责”的要求，重点解决地方政府干扰环境执法问题，认真落实主要领导是第一责任人、分管领导是直接责任人的要求，创建和强化一套行之有效的环境管理制度。落实政府环保责任应确立或者完善的主要法律制度和措施可归纳为 5 大类。

科学决策类 （1）战略环境影响评价。对各级政府和部门编制的区域开发和行业发展规划，必须进行环境影响评价；对各级政府和部门提出的对环境有重大影响的决策，必须进行环境影响论证。（2）按主体功能区划分区开发。根据资源禀赋、环境容量、生态状况、人口数量以及国家发展规划和产业政策，明确不同区域的功能定位和发展方向，分别实行优化开发、重点开发、限制开发和禁止开发。（3）超总量地区暂停开发。国务院将主要污染物总量控制指标逐级分解到地方各级人民政府；对超过污染物总量控制指标、生态破坏严重或者尚未完成生态恢复任务的地区，不得审批新增污染物排放总量和对生态有较大影响的建设项目。（4）环保规划、计划。重点区域、流域生态规划；各级人民政府应当制定环境保护五年规划、年度计划；各级人民政府应当将环境保护目标、任务和措施纳入国民经济社会发展规划，报同级人大审议批准；各级地方人民政府批准的环保规划，须报上一级政府环保部门备案。

实施执行类 （1）环境保护目标责任制。各级政府要和下级政府签订环保目标责任状，确定量化指标、实施措施、分步实施方案，明确考核和责任追究方式。（2）强制淘汰制度。（3）环保基础设施建设。各级政府要组织建设城市污水、生活垃圾、危险废物等环保基础设施。（4）跨界环境责任协调制度。建立跨省界河流断面水质考核制度，省级人民政府应当确保出境水质达到考核目标；国家加强跨省界环境执法及污染纠纷的协调。（5）区域生态补偿。上游省份排污对下游省份造成污染事故的，上游省级人民政府应当承担赔付补偿责任，并依法追究相关单位和人员的责任。（6）环境应急管理及信息通报。各级人民政府要制定突发环境事件应急预案，并组织实施；各级人民政府要建立上、下级人民政府环境应急处理和决策信息通报机制并保证交流渠道畅通。（7）环境教育。各级人民政府应当组织开展环境保护的宣传教育，使公众了解环境保护科学知识和相关信息。

保障措施类 （1）环保公共预算制度。各级人民政府要将环保投入列入本级财政支出预算的重点内容，并逐年增加。（2）制定有利于环境保护的经济政策。国务院和省、自治区、直辖市人民政府应当制定税收、价格、信贷、贸易等经济政策，鼓励、支持单位和个人参与环境保护。（3）建立跨行政区环境问题的监督协调机制。国家设置区域性环保派出机构，协调和督促有关地方政府的环保工作；地方政府应当支持环保派出机构工作；进一步总结和探索设区城市环保派出机构监管模式，完善地方环境管理体制。（4）环保能力建设。各级人民政府应当加强环保执法、监督、监测、风险预警、机构建设，落实职能、编制和经费。（5）政府高层协调机构（环委会）。各级人民政府应当成立环境保护事务的议事协调机构。（6）联合执法机制。（7）政府绿色采购。各级人民政府及有关部门应当优先采购经过环境认证或者其他环境友好的产品。

监督机制类 （1）政府环保工作向人大报告制度。报告内容——环保规划、计划、预算及其执行情况；报告期限——年度报告、中期评估、五年总结；人大监督，政府整改。（2）对政府环保职责的监督制度。上级政府环保部门，代表本级政府对下级政府进行环保考核；同级监察机关对政府的监督。（3）环境行政复议制度。（4）环境法律援助与救济制度。（5）信息公开和公众参与。各级人民政府和有关部门，应当公开环境信息，并为公众环境知情、参与、表达、监督和救济提供便利。（6）行政诉讼制度。

责任追究类 政府环境责任追究，包括：未完成环境责任目标；造成跨界环境纠纷；干预环境执法；决策失误；造成重大环境事故；明显的环境不作为。

环保组织：环境公益诉讼的主力军
——《民诉法》修正案评析与《环保法》修改建议[①]

别 涛[②]

李克强同志2011年12月20日在第七次全国环境保护大会上讲话指出：要“推动环境公益诉讼和法律援助，强化环境司法保障”。目前，推进环境公益诉讼已经成为社会共识，特别是新通过的《民诉法》修改决定增加了“公益诉讼”的规定，更成为环境公益诉讼制度建设的新起点。正在研究之中的《环保法》修正案，应当在《民诉法》新规定的基础上，进一步明确环保部门和环保社会组织提起环境公益诉讼的主体资格。

一、保护环境：为什么需要公益诉讼

何谓“公益诉讼”？顾名思义，是指为了维护公共利益而提起的诉讼。它是公共利益损害的一种民事救济机制，主要适用于出现了民事侵权行为，致使社会公共利益遭受民事性质的损害，但没有合适的原告提起诉讼的特殊情形。

针对民事侵权损害，一般是由直接受害人提起诉讼。在某些特殊情形下，民事侵权行为即使损害了社会公共利益，或者侵害了不特定多数人的共同利益，但没有合乎资格的原告提起诉讼，公共利益也因此难以得到保障。

在我国出现这种情形的根源，在于公有制造成的民事主体缺失，即所谓人人都是主人，但每个人又都不能行使所有权。根据我国宪法规定，我

① 本文原载于《中国环境报》第3版，2012-10-12。
② 别涛，环境保护部政策法规司副司长。

国实行自然资源的公有制。对于水体、海洋、空气、土壤等公共环境要素，普通个人不能行使完整的所有权；行政部门并非环境资源的当然所有者，其行政管理权也是有限度的。

例如，某个企业的排污行为造成环境污染，行政部门固然可以依法对其实施责令限期治理等行政处理，或者依法做出罚款、停产等行政处罚；直接的污染受害人可以就其个人遭受的损害提起赔偿损失等民事诉讼；司法机关还可能对构成犯罪的严重污染行为追究刑事责任。但是，对污染环境造成的社会公共利益损害，行为人还应当承担赔偿国家损失等民事责任。

问题在于，公共利益或者国家利益受损，谁来担当原告角色呢？

对公共环境的民事损害，个人固然可以就其个人遭受的直接损害提起私益性质的民事诉讼，但却不能为了社会公益提起民事诉讼；如无法律特殊授权，行政部门一般无权直接裁决民事赔偿等责任，也不能作为直接受害人向法院提起民事诉讼；司法机关基于“民不告、官不理”原则，对民事案件通常也不会主动干预。因此，我国现行民诉法欠缺的仅仅是自己不是直接受害者，但想以自己的名义，代表公共利益或者不特定多数受害者提起民事诉讼的主体资格。

正是针对公共利益受损而原告主体缺位的情形，公益诉讼制度应运而生。为了保障社会公共利益，国家通过立法授予某些机关、社会组织以原告资格，并通过公益诉讼程序维护公共利益，就是一种法律主体的弥补。

二、环境公益诉讼渐成共识

近年来，在各方面的推动下，建立环境公益诉讼制度，逐步形成了社会共识，特别是全国“两会”代表、专家学者、环保组织持续不断地呼吁，环保部门大力推动，司法机关大胆实践，环境公益诉讼取得积极效果。万鄂湘、梁从诚等全国政协委员，吕忠梅、黄细花等全国人大代表，先后提出多项相关建议和议案，新闻媒体对环境公益诉讼做了大量宣传报道。

2005 年 12 月 3 日，国务院发布的《关于落实科学发展观加强环境保护的决定》指出，“健全社会监督机制，发挥社会团体的作用，鼓励检举和揭发各种环境违法行为，推动环境公益诉讼。”

2011 年 12 月 15 日，国务院印发的《国家环境保护“十二五”规划》规定：“建立健全环境保护举报制度，畅通环境信访、12369 环保热线、网络邮箱等信访投诉渠道，鼓励实行有奖举报。支持环境公益诉讼。”

显而易见，最高行政机关明确鼓励和支持“社会团体”提起环境公益诉讼。

2010 年 6 月 29 日，最高人民法院印发的《关于为加快经济发展方式转变提供司法保障和服务的若干意见》提出，“依法受理环境保护行政部门代表国家提起的环境污染损害赔偿纠纷案件，严厉打击一切破坏环境的行为。”最高人民检察院的态度也非常积极。由此可见，最高司法机关明确认可“环保行政部门”可以提起环境公益诉讼。

正是在这样的背景之下，最高立法机关对《民诉法》的修改也吸纳了环境公益诉讼制度。

三、环境公益诉讼在实践中不断推进

设立环境法庭、受理环境公益诉讼案件，成为司法机关近年来强化环境司法、支持环保事业的重要举措。无论是环境公益诉讼的制度建设，还是司法实践，都取得良好法律效果、社会效果，同时也产生积极的环境效果。

（一）环境公益诉讼的制度建设成果丰富

在国家立法缺乏明确规定的情况下，贵阳市及其所属清镇市法院积极探索，自 2007 年 11 月 20 日正式揭牌以来，在全国最早成立环境法庭，受理和裁判环境公益诉讼案件，并注重环境公益诉讼的制度建设。无锡、昆明等城市和海南、云南、重庆、浙江、江苏等省高级法院领导，高度关注环境保护，联合检察院及公安、环保等行政部门，制定了专门规则，指导环境公益诉讼实践。在这过程中，最高法院、环保部密切协作，对环境公益诉讼实践给予了大力推动和指导，并于2010年5月31日联合印发《水资源司法保护工作座谈会纪要》。

具有代表性的环境公益诉讼指导性文件见表1。

表1　有关环境公益诉讼的规范性文件（12个地方，18份文件）

地方	文件名称（按时间顺序）	发布机关	发布时间
贵阳市	关于环境保护法庭案件受理范围的规定	市中院	2007年11月
	贵阳市促进生态文明建设条例（第23条）	市人大	2010年3月
	关于大力推进环境公益诉讼、促进生态文明建设的实施意见	市法院	2010年3月
无锡市	关于办理环境民事公益诉讼案件的试行规定	市法院 市检察院	2008年9月
	关于在环境民事公益诉讼中具有环保行政职能的部门向检察机关提供证据的意见	市法院 市检察院 市法制办	2008年12月
昆明市	关于建立环境保护执法协调机制的实施意见	市法院 市检察院 市公安局 市环保局	2008年11月
	环境公益诉讼救济专项资金管理暂行办法	市政府	2010年10月
	关于办理环境民事公益诉讼案件若干问题的意见	市法院	2010年11月
云南省	全省法院环境保护审判建设及环境保护案件审理工作座谈会纪要	省高院	2009年5月
青岛市城阳区	关于建立环保执法协调联动工作机制的实施意见	区法院 区检察院 区环保分局	2010年4月
嘉兴市	关于环境保护公益诉讼的若干意见	市检察院 市环保局	2010年5月
湖州市	关于建立环境保护公益诉讼制度的若干意见	市法院 市检察院	2010年8月
浙江省	关于积极运用民事、行政检察职能加强环境保护的意见	省检察院 省环保厅	2010年8月
玉溪市	关于办理环境资源民事公益诉讼案件若干问题的意见	市法院 市检察院	2011年2月
海南省	海南省级环境公益诉讼资金管理暂行办法	省高院 省财政厅	2011年9月

地方	文件名称（按时间顺序）	发布机关	发布时间
重庆市	关于试点集中办理环境保护案件的意见	市高院 市检察院 市公安局 市环保局	2011 年 11 月
	关于试点设立专门审判庭集中审理刑事、民事、行政环境保护案件的意见	市高院	2011 年 11 月
江苏省	关于在我省部分法院开展环境保护案件集中化审判试点工作的通知	省高院	2012 年 4 月

（二）环境公益诉讼的司法实践进展良好

据中华环保联合会不完全统计，我国各级法院近年来已经受理环境民事公益诉讼至少 20 起以上；提起诉讼的原告，主要涉及检察机关、环境保护等行政机关、环保组织三种类型。具体案件情况见表 2。

表 2　主要环境民事公益诉讼案件（21 起）

当事人		判决结果	典型案情
原告	被告		
检察机关	企业或个人	6 起，原告胜诉	2009 年，广州番禺区检察院起诉某皮革厂偷排废水造成海域陆源污染，要求停止侵害并承担环境污染损失费用
环保组织	企业	8 起，原告胜诉	2010 年，中华环保联合会起诉要求贵阳市某造纸厂停止向河道排放污水，并承担原告律师费和诉讼费
环保部门	企业	1 起，原告胜诉	2010 年，昆明市环保局起诉要求某农牧公司停止对环境的侵害，赔偿为大龙潭水污染所发生的全部费用
库区管理局	企业	1 起，原告胜诉	2007 年，某公司产生的废渣堆放污染了红枫湖上游的昌羊河，贵阳市“两湖一库”管理局要求被告停止排污损害
海洋局	企业	1 起，原告胜诉	“塔斯曼海”油轮发生溢油事故，致使渤海渔业资源和生态环境遭受严重破坏。天津市海洋局起诉船东索赔，法院判决被告赔偿原告海洋环境容量损失及调查评估经费等计 10 000 余万元，渔业资源损失和调查评估费等共计 1 500 余万元

当事人		判决结果	典型案情
原告	被告		
环保部门	个人 企业	1起， 原告胜诉	东营市中级人民法院2012年12月14日对东营市环境保护局诉东营市垦利县双河村村民吴某、淄博市周村某溶剂化工厂环境污染责任纠纷一案公开宣判，一审判决被告赔偿原告东营市环境保护局环境污染损失费用742.560 7万元，用于被污染场地的修复治理工作
环保组织	个人	1起， 原告胜诉	2012年2月，肇事者高某某将有毒有害淤泥倾倒在占地12亩的鱼塘内。常州市环境公益协会作为原告，将被告告上了法庭。 7月20日，溧阳市人民法院水资源保护法庭开庭。经过法庭辩论，高某某答应尽快请来从事生态修复的专业环保公司，对污染鱼塘进行生态修复。为此，高某某支付场地修复费用为70万元。 12亩的废弃鱼塘生态修复的情况如何？是否能够重新利用？在常州市环境公益协会的见证下，高某某委托常州市环科院对污染场地进行了技术评估。 11月13日第二次开庭，原被告再次对簿公堂，双方当庭达成了民事调解书： 为了避免这块场地的污染转移，被告答应与拥有这块废弃鱼塘土地使用权的农户，以6 000元的价格签订两年承包合同，以保障短期内不让农户种植或养殖食用类的农作物或鱼类；为进一步推进生态修复，种植芦苇等非食用类的经济作物，使这块场地的污染场得以自然净化
环保组织	企业	未决	原告：中华环保联合会 2013年3月1日 被告：潍坊乐港食品股份有限公司 诉讼请求：（1）依法判令被告立即停止昌乐县五图街道办事处第三商品猪养殖场排放超标废水的违法行为，停止对排污渠沿岸张家庄、宋家庄、胡家庄等地下水和下游潍坊市重要饮用水源庙子水库的污染行为；（2）依法判令被告消除对上述排污渠沿岸地下水及下游水库所造成的危险，并采取合理措施消除和修复对排污渠沿岸地下水及下游水库所造成的污染损害；（3）依法判令被告支付环境污染赔偿款用于治理和修复受其污染的环境，赔偿金额为7 064 064元人民币；（4）依法判令被告承担本案的诉讼费、原告工作人员的交通住宿差旅费用6 772元、律师费5万元及检测鉴定7 110元

当事人		判决结果	典型案情
原告	被告		
环保部门	企业	1 起，胜诉	韩城市人民法院 2013 年 3 月 23 日判决，被告韩城市白矾矿业有限责任公司支付因污染白矾河环境损害费用 100.5 万元

四、《民诉法》修改：环境公益诉讼是亮点

全国人大常委会及其法制工作委员会对环境公益诉讼的社会呼声以及司法实践高度关注，并在研究修改民事诉讼法的过程中给予了积极回应。不过，有关起诉主体的核心措辞经历了重要变化。

[一审稿] 2011 年 10 月 29 日，全国人大常委会第 23 次会议对《民诉法》修正案草案进行一审，随后向社会公开征求意见。草案对公益诉讼制度作了专门规定："对污染环境、侵害众多消费者合法权益等损害社会公共利益的行为，有关机关、社会团体可以向人民法院提起诉讼。"

[二审稿] 2012 年 4 月 24 日，全国人大常委会第 26 次会议对《民诉法》修正案草案进行二审。二审稿中，并将此前规定的公益诉讼的主体由"有关机关、社会团体"修改为"法律规定的机关和有关社会团体"。

[三审稿] 2012 年 8 月 31 日，第十一届全国人大常委会第 28 次会议三审通过了《关于修改〈中华人民共和国民事诉讼法〉的决定》。该决定规定：增加一条，作为《民诉法》第 55 条："对污染环境、侵害众多消费者合法权益等损害社会公共利益的行为，法律规定的机关和有关组织可以向人民法院提起诉讼。"

《民诉法》修改后，有关机关和环保组织，针对污染环境等损害社会公共利益的行为，将可以据此提起诉讼。这是我国"公益诉讼"制度建设的突破性进展，因而也成为这次《民诉法》修改的一大亮点，更成为我国环境公益诉讼制度建设的新起点。

五、环境公益诉讼：谁可起诉是焦点

2011年8月环境保护部向全国人大环资委提交了《环境保护法》修正案建议稿，建议确定环保专业组织的环境公益诉讼资格，并提供了论证材料。环境保护部的建议为："因污染损害公共环境利益的，经依法登记的环境保护社会团体、县级以上地方人民政府环境保护行政主管部门，可以依法向人民法院提起诉讼，要求污染者承担侵权责任。"全国人大环资委研究认为，公益诉讼问题应由全国人大常委会在《民事诉讼法》修订中统一考虑。

在《民事诉讼法》修订过程中，公益诉讼制度成为各方面关注的热点问题之一，全国人大法工委进行了大量认真调研，并通过专家座谈会、部门座谈会等形式听取有关方面意见，通过公开征求意见也收到大量反馈。法工委还专门听取过环保部门的意见和建议。

关于建立公益诉讼制度，事实上存在"一个共识、一个焦点"。一个共识，就是社会各方认为有必要规定公益诉讼制度；一个焦点，就是谁可作为起诉主体。

关于起诉主体，无非行政机关、检察机关、社会团体和公民个人四类。特定国家机关（包括行政部门、检察机关），经过法律规定明确授权，当然作为公益诉讼主体。至于公民个人，由于环境污染等领域的公益诉讼大多涉及复杂的技术，需要配置专用设备，并经过专门技术培训，进行符合标准规范的监测、采样、分析、化验，专用设备和相关费用都很高，这些因素会严重限制普通个人的有效诉讼能力，实际诉讼难度很大。至于环保社会团体，有兴趣，也有能力。据民政部统计已有几十万家，另外还有各种未取得注册登记的草根组织，数量太大，应予适当限定。

因此，争议焦点在于哪些机关和社团组织可以提起环境公益诉讼。

六、修改《环保法》：将环境公益诉讼进行到底

关于公益诉讼，《民诉法》修改决定的表述是："对污染环境、侵害众多消费者合法权益等损害社会公共利益的行为，法律规定的机关和有关组织可以向人民法院提起诉讼。"

但是，哪些"法律"可以规定公益诉讼的主体？哪些"机关"、哪些"社会组织"可以纳入法律规定的主体范围？除了污染环境，破坏资源领域能否适用公益诉讼？这四个问题依然有待环保法律进一步明确。

（一）哪些"法律"可以规定环境公益诉讼主体——《环境保护法》

《民诉法》明确规定了环境公益诉讼、消费者权益保护两类公益诉讼。关于消费者保护公益诉讼，法工委有关领导在《民诉法》修改决定通过之后曾经明确指出：立法机关正在抓紧修改《消费者权益保护法》，并正在研究当消费者权益受到侵害的时候，哪些涉及保护消费者的组织有权提起或适宜提起公益诉讼。

由此可以推想，既然立法机关认为侵害消费者权益的公益诉讼主体由《消费者权益保护法》规定，那么侵害环境权益的公益诉讼主体也就应当由《环境保护法》规定。

因此建议：国家立法机关在研究修改《环境保护法》修正案草案时，积极回应环保要求，顺应社会呼声，并吸收环保司法实践，对环境公益诉讼主体做出明确规定。如能如此，则能普遍适用于水、大气、噪声、固体废物、放射性、海洋等各个环保领域的公益诉讼，其他专项环保法律则无须分别规定。很难设想，在综合性的《环保法》之外，还有哪部其他单项环保法律更适合规定环境公益诉讼。

（二）哪些"机关"适合提起环境公益诉讼——环保行政机关

关于环境公益诉讼，我国个别单项环保法律已经有零星规定。1999 年

修订的《海洋环境保护法》第 90 条规定："对破坏海洋生态、海洋水产资源、海洋保护区，给国家造成重大损失的，由依照本法规定行使海洋环境监督管理权的部门代表国家对责任者提出损害赔偿要求。"

据此，"依照法律行使海洋环境监管权的部门"，可以提起海洋环境公益诉讼。根据海洋环保法的规定，这些部门具体包括五个部门，即所谓"五龙闹海"：国务院环保部门、国家海洋部门、国家海事部门、国家渔业部门、军队环保部门，此外还有沿海地方政府行使海洋环境监管权的部门。

因此建议：目前正在修改综合性的《环保法》，应当在海洋环保法和新的《民诉法》基础之上，对有权提起环境公益诉讼的行政机关，做出统一规定，其他单项环保法律则无须再做分散规定。建议具体表述为："县级以上人民政府环境保护行政主管部门和其他依照法律规定行使环境监督管理权的部门"，对污染环境等损害社会公共利益的行为，可以提起诉讼。当然，法律也可以授权检察机关提起环境公益诉讼。

（三）哪些"社会组织"适合提起环境公益诉讼——合法环保组织

毫无疑问，这是最为敏感，因而也是争议最大的问题。"社会组织"的具体名称林林总总，如社会团体、民间组织、民间机构、公民组织、非赢利组织、非政府组织（NGO）等。根据环境保护部 2010 年发布的《关于培育引导环保社会组织有序发展的指导意见》，"环保社会组织是以人与环境的和谐发展为宗旨，从事各类环境保护活动，为社会提供环境公益服务的非营利性社会组织，包括环保社团、环保基金会、环保民办非企业单位等多种类型。"

社会组织具备四个突出特征：一是非政府性，这使它区别于各种政府组织或者官办团体，因而表现出社会性；二是非赢利性，这使它区别于盈利性组织，因而表现出公益性；三是专业性，这使它得以聚积一定数量的专业人才，因而具有较强的活动能力；四是合法性，这使它区别于各种非法组织，因而具有合法开展活动的主体身份。

根据我国民政主管部门的分类，社会组织包括民办非企业单位、基金会、社会团体三大类。截至2011年年底，全国登记在册的各类社会组织共有45.7万个。其中：社会团体25.3万个，民办非企业单位20.2万个，基金会2 510个。此外，还有大量未经登记注册的社会组织。可见，社会组织包含社会团体；社会团体是社会组织的主要组成部分，但并非其全部。

正因如此，正式通过的《民诉法》修改决定将草案中的“有关社会团体”，修改为“有关组织”，意在包括社会团体之外的其他社会组织。法工委领导在有关修改说明中明确表示：至于哪些组织适宜提起民事诉讼，可以在制订相关法律时进一步明确规定。

因此建议：正在研究修改的《环保法》，应当在民诉法基础上，进一步明确规定：“依法登记的环境保护社会组织”，对污染环境等损害社会公共利益的行为，可以提起诉讼。

目前做出这样的规定，不仅具有诉讼法的基础，而且具有很强的可行性，环保组织必将成为环境公益诉讼的主力军。《2008年中国环保民间组织发展状况报告》显示，全国现有经过正式登记注册的各类环保民间组织3 539个。比较活跃的环保民间组织，有中华环保联合会、自然之友、地球村、污染受害者法律帮助中心、公众与环境研究中心、绿家园、达尔问、绿色流域、阿拉善SEE生态协会等。如中华环保联合会目前每年提起10起左右环境公益诉讼案件。

（四）破坏资源、损害生态能否适合提起环境公益诉讼范围——不应限于环境污染

《民诉法》明确规定的环境公益诉讼范围为污染环境，即“对污染环境……等损害社会公共利益的行为”，可以提起诉讼。事实上，在环保领域，损害公共环境利益的行为，主要有三种基本类型：一是污染水、气等环境要素，二是破坏森林、矿产等自然资源，三是损害湿地、物种等生态系统。可见，民诉法明确界定的环境公益诉讼范围是不完整的；同时，民诉法关于公益诉讼范围的规定又是相对开放的，即“污染环境……等损害社会公共利益的行为”，其适用前提是“损害社会公共利益”。

因此建议：有必要在作为环保领域基本法的《环保法》中，在民诉法基础上，将破坏资源、损害生态行为，纳入环境公益诉讼的范围。具体范围可以表述为：对“污染环境、破坏自然资源、损害生态系统等损害社会公共利益的行为”，可以提起诉讼。

附录：有关环境污染损害诉讼的法条摘录

民事诉讼法（2012 年 8 月 31 日修正）

第 55 条 对污染环境……等损害社会公共利益的行为，法律规定的机关和有关组织可以向人民法院提起诉讼。

侵权责任法（2009 年 12 月 26 日通过）

第 65 条 因污染环境造成损害的，污染者应当承担侵权责任。

环境保护法（1989 年 12 月 26 日通过）

第 6 条 一切单位和个人都有保护环境的义务，并有权对污染和破坏环境的单位和个人进行检举和控告。

第 41 条 造成环境污染危害的，有责任排除危害，并对直接受到损害的单位或者个人赔偿损失。

海洋环境保护法（1999 年 12 月 25 日修订）

第 90 条 造成海洋环境污染损害的责任者，应当排除危害，并赔偿损失；完全由于第三者的故意或者过失，造成海洋环境污染损害的，由第三者排除危害，并承担赔偿责任。

对破坏海洋生态、海洋水产资源、海洋保护区，给国家造成重大损失的，由依照本法规定行使海洋环境监督管理权的部门代表国家对责任者提出损害赔偿要求。

水污染防治法（2008 年 2 月 28 日修订）

第八十八条 因水污染受到损害的当事人人数众多的，可以依法由当事人推选代表人进行共同诉讼。

环境保护主管部门和有关社会团体可以依法支持因水污染受到损害的当事人向人民法院提起诉讼。

《国务院关于落实科学发展观加强环境保护的决定》（2005 年 12 月 3 日）提出：“健全社会监督机制，发挥社会团体的作用，鼓励检举和揭发各种环境违法行为，推动环境公益诉讼。”

《国家环境保护“十二五”规划》（2011 年 12 月 15 日）规定：“建立健全环境保护举报制度，畅通环境信访、12369 环保热线、网络邮箱等信访投诉渠道，鼓励实行有奖举报。支持环境公益诉讼。”

《最高人民法院关于为加快经济发展方式转变提供司法保障和服务的若干意见》（2010 年 6 月 29 日）提出：各级人民法院应当“依法受理环境保护行政部门代表国家提起的环境污染损害赔偿纠纷案件，严厉打击一切破坏环境的行为。”

《2008 中国环保民间组织发展状况报告》

中国环保民间组织总量已达 3 500 余家

根据中华环保联合会发布的《2008 中国环保民间组织发展状况报告》，由于中国各级政府的大力扶植，中国环保民间组织近年来发展迅速，截至 2008 年 10 月，全国共有环保民间组织 3 539 家。其中，由政府发起成立的环保民间组织 1 309 家，学校环保社团 1 382 家，草根环保民间组织 508 家，国际环保组织驻中国机构 90 家，港澳台地区的环保民间组织约 250 家。

随着环保民间组织的壮大和发展，环保民间组织在从事环境宣传教育、推动公众参与、监督企业履行社会责任、参加环境维权等方面都起到了积极的作用，成为政府环境保护工作的有益补充。

论规范和制约有关环境的政府决策的必要性[①]

王　曦[②]

近年来，笔者领导的跨校联合研究组结合对《中华人民共和国环境保护法》修改的研究，发表了一批论文，初步探讨了我国环保事业和环境法制建设中的一个重大问题——规范和制约有关环境的政府决策。本文拟对这个问题做进一步探讨。本文所称“有关环境的政府决策”，指的是以政府的名义做出的，可能对环境带来重大影响的产业发展规划和招商引资决策，尤其是各级地方政府有关地方产业发展规划和招商引资的决策。

为什么要规范和制约有关环境的政府决策？对这个问题可以从现实和理论两个方面给予回答。从现实来看，政府行为对环境带来的巨大压力和破坏已经显现，现阶段频繁爆发的环境群体性事件更把这个问题尖锐地提到了我们的面前。人民的生命和健康、环境和生态的安全、政权的稳固，都需要我们规范和制约有关环境的政府决策。从理论上看，处于经济学、政治学和法学交界之处的宪政经济学对规范和制约有关环境的政府决策做出了有力的论证，给我们以很多有益的启示。

一、规范和制约有关环境的政府决策的必要性：现实的迫切要求

笔者根据《中国环境年鉴》（1996—2010年）中的《中国环境统计公报》等资料，做成“表1　1996—2010年环境污染与破坏事故情况[③]”如下：

① 本文原刊于《法学评论》，2013年第31卷第2期。

② 上海交通大学凯原法学院教授，博士生导师。

③ 《中国环境年鉴》中统计指标“环境污染与破坏事故”的定义如下：“环境污染与破坏事故指由于违反环境保护法规的经济、社会活动与行为，以及意外因素的影响或不可抗拒的自然灾害等原因，致使环境受到污染，国家重点保护的野生动植物、自然保护区受到破坏，人体健康受到危害，社会经济和人民财产受到损失，造成不良社会影响的突发性事件。”

表 1 1996—2010 年环境污染与破坏事故情况

年份	环境事故发生次数	事故造成伤亡人数	污染与破坏事故直接经济损失/万元
2010	420※	241	2 256.9
2009	418※	36	43 354.4
2008	474※	31	18 185.6
2007	462※	358	3 016
2006	842※	85	13 471.1
2005	1 406	2 400	10 515
2004	1 441	339	36 365.7
2003	1 843	416	3 374.9
2002	1 921	97	4 640.9
2001	1 842	187	12 272.4
2000	2 411	578	17 807.88
1999	1 614	261	5 710.59
1998	1 422	152	19 843.7
1997	1 992	188	8 366.1
1996	1 446	33	16 929.1

※：环境事故发生次数项中 2006—2010 年为突发性环境事件发生次数，1996—2005 年为各类环境事故。

表 1 告诉我们：环境污染和生态破坏事故频发，经济和社会代价十分高昂。首先，环境污染事故频发。1996—2005 年，平均每天发生环境事故 4.8 起。2006—2010 年开始，平均每天发生突发性环境事件 1.5 起。另据环保部原总工程师、中国环境科学学会副理事长杨朝飞 2012 年 10 月 26 日在第十一届全国人大常委会所做的专题讲座，我国重特大环境事件高发频发。2005 年以来，环保部直接接报处置的事件共 927 起，重特大事件 72 起，其中 2011 年重大事件比上年同期增长 120%，特别是重金属和危险化学品突发环境事件呈高发态势。①其次，环境污染事故严重危害公民生命健康。据统计从 1996—2010 年，环境事故造成伤亡人数共计 5 410 人，平均每年伤亡人数 360 人。最后，环境污染和生态破坏事故带来巨大经济损失。从 1996

① 《我国环境群体事件年均递增 29% 司法解决不足 1%》，http://politics.caijing.com.cn/2012-10-27/112233970.html, 2012 年 10 月 29 日访问。

—2010 年污染与破坏事故直接经济损失高达 14.519 6 亿元。据原国家环保总局副局长披露，“20 世纪八九十年代，世界银行、原国家环保总局以及一些科研单位曾经分别做过研究。环境损失（财产性损失和健康损失）占中国 GDP 的比重少则为 3%～4%，多则达到 11%左右。这两年没进行过相关研究，但我估计，环境损失占中国 GDP 的比重可能达到 5%～6%。2011 年中国 GDP 为 47 万亿多元，据此折算，环境污染造成损失将达到 2.35 万亿～2.82 万亿元，也就是超过 2 万亿元。”①

近年来，笔者在平常浏览中央电视台、新华网、人民网、凤凰网等主要网络媒体和书面媒体时，随机地记录下了一些有关重大环境污染或生态破坏事件的报道。现根据这个记录做成“表 2　主要网络媒体披露的环境事件（2004—2012，不完全统计）”如下：

表 2　主要网络媒体披露的环境事件（2004—2012，不完全统计）

年份	环境事件	总件数
2012	上海松江区垃圾焚烧场群体性事件；四川什邡市环境群体性事件；江苏启东市王子制纸排海工程环境群体性事件；广西龙江镉污染事件；广东中石化炼油企业违法排污事件；辽宁锦州凌海市国电、中石化侵占湿地事件；山西汾阳市文峪河农田污染事件；浙江宁波镇海区 PX 项目环境群体性事件；安徽马鞍山会山县企业被逼迁事件；浙江湖州吴兴区八里店镇官员阻扰记者采访事件	10
2011	浙江海宁环境群体性事件；湖北荆州市长江大学教授因污染集体请愿事件；浙江德清县铅污染群体性事件；云南曲靖铬污染事件；康菲渤海湾漏油事件；广东河源临江镇紫金村铅污染事件；河南省灵宝市豫灵镇铅污染事件；湖南石门县壶瓶山国家级自然保护区内建小水电建设事件；广西阳朔县兴坪镇镉米事件；浙江台州电子垃圾事件；安徽蚌埠鲍家沟“毒沟”事件；河南舞阳县小马庄化工污染事件；上海浦东新区康桥镇铅污染事件；广西南丹县东河镇铅污染事件；安徽怀宁县高河镇铅污染事件；浙江海宁市袁花镇晶科能源公司污染群体性事件；大连市 PX 项目群体性事件；江西德兴市江西铜业集团水污染事件；江西修水县上市乡金矿尘肺病事件；胶济铁路客运专线违反环评制度事件；江苏常州市春江镇化工区污染事件	23

① 《原环保局副局长：环境损失占 GDP 比重可能达 6%》，新华网，http://finance.qq.com/a/20120313/002380.htm，2012 年 10 月 30 日访问。

年份	环境事件	总件数
2010	湖南嘉禾县铅污染事件；安徽固镇县 6 名环保干部被停职事件；广西百色市靖西县铝厂污染群体性事件	3
2009	陕西凤翔县铅污染事件；湖南武冈市铅污染事件；江苏仪征市扬州化工园区污染事件；河北廊坊市夏垫村癌症村事件；广东广州市南沙炼化一体化项目迁离事件；黑龙江环保厅“保密风波”事件	6
2008	云南昆明市阳宗海砷污染事件；云南滇池水污染事件；广西河池砷污染事件；国家审计署渤海水污染防止审计调查事件	4
2007	太湖流域水污染事件；厦门 PX 项目群体性事件；环保部“流域限批”事件；环保部“行业限批”事件；环保部“区域限批”事件；湖北武汉赫山地块“毒地”事件	7
2006	湖南岳阳市饮用水源砷超标事件；甘肃徽县铅污染事件；河南卢氏县铅污染事件；湖北省清理妨碍环保“土政策”事件	4
2005	湘黔渝“锰三角”重金属污染事件；吉林松花江吉林石化污染事件；福建屏南县化工厂污染案	2
2004	四川沱江废水水污染事件；四川盐边县磷污染事件；广东翁源县癌症村事件；云南怒江水电开发事件；原广州环保局长腐败事件；北京市东五环外朝阳区管庄乡康泉新城二期“毒地”事件	6
总计		65
信息来源：中央电视台、新华网、人民网、凤凰网等		

表 2 告诉我们：一些地方政府（和一些基层群众自治组织，如村民委员会）沦为“环境问题的制造者”。[①]在这些事件中，地方政府的产业发展规划和招商引资决策对人民生命健康和环境生态带来了严重危害。表 2 所列各种事件中，几乎都与地方政府的产业发展规划和招商引资没有对人民健康和环境给予足够的重视有关。在这些事件中，危害当地群众健康和环境的企业，都是由当地政府（和村民自治组织）通过招商引资“招”、“引”来的。例如，在表 2 中反复出现的铅污染事件中，引起大量儿童铅中毒的铅厂几乎都是响应当地政府的产业发展规划，由当地政府邀请而来。有的铅厂原本在另外的地方遭到拒绝，而后转来当地。揭示地方政府沦为“环境问题的制造者”的另一个典型的例子，是环保部在 2007 年掀起的“环保风

① 王曦：《环保主体互动法制保障论》，载《上海交通大学学报（哲学社会科学版）》，2012 年第 1 期（中国人民大学《复印报刊资料——经济法学、劳动法学》2012 年第 7 期全文转载）。

暴”。在那场“环保风暴”中，一批相当高层次的地方政府和国有企业遭遇环保部的“行政限批”（包括“流域限批”、“行业限批”和“区域限批”）。[①]环保部决定在规定的期限内不受理这些地方和国企的环境影响评价报告申报。遭遇此“行政限批”是由于这些地方政府和国企存在着严重违反《环保法》、《环评法》等法律的情况。在那场“环保风暴”之后，不少省份也仿效环保部，在省内动用了“行政限批”手段。这些“行政限批”的对象，是省级以下的地方政府。其所涉违法违规事实多于当地的经济或产业发展规划或招商引资决策中的失误有关。大量的事例表明，由于这种决策失误，不少地方的政府成了“间接的环境污染者或生态破坏者”。[②]

笔者根据《中国环境年鉴》（1996 — 2010 年）中的《中国环境统计公报》等资料，还做成“表 3　1989 —2009 年群众环境信访及环境群体性事件情况”如下：

表 3　1989 — 2009 年群众环境信访及环境群体性事件情况表

年份	群众因污染来信数/封	群众因污染来访数	环境问题引发群体性事件/起
2009	2 638	407 批/1 231 次	3
2008	3 789	498 批/1 382 次	1
2007	4 658	548 批/1 270 次	7
2006	616 122	71 287 人	
2005	608 245	88 237 人	
2004	595 852	86 414 人	
2003	525 988	85 028 人	
2002	435 020	90 746 人	
2001	367 402	80 329 人	

① 那次“流域限批”针对的是：长江、黄河、淮河、海河四大流域的内蒙古自治区巴彦淖尔市、河南省周口市、陕西省渭南市、山西省襄汾县、安徽省芜湖市经济技术开发区、甘肃省白银市，安徽省巢湖市、蚌埠市，河北省邯郸经济开发区，山东省莘县工业园区、河南省濮阳经济开发区、兰州市高新技术产业开发区、山西省河津市。“行业限批”针对的是大唐国际、华电集团、华能集团、国电集团、云南华电鲁地拉水电有限公司、华能龙开口水电有限公司、山东省钢铁行业（日照钢铁控股集团有限公司、潍坊钢铁集团有限公司）。“区域限批”针对的是河北省唐山市、山西省吕梁市、贵州省六盘水市、山东省莱芜市。

② 王曦：《“环保事业基础法”：让特殊的〈环保法〉特殊起来！》，载《绿叶》2011 年第 1 期。

年份	群众因污染来信数/封	群众因污染来访数	环境问题引发群体性事件/起
2000	247 741	13 942 人	
1999	230 346	89 872 人	
1998	147 630	93 791 人	
1997	106 210	71 528 人	
1996	67 268	47 714 人	
1995	58 678	94 798 人	
1994	59 499	95 061 人	
1993	53 752	84 743 人	
1992	55 340	79 112 人	
1991	55 775	79 313 人	
1990	60 099	80 582 人	
1989	52 786	78 122 人	

表 3 告诉我们：环境群体性事件成为对基层党和政府执政能力的一个新考验。自 1989 年以来，我国环境信访数量很大。1989—2006 年群众因污染的信访信件和信访人数一直保持高位。尽管表 3 所列的环境群体性事件甚少，但根据表 2 显示实际生活中的环境群体性事件大大超过表 3 的统计。仅 2012 年 1—10 月，媒体上广泛报道的环境群体性事件就有四川什邡市环境群体性事件；江苏启东市王子制纸排海工程环境群体性事件和浙江宁波镇海区 PX 项目环境群体性事件。另据杨朝飞介绍，自 1996 年来以来，环境群体性事件一直保持年均 29%的增速。①

在 2013 年发生的四川什邡市环境群体性事件、江苏启东市王子制纸排海工程环境群体性事件和浙江宁波镇海区 PX 项目群体性事件中，在当地民众的强烈抗议下，当地政府被迫改变原来的招商引资决策。在前两起事件发生后，人民日报的评论指出我国政府面临"'环境敏感期'的新考题"："在环境问题日益突出、公民维权意识日益增强的社会环境敏感期，怎样才能避免民众非理性情绪之下的极端行为？政府与民众如何理性互动，求得解

① 《我国环境群体事件年均递增 29% 司法解决不足 1%》，http://politics.caijing.com.cn/2012-10-27/112233970.html, 2012 年 10 月 29 日访问。

决社会矛盾的最佳途径？”[①]中国青年报的评论指出：“理性克制、反应迅速、尊重民意……就事论事，‘启东事件’确实是‘理性与双赢’，但从更宽广的视域来审视，民众以如此方式‘参与’到重大项目的走向中来，这显然有值得省思处。正如有媒体人在微博中梳理出来的逻辑：从什邡到启东，某些地方政府给社会的印象是，他们在背着公众做违反公共利益的决定，只要出现大规模抗议，就会立刻改变之前的决定，‘这样的政府形象如果从点连成片，对社会稳定将是灾难性的。’”[②]长江日报的评论发人深省：“对于不断发生的群体性冲突事件，现在到了从政治和道义合法性方面来思考问题的时候了。目前许多地方政府的种种不当行为，以及‘捂盖子’、‘不出事就是没问题’、‘花钱买平安’等错误做法，就是在回避问题，主动制造与社会的紧张与对抗，实际上就是在耗损合法性资源，与民心渐行渐远。经济发展的成就，不能等同或代替合法性资源的获取。新的政治和道义合法性资源从哪里来，政府将如何重新树立公共权威性，都是重大的时代问题，关系到中国社会的前景”、“合法性资源不是可以无限透支，修复合法性的时间也不是无限多。当务之急，是赶快收拾人心，重塑合法性，这是对人民、国家和历史负责的正确做法。”[③]在宁波镇海区 PX 项目环境群体性事件发生后，齐鲁晚报的评论指出：“对预期利益的难以割舍，或许才是宁波有关部门与民意沟通的最大障碍。因为公信力不足，面对民意难以过关，因为民意关难过，索性绕道和回避，这似乎成了一些地方在决策中的死循环。……这个事件也再次提醒各地政府部门，重大决策必须与民意做及时、顺畅的沟通，否则就会在以后遇到难以克服的阻力，并为之付出巨大成本。从厦门、大连到什邡、启东，各地上马的项目不尽相同，但暴露的问题却是一样的，那就是重视‘环评’却忽略民意。以‘科学’的名义为民做主，实质上损害了民众的知情权、参与权、决策权，而等到民众发现事与愿违

① 郝洪：《“环境敏感期的新考题”》，人民网—人民日报，http://news.sina.com.cn/pl/2012-07-30/053424868476.shtml，2012 年 7 月 30 日访问。
② 毕诗成：《让温和“参与”释放更多正能量》，载《中国青年报》2012 年 7 月 31 日，http://news.ifeng.com/opinion/politics/detail_2012_07/31/16431481_0.shtml，2012 年 7 月 31 日访问。
③刘敏：《赶快收拾人心》，载《长江日报》2012 年 7 月 31 日，http://news.ifeng.com/opinion/politics/detail_2012_07/31/16431109_0.shtml，2012 年 7 月 31 日访问。

要行使监督权的时候，一些重大项目已经开弓没有回头箭，矛盾也由此激化。如果这些项目决策过程中有民意的广泛参与，事情也未必都是这般结果。”[①]这些评论，无不提醒我们：有关环境的政府决策绝不仅仅是一个经济上的事，而是一个有政治影响的事。有关环境的政府决策与政府的民意基础和执政合法性紧密相关。如果继续推行过去那种以牺牲环境、资源甚至人民生命和健康来换取经济一时的高速增长的做法，政府的民意基础和合法性将受到极大的减损。

总之，这三个表格包含的事例都证明：我国在资源环境问题上存在着严重的“政府失灵”（governmental failure）。[②]

“政府失灵”是违背政府存在的理由的。政府存在的基本理由之一是通过行政干预防止和克服“市场失灵”（market failure）。政府是为了克服市场失灵而存在的。如果政府也“失灵”，市场失灵何能被纠正和消除？因此，规范和制约有关环境的政府决策，纠正这方面的“政府失灵”，实际上是克服市场失灵的逻辑需要。只有克服了这种“政府失灵”，才能克服市场失灵，资源才能够得到高效的配置，发展才能平衡、协调、可持续。只有克服了这种“政府失灵”，发展的资源环境代价才能回归正常，政府才能发挥其应当发挥的公共职能，党和政府才能保持人民的信任。

二、规范和制约有关环境的政府决策的必要性：宪政经济学的启示

处于经济学、政治学和法学交界之处的公共选择理论中的宪政经济学为我们认识规范和制约有关环境的政府决策的必要性提供了十分有益的启示。公共选择理论是一种用经济学的方法来研究政治关系的理论。公共选择理论的代表人物詹姆斯·布坎南[③]曾说，公共选择理论是关于“政府失灵

①沙元森：《PX 上也得明白下也得明白》，载《齐鲁晚报》2012 年 10 月 29 日，人民网，http://cpc.people.com.cn/pinglun/n/2012/1029/c78779-19419260.html，2012 年 10 月 31 日访问。

② 政府失灵，指的是“政府为纠正市场失灵而进行的干预措施无法提高资源配置效率的现象”。引自《大辞海》（环境科学卷），上海世纪出版股份有限公司、上海辞书出版社 2006 年版，第 264 页。

③詹姆斯·M·布坎南（James M Buchanan，1919—），美国乔治·梅森大学公共选择研究中心教授，曾任美国经济学会会长，1986 年诺贝尔经济学奖获得者。

的理论”，[①]“在一些情况下，我把20世纪六七十年代成形和发展了的公共选择理论作为一种‘政府失灵理论’……公共选择理论（曾被保罗·萨缪尔森称为‘福利政治学’）中含有这样的例证，即在履行纠正措施的时候，政府的政治过程无法达到配置效率的要求。”[②]公共选择理论著名学者——戈登·塔洛克（Gordon Tullock）[③]认为，“政府是某些问题的解决办法，也是另一些问题产生的根源。”[④]公共选择理论的另一著名学者丹尼斯·C·缪勒（Dennis C.Mueller）说到，“在争论当公共物品、外部性和其他种类的非纯私人物品出现时，国家对于纠正市场失灵具有必要性的时候，经济学文献作者总是隐含的假设这些失灵可以没有成本地得到纠正。政府被视为万能的和仁慈的机构，以税收、补贴等手段实现配置资源的帕累托最优。[⑤]在20世纪60年代，大部分公共选择理论文献开始挑战者中关于政府的‘天堂式模型’，这些文献并不是检验政府如何或应当怎么行为，而是它们实际上是如何行为的。这揭示了政府同样可以以特定的方式失灵。”[⑥]

（一）时间维度对政府行为的影响

在研究政府失灵的过程中，杰弗瑞·布伦南和詹姆斯·布坎南通过引入时间维度，以下成对选择序列图，论证了在缺乏约束的情况下政府官员做出眼光短浅之选择的必然性。而决策眼光短浅，正是一种常见的政府失灵。

在图1中，选择者在 t_0、t_1 和以后的每个时间节点上都面对两种选择或

---

① [美]詹姆斯·M·布坎南：《宪政的经济学阐释》，贾文华、任洪生译，中国社会科学出版社2012年版，第20页。

②前注③，[美]詹姆斯·M·布坎南书，第21页。

③戈登·塔洛克（Gordon Tullock，1922—），美国乔治·梅森大学公共选择研究中心教授，曾任美国公共选择学会会长。

④ [美]戈登·塔洛克：《公共选择——戈登·塔洛克论文集》，柏克、郑景胜译，商务印书馆2011年版，第28页。

⑤这段话的原译文是：“在争论当公共物品、外部性和其他种类的非纯私人物品出现时，国家对于纠正市场失灵具有必要性的时候，经济学文献总是作者隐含的假设，即这些失灵可以没有成本地得到纠正。政府被视为万能的和仁慈的机构税收、补贴和数量以实现配置资源的帕累托最优。”其中多处语句不通。由于没有找到英文原著，笔者只好就这段译文整理了语句。正确的译文，需要核对原著。笔者注。

⑥ [美]丹尼斯·C·缪勒：《公共选择理论》（第三版），韩旭等译，中国社会科学出版社2012年版，第5页。

两种预期，即 A、B，a_1、a_2，b_1、b_2。当选择者在时间节点 t_0 做选择时，如果是私人选择，他会选择 A，得到图中所示 1 000 个单位的报酬。这是因为从 t_0、t_1 到 t_2，即选择路线 Aoa_1 是他的私人事务，在他的认识和控制范围以内。这 1 000 个单位的报酬是他所能够预见到并有十足把握得到的。但如果是公共选择，情况就不同了。在公共选择的情况下，选择者作为众多选择者之一，不知道别人会作何选择，也无法预见 1 000 个单位报酬的选项 a_1。他的视野只及于眼下的第一个时间段即从 t_0 到 t_1。他所面对的只是 t_1 时间段的两种选项 A 和 B。如果他选择 A，将一无所获；如果选择 B，则可获 600 个单位的报酬。在这种情况下，作为一个理性人，他必然选择 B。他会认为这样的选择于私于公都是最佳选择。然而对于共同体而言，相对于选项 A 的 1 000 个单位报酬，B 无疑是一个眼光短浅的次佳选择。布伦南和布坎南用这个图例说明，由于时间节点这个条件的限制，政府官员的视野自然地倾向于短浅。在缺乏必要约束（例如外部监督和内在道德）的情况下，政府官员做公共选择的结果必然是短视的和从公共利益看并非最佳的。如果我们把图中的各个时间段看成政府官员的任期，对这种政府失灵就更容易理解了。

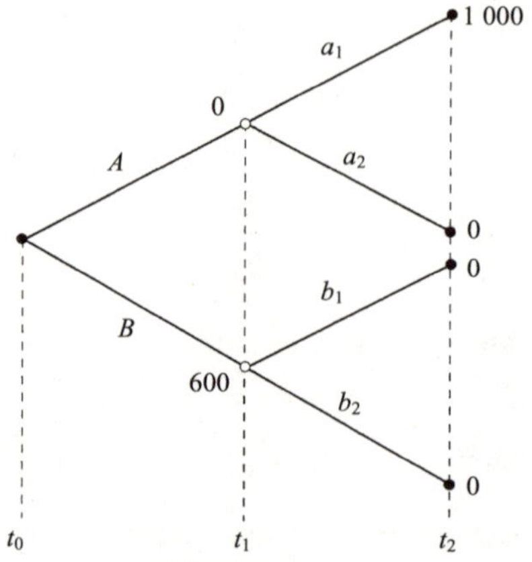

图 1　时间维度对公、私选择的影响

信息来源：Geoffrey Brennan and James M. Buchanan，The Reason of Rules：Constitutional Political Economy，Liberty Fund，Inc.，2000，page 88

（二）政府失灵的背后：缺乏矫正社会贴现率的动机

在论证了时间维度对政府行为的重要影响之后，布伦南和布坎南继而探讨了政府失灵现象背后一个更为重要的问题——政府缺乏矫正社会贴现率的动机。政府的存在本来是为了矫正社会贴现率过高，确保社会发展的可持续性。如果政府缺乏这种动机，问题岂不大耶？

贴现和贴现率本是银行业务术语。贴现，本指“银行的一种放款形式。以未到期票据向银行通融资金，银行扣取自贴现日至到期日的利息后，以票面余额付给持票人。”[①]贴现率，本指“将未来支付改变为现值所使用的利率，或指持票人以没有到期的票据向银行要求兑现，银行将利息先行扣除所使用的利率。”[②]社会贴现率是贴现和贴现率概念在经济学、伦理学和环境法学领域里的延伸应用。社会贴现率指的是社会贴现未来的比例。布伦南和布坎南指出，“长期以来，尤其是自庇古的《福利经济学》21世纪初出版以来，经济学家一直关注下面的规范性问题：社会应该以多大比例去贴现未来？在做出当期决策的时候，‘应当’如何权衡后代的效用？”[③]社会贴现率问题实际上是社会可持续性（sustainability）问题。社会贴现率越高，这个社会就越短视，对未来的透支就越大，社会的可持续性就越低，就越快接近社会危机。

布伦南和布坎南用“高征税陷阱”、“通货膨胀陷阱”、“公债陷阱”等美国和其他西方国家实行的宏观经济政策中的问题为例，证明了由于受到时间维度的限制，政府官员难以做出眼光长远的、符合共同体的长远利益的政策选择。如果不对政府行为加以“宪法”的约束，政府必然陷入这些“陷阱”，不仅不能解决社会贴现率过高问题，反而会使之恶化。

他们所谓“高征税陷阱”指的是由于纳税人无法在短期（例如某届政

---

① 《辞海》（第6版，世博会珍藏版），上海世纪出版股份有限公司、上海辞书出版社2010年版，第1876页。

②曾艳玲主编：《英汉西方经济学词典》，机械工业出版社2003年版，第193页。

③ [美]杰弗瑞·布伦南、詹姆斯·布坎南：《规则的理由——宪政的政治经济学》，秋风等译，中国社会科学出版社2004年版，第94页。载布伦南、布坎南：《宪政经济学》，冯克利等译，中国社会科学出版社2004年版。

府的任期）内调整自己的涉税行为以适应某项新的税收，政府在该税收的初始短期内每期收到的税收要多于更长期间内该税收每期征收的税收。“比起体现着等于或长于纳税人调整周期的时间视野的过程来说，体现着较短时间视野的财政过程，能够更充分地盘剥纳税人。比起具有真正长远打算的过程，仅仅关注短期政府税收流的政府决策过程，对纳税人的压榨更彻底。”[①]政府征税的本来目的是为了给纳税人提供更好的公共产品和公共服务，使纳税人享受更多的利益。但这种情况却事与愿违，纳税人的利益受到不应有的盘剥。这就是所谓“高征税陷阱”。布伦南和布坎南的高明之处，不在于指出“高征税陷阱”这个现象，而在于揭示出现这个现象的原因。原因就是在缺乏对政府征税权的约束的情况下，政府官员对短期（例如该届政府的任期）财政收入的关心必然超过对纳税人所需的更长的税收调整期的关心。他们指出，“参与政治决策的个人，即使完全理解他们的处境，也不可能轻松地摆脱这一两难困境。如果缺乏对集体财政倾向的约束，而仅靠形成财政决策的现有规则和程序，即使在其私人活动中具有长远眼光的人，在作为政治的参与者行为时，也是非理性的。”[②]

他们所谓“通货膨胀陷阱”指的是虽然短期的、轻微的通货膨胀可引起就业增加和经济增长，但长期的通货膨胀必然导致经济衰退。在缺乏有效规则约束的情况下，政府官员由于其看待此问题的眼光受时间维度（例如其任期）所限，必然会不断容忍任期内的“轻微的通货膨胀”，而不考虑其长远的糟糕后果。布伦南和布坎南指出，“1981 年和 1982 年的美国就出现过这种局面，并且相当严峻。政治决策参与者通常据以作出决策的时间视野不够长，无法使他们相信降低或消除通货膨胀是理性的，即使他们完全承认这种措施能使他们得到长远收益。”[③]

他们所谓“公债陷阱”指的是：虽然发行公债有助于政府推行其主张的项目或“利益”，但从长远看，债台高筑的政府将面临极大的财政风险。

---

① 第 209 页注③，[美]杰弗瑞・布伦南、詹姆斯・布坎南书，第 100 页。
② 第 209 页注③，[美]杰弗瑞・布伦南、詹姆斯・布坎南书，第 101 页。
③ 第 209 页注③，[美]杰弗瑞・布伦南、詹姆斯・布坎南书，第 105 页。

对于政府官员而言，“即使有人已经意识到，从长远看来，没有负债的财政结构要比负债的财政结构更可取，他们依然会认为这种计算（即关于发行公债的考虑，笔者注）是正确的。人们不可能放弃债务支撑的开支项目带来的收益，也不可能采取措施防止出现支付利息和分期偿还所要求承受的长期税收负担。”①政府官员之所以会陷入这个陷阱或悖论，还是因为其眼光受到了其时间维度（如任期）的限制。这正如布伦南和布坎南所说，“即使政治组织中的所有成员都认识到了发行公债的后果（当然这可能是个很成问题的假设，不好在对于我们这儿的讨论这一点不太要紧），但政治活动中短浅的时间视野，会使这种筹资手段在某种开支的初期范围内较之征税更为可取，除非举债受着宪法或道德的限制。政治参与者通过借钱为当前享受的‘利益’提供资金，这等于推迟了付款期。政府可以以相当于或低于市场水平的利率水平借钱。”②

“高征税陷阱”、“通货膨胀陷阱”和“公债陷阱”问题都是需要政府代表人民用正确的公共选择来解决的社会贴现率问题。尤为值得注意的是，布伦南和布坎南所关注的，不是社会贴现率过大问题本身，而是政府是否具有解决这个问题的能力的问题。同社会贴现率问题相比，这个问题更为重大。他们说到，“这些问题（指社会贴现率问题，笔者注）本身当然都很有意思。不过，对我们的讨论而言，促使经济学家提出这些问题的隐含的假设则更加发人深省。提出这些问题的经济学家几乎毫无例外地假定：只要学者们能就某个令人满意的规范性解决方案达成一致，则一个仁慈的政府就能够，大概也会乐意实施这一方案。这些经济学家从来也没有抬起头来问一声，我们在现实中所观察到的政府，是否能够或乐意执行从规范性处方的仔细操练中形成的这一‘最优’贴现率。”③布伦南和布坎南就是这样一种少有的，能够“抬起头来问一声”“政府是否愿意实行最优社会贴现率”的人。

---

① 第 209 页注③，[美]杰弗瑞·布伦南、詹姆斯·布坎南书，第 106 页。
② 第 209 页注③，[美]杰弗瑞·布伦南、詹姆斯·布坎南书，第 105 页。
③ 第 209 页注③，[美]杰弗瑞·布伦南、詹姆斯·布坎南书，第 95 页。

时间维度对于政府官员行为的影响，不容忽视。在上述“高征税陷阱”、“通货膨胀陷阱”和“公债陷阱”的例子中，一个重要的共性问题是政府官员由于“时间视野”的短浅，甚至在承认其短期行为（如征税、容忍通货膨胀和发行公债）的长期不合理后果的情况下，仍然要采取短期行为。他们指出，“我们根据人们——很有可能是同一个人——用于公共选择和私人选择的时间贴现率之间存在差异的观点，来说明政治仅仅考虑暂时或短期收益，这种倾向是不受约束的多数至上政治内在所固有的，也是其他类型不受约束之政府决策程序所不可避免的，而对于长期考虑的相对忽视所导致的结果，是共同体中的任何人或集团所不想看到的……这也正是‘陷阱’或‘两难困境’这两个词的用意。简而言之，现代政治中的短视所导致的结果可能是‘帕累托最劣’”。①这种情况迫使人们质疑政府应对社会贴现率过高问题的能力。政府存在的理由之一，是防止社会出现社会贴现率过高以致社会发展不可持续。而“高税收陷阱”、“通货膨胀陷阱”和“公债陷阱”这些例证都告诉我们，由于政府官员的视野短浅，政府似乎不可避免地都掉入了这些“陷阱”，其政策都是虽短期“利好”却同人们的长远利益相悖。在这些例子中，政府从社会贴现率过高的矫正者不幸沦为社会贴现率过高制造者或推动者！

（三）“时间维度”的启示

应当承认，“时间维度对政府行为的影响”问题和相应的“政府缺乏矫正社会贴现率的动机”问题，不仅存在于布伦南和布坎南所生活的美国，也存在于当下的中国。在某种意义上，这些问题在当下中国表现得更加严重。本文第一部分表 2 所列各种环境事件几乎都是这些问题的中国版本。这些环境事件告诉我们，当下我国经济发展模式的社会贴现率高得极不合理。在不少地方，负有责任矫正这个社会贴现率的地方政府还没有切实担负起这个责任。

在我国，政府官员五年一届的任期，就同美国等西方国家一样，是一

① 第 209 页注③，[美]杰弗瑞·布伦南、詹姆斯·布坎南书，第 107-108 页。

个影响官员行政“视野”的重要因素。本文第一部分表 2 所列各种环境事件，几乎都是当地政府为了追求任期内的 GDP 增长而忽视环境代价所引起。有学者指出前些年中国存在一种以 GDP 增长数字为中心指标的“政治锦标赛”模式的政府治理。①在这种政府治理模式下，上级政府以地方 GDP 增长数字作为考核政府主要领导的指标。GDP 增长数字高的地方政府的主要领导比起这个数字低的地方的主要领导，更容易得到晋升。我认为，这种情况是存在的。在这种“政治锦标赛”中，一个基本的竞赛规则是官员任期的相同性。只有在相同的任期内，官员的 GDP 增长业绩才有可比性。而这个任期就是布伦南和布坎南所说的“时间维度”。只有在相同的时间维度内，官员的 GDP 增长业绩才可进行“公平的竞赛”。在这种政府治理模式下（尽管政府从未认可过这种模式），各地政府主要领导不可避免地陷入在任期内提高地方 GDP 增长率的怪圈。而最快地提高地方 GDP 增长率的方式就是粗放型的发展方式。在这种发展方式下，环境、生态甚至人民的生命和健康都成了官员追求任期内经济政绩的牺牲品。同布伦南和布坎南所论述的“高征税陷阱”、“通货膨胀陷阱”和“公债陷阱”一样，我国的这种“唯 GDP 陷阱”也是一种政府短视的表现。布伦南和布坎南引入时间维度揭示美国政府短视现象的方法，对于我们认识我国有关环境的政府决策，颇有裨益。

三、结语

大量的事实证明，有关环境的政府决策的失误是很多环境污染事件的主要原因。宪政经济学的“时间维度”理论对我国资源环境领域里的“政府失灵”做出了有力的论证。问题在于如何克服这种“政府失灵”，使政府官员由“视野短浅”变成“眼光远大”。办法是有的。办法就在于以法律建立足以制约政府行为的规则，为政府按照科学发展观的要求来从事有关环

①参见周黎安：《转型中的地方政府：官员激励与治理》，格致出版社、上海人民出版社 2008 年版，第 87-122 页。

境的决策建立最低的行为规则。正如布伦南和布坎南所说，“只有对政治联盟（政府）的权力施加某些限制，使其无法抵消或破坏人们在当下做出都具有长期‘投资性质’的选择的果实，才能够形成某种激励，诱导参与政治的个人，按照符合他（和共同体）的长远利益的方式行事。”[①]规范和制约有关环境的政府决策已经成为摆在我们面前的一个严肃的挑战。唯有给政府这个“有形的手”规定完善的规则，它才会以符合人民长远根本利益的方式去运行，切实履行矫正社会贴现率的政府职能。而当前全国人大正在进行的《环保法》修改，为建立有关环境的政府决策规则提供了一个极其宝贵的机会。我们应当利用好这个机会，把《环保法》“改造”成为一部规范和制约有关环境的政府决策的法律。《环保法》的一个不可替代的特殊功能就在于此。我再次呼吁：让特殊的《环保法》特殊起来！[②]

① 第 209 页注③，[美]杰弗瑞·布伦南、詹姆斯·布坎南书，第 106 页。
② 笔者曾在中国环境文化促进会主办的刊物《绿叶》2011 年第 1 期上发表文章《“环保事业基础法”：让特殊的〈环保法〉特殊起来！》。

论《环保法》的功能改造和提升
——兼释上海交通大学《环保法修订建议稿》[①]

王　曦[②]

2011年4月，上海交通大学环境资源法研究所《中华人民共和国环境保护法》（以下简称《环保法》）修订联合研究组[③]在武汉向全国人大环境与资源保护委员会《环保法》修改调研组全面汇报并提交了一份《中华人民共和国环境保护法修订建议稿》（以下简称《环保法修订建议稿》或《建议稿》）。通过对大量国内环境污染和生态破坏事件、政府履行环保职能的经验和教训和外国的同类立法经验的研究，综合运用法学和相关学科的原理，研究组对我国《环保法》的特殊功能有了比较清楚的认识。研究组认为我国《环保法》应当具备以下三项特殊功能：一，为环保事业奠定法律基础和组织保障；二，规范和约束有关环境的政府行为；三，规定一般性环境监管制度。总起来看，这三项功能都服务于“为环保主体良性有效互动提供法律保障”这个环境法的基本任务。这种对《环保法》特殊功能的认识，既为《环保法》修改提供了思路，又是我国环境法学研究的新成果。本文结合上海交通大学环境资源法研究所起草的《环保法修订建议稿》，对我国《环保法》的功能改造和提升作一阐释。[④]

---

① 本文系环境保护部《环境行政立法与政策研究——环境法制定研究》（项目编号：二~1）的阶段性成果。

② 王曦，上海交通大学法学院环境资源法研究所所长、法学博士、教授、博士生导师，美国华盛顿大学法学硕士，第九、十、十一届全国政协委员，上海市人民政府参事，湖北襄阳人。

③ 这个研究组的成员有吉林大学王小钢副教授、中山大学谷德近副教授、深圳大学周卫副教授、中南林业科技大学徐丰果副教授、华北电力大学陈维春副教授、上海政法学院赵俊副教授、浙江嘉兴学院杨华国博士、湖北第二师范学院罗文君博士和上海交通大学法学院环境法专业部分博士研究生和硕士研究生。这项研究得到了环境保护部政策法规司、美国 Pace 大学法学院环境法教学研究中心、芝加哥 Kent 法学院、日本京都龙谷大学等机构的大力支持和帮助，在此顺致衷心感谢！

④ 《环保法修订建议稿》的目录，登载在《上海交通大学学报（哲学社会科学版）》，2012年第1期，第20-21页。

一、《环保法》是一部特殊的法律

我曾将现行《环保法》与《大气污染防治法》等其他环境资源保护类法律做了比较，从立法目的、法律内容、立法史和《环保法》的“空心化”问题四个方面辨析了《环保法》的特殊性和特殊功能。①

（一）从立法目的看《环保法》的特殊性

通过比较立法目的，我得出的认识是：一，《环保法》的立法目的是上位的、总体的，其他环境资源保护法律的立法目的是下位的、局部的，从属于《环保法》的立法目的。二，《环保法》标题中的“环境保护”是一个上位概念，它涵盖其他环境资源保护法律所调整的那些领域如大气污染防治、环境影响评价、森林、防沙治沙等。相对而言，其他法律的标题中的“大气污染”等污染、“森林”等自然资源、“环境影响评价”和“防沙治沙”等专门事项，都属于《环保法》标题中“环境保护”概念的下位概念。三，《环保法》与其他环境资源保护法律在立法目的上的差异，显示它们在功能上的差异：《环保法》着眼于整体环境的保护和改善；相应地，它的主要功能是为环保事业提供总的法律基础和制度框架。其他环境资源保护法律则在《环保法》所提供的法律基础上和制度框架中，为各自所涉环境因子的保护和专门事项建立具体的制度。②

（二）从法律内容看《环保法》的特殊性

通过法律内容的比较，我得出的认识是：一、其他环境资源保护法律基本上是《环保法》的延伸和细化；二、这种延伸和细化表明《环保法》具有某种基础性；三、这种“基础性”是其他的环境资源保护法律所没有

① 详见王曦：“环保事业基础法”：让特殊的《环保法》特殊起来！《绿叶》，2011 年第 1 期，第 9-19 页。
② 详见王曦：“环保事业基础法”：让特殊的《环保法》特殊起来！《绿叶》，2011 年第 1 期，第 10-11 页。

的，它体现《环保法》的特殊性和特殊功能。[①]

（三）从立法史看《环保法》的特殊性

通过研究1979年《中华人民共和国环境保护法（试行）》（以下简称《环保法（试行）》及其继承者——1989 年修订的《环保法》之间的关系，我得出的认识是：《环保法（试行）》的“主要功能是在法律层面上落实1978年《宪法》中首次规定的有关环境保护的条款，[②]为我国环保事业进一步奠定法律基础，为政府履行宪法规定的环保职能做出基本的制度安排，并为后来各项其他的环境资源法律的制定提供法律。现行《环保法》继承了《环保法（试行）》的这个特殊功能，仍然是一部环境资源保护领域里的“基础性”法律。[③]

（四）从《环保法》的“空心化”看其特殊性

《环保法》的“空心化”问题是我国环境法的发展带来的问题。在《环保法（试行）》和《环保法》颁布之后，我国陆续制订了一批其他的关于环境资源保护的法律。这些法律可以分为三种类型即污染防治法律（如《大气污染防治法》等法律）、自然保护型法律（如《森林法》等法律）和环保专门事项型法律（如《环评法》等法律）。这些法律基本上都是《环保法》中有关条款的延伸和细化。这种延伸和细化，给《环保法》带来了“空心化问题”。“这个‘空心化’指的是《环保法》中的一些条款被后来的其他环境资源保护法律所延伸和细化，因而与后来的那些法律相重复。假如删除处于这种状态的条款，《环保法》就会出现很多‘空洞’。‘空心化’就是对这种情况的形象化描述。”[④]《环保法》的“空心化”问题主要存在于该法的第三章（保护和改善环境）和第四章（防止环境污染和其他公害）。这两章关于防治污染和保护自然资源和生态系统的种种原则性规定，大都在后来被专门的污染防治法律、自然保护型法律和环保专门事项型法律所延

① 王曦：“环保事业基础法”：让特殊的《环保法》特殊起来！《绿叶》，2011年第1期，第11-12页。
② 1978年《宪法》第11条规定：“国家保护环境和自然资源，防治污染和其他公害。”
③ 王曦：“环保事业基础法”：让特殊的《环保法》特殊起来！《绿叶》，2011年第1期，第12-13页。
④ 王曦：“环保事业基础法”：让特殊的《环保法》特殊起来！《绿叶》，2011年第1期，第12-14页。

伸和细化，从而处于“空心化”状态。[①]

通过对《环保法》“空心化”问题的研究，我得出的认识是：“《环保法》‘空心化’了的条款反证那些未被‘空心化’的条款的特殊性和必要性。正是那些没有被‘空心化’的条款保存着《环保法》的特殊基因，显示《环保法》的特殊功能和存在价值。”[②]这些条款大都是《环保法》总则部分的条款。例如，关于“环境”定义的第二条，关于将国家制定的环境保护规划纳入国民经济和社会发展计划的总体要求的第三条，关于单位和个人的保护环境的义务和对污染或破坏环境者的检举和控告权的第六条，关于国家和地方人民政府环境保护行政主管部门的第七条等。这些条款有一个共性，我称之为“基础性”，即它们都是关于环境保护事业基本事项的规定，具有为环境保护事业提供制度基础和管理框架的作用。这个“基础性”是其他环境资源保护类法律所不具有的。

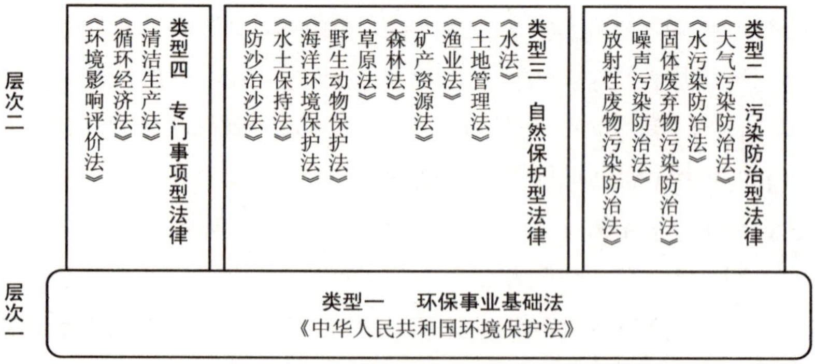

作图：上海交大王曦，2012 年 11 月

图 1 国家环境资源保护类法律类型

总而言之，通过以上四方面的比较研究，可以看出我国环境资源保护

① 因此《环保法修订建议稿》将那些“空心化”了的条款予以删除，只规定那些属于为环保事业奠定法律基础的事项。把关于污染防治、自然资源保护和环境影响评价、循环经济等事项留给相关法律去规定，既突出了《环保法》的特殊功能，又照顾到了《环保法》同其他的环境资源保护类法律的协调，从整体上提高了我国环境资源保护类法律的效率。

② 王曦：“环保事业基础法”：让特殊的《环保法》特殊起来！《绿叶》，2011 年第 1 期，第 12-14 页。

类法律从功能上可以分为两个层次和四种类型（见图 1——国家环境资源保护类法律类型）。《环保法》就是图 1 中位于下层的那个“环保事业基础法”。它具有独特的、不可替代的功能。

二、《环保法》特殊功能之一：为环保事业奠定法律基础和组织保障

综合考察《环保法（试行）》和《环保法》，可以看出“为环保事业奠定法律基础和组织保障”是《环保法》的一个特殊功能。例如，《环保法（试行）》和《环保法》都在总则部分规定了“环境”的法律定义，确定了我国环境法律关系客体的范围。又如，这两部法律都有关于“单位和个人”的环保义务和权利的原则性规定。《环保法（试行）》第八条规定“公民对污染和破坏环境的单位和个人，有权监督、检举和控告。被检举、控告的单位和个人不得打击报复”。《环保法》第六条规定“一切单位和个人都有保护环境的义务，并有权对污染和破坏环境的单位和个人进行检举和控告”。这些规定都是对环境法律关系主体的基本权利和义务的规定，从一个方面确定了环境法律关系的内容即权利义务关系。再如，这两部法律都有关于创设国家环境保护行政管理体制的规定，分别授予国务院环境保护行政主管部门、县级以上地方人民政府环境保护行政主管部门、国务院相关部门和县级以上地方人民政府相关部门不同的环境保护监管职责。这些规定为我国政府履行环保公共职能提供了组织和机构安排。还如，这两部法律都有关于将环境保护工作纳入国民经济和社会发展计划的规定，使政府环保工作成为有计划和资金保障的政府职能工作。所有这些规定，都为新生的环保事业从整体上提供了合法性和基本制度保障。这个功能是《大气污染防治法》等其他环境资源保护类法律所没有的。又如，《环保法（试行）》和《环保法》都以专章规定了“法律责任”，对有关环境问题的民事、行政和刑事责任和问责程序做了规定，其中有些规定如环境损害民事赔偿诉讼的诉讼时效，还具有特殊性。这些规定都属于为环保事业奠定法律基础的范畴，具有普遍性，不宜由《大气污染防治法》等其他环境保护类法

律来规定。

为了更好地发挥《环保法》的这个特殊功能，《环保法修订建议稿》提出了以下几个方面的建议。

（一）宣示环保基本理念

《环保法》没有用专门条款宣示环保基本理念。相比于它的前身《环保法（试行）》和外国同类法律，这是一个不足。例如，《环保法（试行）》第四条规定“环境保护工作的方针是：全面规划，合理布局，综合利用，化害为利，依靠群众，大家动手，保护环境，造福人民”。它虽称之为“方针”，但其中“保护环境，造福人民”一语无疑是对一种理念的宣示。

工业化国家由于较先遭遇工业化带来的环境危机，从而较先引发对于人类与环境关系的反思。这种反思引起了它们的理念更新。例如美国和日本都用法律宣示环保基本理念。1969 年美国《国家环境政策法》第 102 条宣布美国的国家环境政策是：“联邦政府与各州和地方政府以及有关的公共和私人团体合作，运用包括财政和技术援助在内的一切切实可行的手段和措施，以旨在发展和促进普遍福利的方式，创造和保持人类与自然得以在建设性的和谐生存的各项条件，实现当代美国人及其子孙后代对于社会、经济和其他方面的要求。”[①]在这项宣示中的最后一句话即“创造和保持人类与自然得以在建设性的和谐生存的各项条件，实现当代美国人及其子孙后代对于社会、经济和其他方面的要求”，反映的是一种新的基本理念。这种理念与 20 多年后的 1992 年联合国环境与发展大会上宣布的可持续发展理念是一致的。它代表了美国人民对人与环境关系的新认识，成为治国理念的新内容。该法明文要求联邦政府各个部门和机构都对照这个新理念来检查本部门的现行职责。如发现本部门的现行职责有同这个理念不一致的地方，就要向总统提出修改现行职责的建议。不仅如此，该法还创造了环境影响评价制度来确保这个新理念的实现。[②]美国国内环境状况的改善，同

① 王曦，“美国国家环境政策法和有关机构”，《法学评论》，1984 年第 3 期，第 58 页。
② 详见王曦.，论美国《国家环境政策法》对完善我国环境法制的启示，《现代法学》，2009 年第 4 期。

政府的理念更新有很大关系。1993年日本《环境基本法》第3条规定“把环境作为得天独厚的资源维持在正常的水平上，是人类健康的文化生活所不可缺少的。但是，由于人类的活动增加了环境的负荷，从而使人类存续基础限度的生态平衡出现被破坏的危险。因此，必须妥善实施环境保护，使当代人和后代人能在世世代代地正常享受得天独厚的环境资源的同时，把作为人类存续基础的环境维持到永远的将来。”[①]该法随后的条文将这个条款称之为“基本理念”并要求政府、企业和国民理会和贯彻。

对于我国，以法律宣示环保基本理念的必要性有三。

其一，依法行政的逻辑要求。依法行政的逻辑前提是法律为政府的行政提供行为准则，政府依据这些准则施政。这种行为准则中最高层次的准则就是指导行为的基本理念。在当代中国，这种理念就是科学发展观。如果法律上没有明确规定科学发展理念，政府有关经济和环保的行政就可能出现无所适从或继续因循粗放式经济增长方式的情况。这种漏洞是不能容许的。以法律宣示科学发展理念就是为了弥补这个制度漏洞，使科学发展观同依法行政有机地结合起来，使科学发展观真正成为指导政府履行环保职能的基本理念。

其二，统一环保事业各方主体思想的需要。环保事业的顺利开展和最后胜利，离不开环保事业各方主体如行政机关、企业、公民、法院、立法机关、新闻媒体等对人与自然的关系怀有高度科学而统一的认识。在当代社会，这种高度科学和统一的认识，在国际社会集中体现为联合国自1992年环境与发展大会以来所提倡的“可持续发展”理念；在我国，集中体现为中国共产党提出的“科学发展观”。以法律宣示先进的关于人与自然关系的理念，就是利用法律的教育和引导作用，提升各类环保主体的思想境界和环境伦理水平，使环保事业各类主体在一个共同的、更高的精神境界上进行互动和合作。应当承认，不少地方的政府和不少企业对科学发展理念的认识还有待提高。“徒法不足以自行”，各类环保主体思想境界和环境伦理水平的统一，无疑是环境保护法律得以顺利施行的必要条件，也是环保

① 赵国青主编，《外国环境法选编》，中国政法大学出版社，2000年10月，第1版，第978页。

事业成功的必要条件。以法律宣示这种先进理念，就是利用法律的教育作用为环保事业的成功培育理念这个至关重要的“土壤”或必要条件。

其三，加快发展方式转变的要求。在当代中国，政府，尤其是地方政府具有的强烈的发展冲动。在强烈的发展冲动面前，发展观或发展理念的提升具有决定性的意义。如果不用科学发展观来引导发展冲动，发展必然会是短视的、粗放的、以牺牲环境和资源为代价的。当前的中国，粗放型发展方式弊端尽显。大量的数据和环境群体性事件表明，不仅资源和环境已经难以维持粗放型发展方式，而且国家的长治久安也不允许粗放型发展方式的继续。最近党的十八大报告一方面提出“在当代中国，坚持发展是硬道理的本质要求就是坚持科学发展。以科学发展为主题，以加快转变经济发展方式为主线，是关系我国发展全局的战略抉择”，另一方面指出“资源环境约束加剧”、“一些干部领导科学发展能力不强”。在这样的情况下，利用《环保法》修改的机会，以《环保法》来宣示科学发展理念，无疑将极大地教育和推动政府和企业走科学发展之路。

为了推动我国环保事业各方主体，尤其是政府、企业和公民的理念更新，《环保法修订建议稿》宣示了科学发展理念并要求各级政府对照这个理念检查现行职责。[①]相关的条文如下：

第3条 （基本理念）

环境是人类的生存和发展所依赖的基本物质基础。

为了满足当代人及其子孙后代的需求，经济和社会发展应当与环境相协调。

以人为本，全面协调可持续的科学发展是人与自然和谐的发展方式，符合人民的当前和长远利益。

必须在科学发展观的指导下，以环境保护优化经济发展，加快经济发展方式的转变，建设资源节约型、环境友好型社会。

第9条 （行政职责的检查和调整）

国务院和省、自治区、直辖市人民政府应当分别要求国务院各部门和

① 参见唐瑭，更新立法理念，完善环境法律制度，《绿叶》，2011年第1期，第20-23页。

省、自治区、直辖市人民政府各部门对照本法，检查其现行职责和行政程序同本法的一致性。对检查所发现的现行职责和行政程序同本法的不一致之处，应提出将现行职责和行政程序同本法保持一致的整改建议。国务院各部门和省、自治区、直辖市人民政府各部门应就此项检查分别向国务院和省、自治区、直辖市人民政府做出报告。国务院和省、自治区、直辖市人民政府应当将该报告汇总后抄送国务院环境咨询委员会并听取其意见。

省、自治区、直辖市人民政府应当要求省级以下各级地方人民政府开展前款规定的检查，并提出检查报告。省、自治区、直辖市人民政府应将该报告汇总后抄送省、自治区、直辖市人民政府的环境咨询委员会并听取其意见。

国务院和省、自治区、直辖市人民政府应当在本法生效后24个月内完成此项检查和整改。

（二）明确环保主体各方在环保事业中的地位和作用

对于一个新兴的公共事业，以法律明确界定参与这个事业的各方主体在事业中的地位和作用，有助于各方主体明确自己的相关权利和义务，更好地为这个公共事业作出自己的贡献。环保事业靠环保事业各方主体的共同参与和推动。在环保事业中各方主体的地位和作用是不一样的。只有它们明确了自己的地位和作用，它们才能更好地发挥自己应当发挥的作用。对于我国这样一个民主和法治发展水平不够高的国家，以法律做出这样的界定更有必要。

在国内环保事业发展较好的工业化国家如美国和日本，都有法律对于环保事业主体在环保事业中的地位和作用做出原则性的宣告。1969年美国《国家环境政策法》第102条所宣布的国家环境政策中就要求“联邦政府”与“各州和地方政府”、“有关的公共和私人团体”进行合作以实施这项政策。[①]该法还规定对公民在环保事业中的地位和作用做了规定。该法规定“每个人都可以享受健康的环境，同时每个人也有责任参与对环境改善与

① 王曦，“美国国家环境政策法和有关机构”，《法学评论》，1984年第3期，第58页。

保护”。[1]1993年日本《环境基本法》就规定得更加清楚。该法以第6、7、8、9条分别对国家、地方公共团体、企业和国民的环保责任和义务做了规定。[2]其中国家的责任和义务是根据第3条规定的环境保护基本理念，“制定和实施有关环境保护的基本的且综合性的政策和措施的职责”。地方公共团体（即地方政府，笔者注）的责任和义务是根据基本理念，“制定和实施符合国家有关环境保护政策的地方政策，以及其他适应本地方公共团体区域自然社会条件的政策和措施”。对企业，该法规定了四项责任和义务，分别是根据环保基本理念，采取必要措施，妥善处理企业产生的污染物的义务；妥善处理因企业活动而变成废弃物的物品的义务；努力降低资源消耗、环境负荷和资源再利用的义务；以及协助国家和地方政府实施环保政策和措施的义务。国民的义务是“根据基本理念，努力降低伴随其日常生活对环境的负荷，以便防止环境污染”和“根据基本理念，有责任在自身努力保护环境的同时，协助国家或者地方公共团体实施有关环境保护的政策和措施”。

我国环保事业的主体主要有三方，即政府、企业和第三方主体。这三方主体在环保事业中分别起着管制者、被管制者、监督者、被监督者的作用。管制者指的是政府，政府通过执行环境保护法律和环境政策来进行环境管制。被管制者，又称为管理相对人，指的是根据环境保护法律和政策的要求，承担环境保护义务的自然人、法人和其他组织，其中主要的是企业。监督者，指的是依法享有对政府和被管制者的影响环境的行为进行监督的权利的主体，包括立法机关、检察机关、法院、公众、公民团体等除管制者和被管制者以外的所有“第三方主体”。被监督者，指的是政府和企业等环境污染者和生态破坏者。在这三大主体之间存在着两种互动关系，即管制关系和监督关系。在监督关系中包含第三方主体与政府和企业之间两种监督关系。笔者曾经以图2——环保主体互动等边三角形模型来表示我

① 赵国青主编，《外国环境法选编》，中国政法大学出版社，2000年10月，第1版，第6页。
② 详见赵国青主编，《外国环境法选编》，中国政法大学出版社，2000年10月，第1版，第979-980页。

国环保事业三方主体之间的地位、作用和互动关系。①

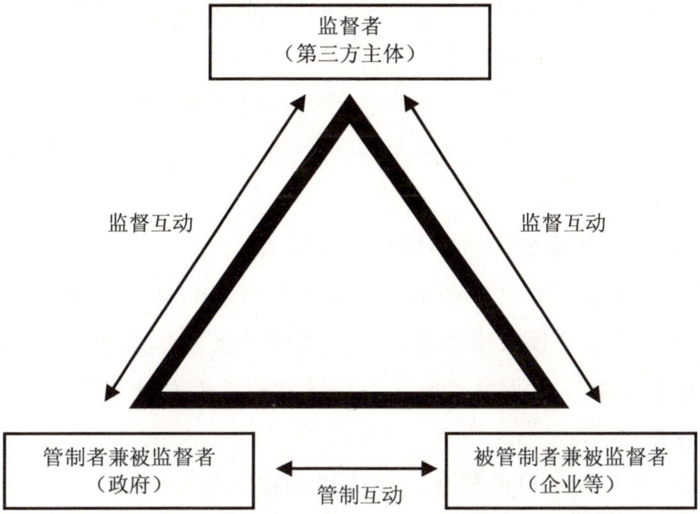

设计者：王曦教授，上海交通大学法学院环境资源法研究所
2011 年 12 月

图 2　环保主体互动等边三角形模型

现行《环保法》关于环保事业主体在环保事业中的地位和作用的规定不够全面和清楚，不能起到应有的教育各方主体的作用。该法仅以第六条规定“一切单位和个人都有保护环境的义务，并有权对污染和破坏环境的单位和个人进行检举和控告”，第十六条中规定“地方各级人民政府，应当对本辖区的环境质量负责，采取措施改善环境”。为了进一步明确我国环保事业主体在环保事业中的地位和作用，《建议稿》做出以下规定：

① 关于环保事业主体之间的互动关系和法律对这种互动关系的保障，详见王曦，环保主体互动法制保障论，《上海交通大学学报（哲学社会科学版）》，2012 年第 1 期，第 5-22 页。还可参见王曦的博客：wangxi7701.blog.163.com。

第 4 条 （政府环境保护职责）

保护环境是政府的公共职能和政府各部门的共同责任。

国务院对全国环境保护工作负责。地方各级人民政府对其管辖范围内的环境保护工作和环境质量负责。

各级政府应当依法保障公民在良好的环境中生活的权利和公民有关环境的知情权、参与权、表达权和监督权，督促公民、法人和其他组织履行环境保护义务，严格执法。

第 5 条 （企事业单位的环保权利和义务）

企事业单位享有依法从事生产、经营等活动的权利，同时负有保护环境的义务。企事业单位应当积极预防和治理其生产、经营等活动造成的环境污染和生态破坏，依法对其造成的环境污染或生态破坏承担修复、治理、赔偿等法律责任。

第 6 条 （公民和社会团体的环保权利和义务）

公民享有在良好的环境中生活的权利，同时负有保护环境的义务。公民应当选择和践行资源节约、环境友好的生活方式。

公民和社会团体享有依法从政府获取环境信息，参与和监督政府环境决策，就污染和生态破坏事项提出申诉、检举和诉讼的权利。

这三条规定有以下三个特色。

特色之一是对环保事业所有主体的环保权利和义务都做了原则性规定，做到了对主体权利义务的均衡“覆盖”。相比之下，现行《环保法》对主体权利义务的规定是不均衡的。它偏重于对政府与企业之间的环境管制关系主体的权利（和权力）义务的规定，对第三方主体与政府之间的监督关系主体的权利义务规定严重不足。

特色之二是对各个主体的环保职责或权利义务都做了原则性规定，比较好地告诉各个主体在环保事业中应当做什么和不应当做什么。其中尤为突出的是对公民与政府之间的监督互动关系的规定。它一方面规定“各级政府应当依法保障公民在良好的环境中生活的权利和公民有关环境的知情权、参与权、表达权和监督权”，另一方面规定“公民和社会团体享有依法从政府获取环境信息，参与和监督政府环境决策，就污染和生态破坏事项提出申诉、检举和诉讼的权利”。这种规定是对现行《环保法》第六条“一切单位和个人都有保护环境的义务，并有权对污染和破坏环境的单位和个人进行检举和控告”的合理细化，操作性更强。

特色之三是强调政府环境保护职能的统一性。这个特色尤其符合现阶段我国的国情。第 4 条第 1 款规定环保是政府的公共职能和政府各部门的共同责任。长期以来，在很多情况下，环保被看做只是环保部门的职能，而不是作为整体的政府公共职能的有机组成部分。在经济增长或 GDP 面前，环保往往被看成是可以“博弈”或“让步”的事。政府的环保职能没有在政府各部门中得到统一的承认和尊重，更谈不上统一的履行。“我们的政府中，一部分政府，如环保局，努力地执行环境法律，保护环境，保护公共品。但同时另一部分政府，如负责经济发展和资源开发的部门，却无视环境法，从事着牺牲环境和生态，谋求短期 GDP 增长的事情。这两类政府部门在对待环境这个公共品上的态度截然相反。在有些地方，由于地方行政首长单打一的经济发展观，环保部门甚至不能有效行使其法定的职能。……‘环保风暴’揭示我们的政府在完整地、统一地履行公共职能方面存在比较大的问题。”① “事实表明，各级政府和政府各部门履行环保职能的不统一是引发或加重环境问题的重要原因之一。政府环保履职存在三个‘不统一’，它们是中央政府与地方政府环保履职不统一、地方政府间环保履职不统一和政府各部门之间环保履职不统一。”② “要真正实现可持续的经济发展，必须以法律的形式明确和统一各级政府和政府各部门的环保职能的履行，彻底改变过去那种环保职能的履行在一部分政府部门中‘硬’，在另一部分政府部门中‘软’；在中央政府中‘硬’，在地方政府中‘软’的局面。”③政

① 王曦，论我国《环保法》的修改与政府环境保护公共职能的统一性——在全国人大环资委“中国环境立法座谈会”上的发言（2005 年 2 月 21 日），载于王曦主编，《国际环境法与比较环境法评论》（2008 年卷），上海交通大学出版社，2008 年 3 月第 1 版，第 202 页。

② 邓旸，理顺职能，确保政府环保履职的统一性，《绿叶》，2011 年第 1 期，第 24-25 页。

③ 邓旸，理顺职能，确保政府环保履职的统一性，《绿叶》，2011 年第 1 期，第 24 页。

府的环保职能，应当像政府的计划生育管理、土地管理甚至国防职能那样，在各级政府和政府各部门中都得到一致承认和尊重。上述美国《国家环境政策法》明确要求联邦政府的各部门对照该法宣布的国家环境政策，检查本部门的行政职能，并提出使该职能同国家环境政策保持一致的整改措施，[①]其目的也是为了确保政府的环保职能同政府的其他职能有机地统一起来。

（三）改进环境行政管理体制

我国环保部门的职能实际上已经发生重大变化。“自 1998 年，原国家环境保护总局承担了原国务院环境保护委员会的全部职能后，其《‘三定’方案》新增了主要职责：‘指导和协调解决各地方、各部门以及跨地区、跨流域的重大环境问题；协调省际环境污染纠纷；组织和协调国家重点流域水污染防治工作。’这是中国环保部门职能定位的一个重要变化——由原来单纯的执法监督，逐步转变为综合管理与执法监督并重。这一变化的目的在于，一方面弱化‘统管’带来的负面作用，另一方面强化环保部门的综合协调能力。2008 年环境保护部《‘三定’方案》在其‘职责调整’中进一步强调：‘加强环境政策、规划和重大问题的统筹协调职责；加强环境治理和对生态保护的指导、协调、监督的职责’。这明确表示环保部门的职能已由‘统一监督管理’转向‘综合协调’，其主要职责在于统筹协调、指导、监督和服务。环境保护部部长周生贤也指出，环境保护部今后的职能配置将朝着统筹协调、宏观调控、监督执法和公共服务四个方向强化。”[②]现行《环保法》关于环保行政体制的规定已经远远落后与现实中环保部“三定”方案的规定。根据实际情况的变化，《建议稿》将中央和地方人民政府环保行政主管部门的职责改为“综合管理，包括监督、指导、协调和服务”。具体规定如下：

---

① 美国《国家环境政策法》第 103 条规定：“所有联邦政府机构均应当对其现行法定职权、行政法规定以及各项现行政策和程序进行一次清理，以确定其是否存在妨碍充分执行本法宗旨和规定的任何缺陷或矛盾，并应当就清理结果在不迟于 1971 年 7 月 1 日以前，向总统报告其职权和各项政策符合本法所规定的意图、宗旨和程序。”该法第 104 条进一步规定：“本法规定的政策和目标（指国家环境政策和环保目标，本文作者注。），性质上属于对联邦各机构现行职权的补充。”

② 邓旸，理顺职能，确保政府环保履职的统一性，《绿叶》，2011 年第 1 期，第 28 页。

第7条 （国务院环保行政体制）

国务院环境保护部门负责全国环境保护工作的综合管理，对国务院各部门和地方人民政府的环境保护工作进行监督、指导、协调和服务。

国务院环境保护部门可以设立区域性环境保护派出机构，协调和督促地方人民政府的环境保护工作，协调解决跨行政区环境纠纷。地方人民政府应当支持区域性环境保护派出机构的工作。

国务院其他有关主管部门依照本法和有关法律的规定对环境保护工作实施监督管理。

第8条 （地方人民政府环保行政体制）

县级以上地方人民政府环境保护部门负责本辖区环境保护工作的综合管理，对本级人民政府各部门和下级人民政府的环境保护工作进行监督、指导、协调和服务。

县级以上地方人民政府其他有关主管部门依照本法和有关法律的规定对环境保护工作实施监督管理。

三、《环保法》特殊功能之二：规范和约束有关环境的政府行为

我曾经提出，当前我国环境法制建设的战略突破口是在法律上建立规范和制约有关环境的政府行为的制度。①之所以将规范和制约有关环境的政府行为作为突破口，是因为政府，尤其是地方政府，除了担负环境管理职责以外，还往往成为“间接的环境污染者或生态破坏者”。②首先，“中国政府不是单纯的环境管理者。在中国的特殊国情下，政府不仅是环境管理者，而且是经济建设的主导者和主要驱动力量。政府的这个主导和驱动作用主要体现在它的经济开发规划，经济计划、投资和招商引资活动中。换言之，政府是经济建设的规划者、计划者、投资者和招商者。也就是说，政府不

① 参见王曦，论新时期完善我国环境法制的战略突破口，《上海交通大学学报（哲学社会科学版）》，2009年第2期。

② 王曦，“环保事业基础法”：让特殊的《环保法》特殊起来！《绿叶》，2011年第1期，第14页。

仅是‘裁判员’，也是‘运动员’。作为经济建设的规划者、计划者、投资者和招商者，政府的规划、计划、投资和招商引资如果没有协调好发展经济与保护环境的关系，没有充分考虑环境资源的支撑能力，从而做出有违科学发展的错误决策的话，政府就成了环境问题的制造者。”[①]其次，“执法不力和行政懈怠”也可能使政府成为“间接的环境污染或生态破坏者”。[②]在政府自身也成为环境问题的制造者的情况下，它如何能够管好市场主体的污染呢？因此，规范和约束有关环境的政府行为是《环保法》修订工作的当务之急。

可以将有关环境的政府行为分为两类。一类是有关环境的政府决策。这类政府行为的典型例子是政府的产业发展规划和招商引资决策，尤其是地方政府的产业发展规划和招商引资决策。大量的环境群体事件证明，有关环境的政府决策上的失误是引起当地环境群体事件的根本原因。最近在江苏省南通市、四川省什邡县和浙江宁波市发生的环境群体事件，都属于这类事件。这类决策上失误的主要原因是当地政府只看到有关产业或招商引资项目的经济效益，忽视了这些产业或招商引资项目所可能造成的污染或生态破坏。人们常常将这种决策失误称之为政府的“乱作为”。

另一类是有关环境的行政执法。政府环境执法懈怠和对环境执法的不当干预是这方面的主要问题。这方面的例子也很多。“长期以来，一些地方仍是重经济发展，重速度、重规模、重眼前；轻资源环保，轻效益、轻创新、轻长远，以 GDP 论英雄，急功近利，导致环境与经济综合决策失误、行政不作为和行政干预环境执法等现象长期存在。环保部门面对地方保护主义的干扰，在执法中‘顶得住的站不住，站得住的顶不住’的问题尚未得到解决。一些地方片面强调营造‘宽松’的发展氛围，有的对工业园区、重点企业实行‘封闭式管理’、‘挂牌保护’，出台‘企业宁静日’等土政策，

---

① 王曦，“环保事业基础法”：让特殊的《环保法》特殊起来！《绿叶》，2011 年第 1 期，第 15 页。

② 王曦，“环保事业基础法”：让特殊的《环保法》特殊起来！《绿叶》，2011 年第 1 期，第 14-16 页；又见王曦、罗文君，论环境管理失效的制度原因，载于高鸿钧、王明远主编：《清华法治论衡》，第 13 辑，清华大学出版社 2010 年 6 月第 1 版，第 300-310 页。

不准执法部门进园区、厂区检查，干扰正常执法；有的在进行决策时，未严格依法行政，环境信息不透明、忽视公民的环境知情权、参与权，引发一系列群体性事件；有的对环境违法行为睁一只眼、闭一只眼，遇到问题相互推诿，避重就轻，行政不作为或者乱作为。一些地方以牺牲环境换取经济发展，片面追求 GDP，不履行环境责任或履责不到位，已经成为制约资源环境保护的重要原因。”[①]

《建议稿》从规范有关环境的政府决策和政府环保履职监督两方面对规范和约束有关环境的政府行为作出了规定。

（一）规范有关环境的政府决策

由于政府施政的信条是依法行政，因而法律应当在决策这个最重要的环节上为政府规定完善的制度。从《环保法（试行）》到《环保法》，都没有在这方面做出完善的规定。虽然《中华人民共和国环境影响评价法》在规划环评方面做出了开创性规定，但法律对有关环境的政府决策的规范和约束仍然存在很大的缺陷。在这种情况下，牺牲环境和资源，甚至牺牲人民的生命和健康，换取当地经济的发展的做法在决策阶段得不到制度的约束，因而引出很多环境和社会问题。落实科学发展观，加快发展方式的转变，要求我们把政府有关环境的决策规范起来，使之走上科学、民主决策的轨道。[②]为此，《建议稿》对有关环境的政府科学民主决策以专章做了规定。其中主要的制度如下：

环境与发展综合决策。环境与发展综合决策是 1992 年联合国《里约环境与发展宣言》和《21 世纪议程》的要求。我国不仅签署了这些国际文件，而且从那时以来一直通过《中国 21 世纪议程》和历次国民经济和社会发展计划或规划来落实这项要求。这次《环保法》修订为环境与发展综合决策成为规范的政府决策制度，提供了宝贵的机会。为此，《建议稿》对环境与

① 杨朝飞，我国环境法律制度和环境保护若干问题，中国环境报，2012 年 11 月 5 日第 3 版。

② 参见罗文君，建立科学决策制度，从源头上规范政府环保履职，《绿叶》，2011 年第 1 期，第 30-34 页。

发展综合决策做了规定。这个制度的核心是协商。具体表现为政府在决策之前的内部协商和外部协商。内部协商指的是政府各部门在做出对环境可能有重大影响的决策前同环保部门的协商。外部协商指的是政府各部门在做出对环境可能有重大影响的决策要听取相关级别的政府环境咨询委员会的意见。相关条文如下：

第 16 条 （环境与发展综合决策）

县级以上人民政府各部门在做出可能对环境产生重大影响的决策之前，应当书面征求本级政府的环境保护部门的意见。环境保护部门在做出涉及经济社会发展问题的决策之前，应书面征求本级政府相关部门的意见。各部门之间应相互协商，共同促进环境与经济、社会的协调发展。如经协商，决策部门的意见与环境保护部门的意见没有达成一致，决策部门或者环境保护部门应将争议的问题和解决问题的建议提交本级政府环境保护联席会议审议。环境保护联席会议应当针对所审议的问题提出对策建议，报请本级人民政府决定。

国务院各部门在做出可能对环境产生重大影响的决策之前，应当书面征求国务院环境咨询委员会的意见。县级以上地方人民政府在做出可能对环境产生重大影响的决策之前，应当书面征求省、自治区、直辖市人民政府环境咨询委员会的意见。

政府环境保护联席会议。将发展经济和环境保护协调一致，说起来容易，做起来难。政府在实际工作中经常遇到两者的对立，出现经济职能部门和环境保护职能部门之间意见不一致的情况。为此，有必要建立政府环境保护联席会议制度，为环境与发展综合决策提供一个协调的平台。《建议稿》将政府环境保护联席会议设计为一种协调工作的组织形式。它的任务是审议政府部门对有关环境的决策的争议，并向本级政府提出对策建议。相关的条文如下：

第17条 （政府环境保护联席会议）

县级以上人民政府应当建立环境保护联席会议制度。

国务院环境保护联席会议的职能是：

1. 研究审议国家环境保护法律、法规、政策、标准、规划和计划的草案；

2. 研究审议国家环境保护法律、法规、政策、标准、规划和计划的贯彻和执行情况；

3. 研究审议由国务院部门提请审议的事项；

4. 研究审议国务院交办的其他事项。

县级以上地方人民政府环境保护联席会议的职能是：

1. 研究审议本行政区环境保护法规、政策、标准、规划和计划的草案；

2. 研究审议国家和地方环境保护法律、法规、政策、标准、规划和计划在本行政区的贯彻执行情况；

3. 研究审议由省、自治区、直辖市人民政府部门提请审议的事项；

4. 研究审议国务院和本级政府交办的其他事项。

县级以上人民政府环境保护联席会议应当邀请同级环境咨询委员会列席会议。

县级以上人民政府环境保护联席会议由本级政府的环境保护部门负责召集。

县级以上人民政府环境保护联席会议下设秘书处。秘书处的工作由本级政府环境保护部门承担。

国务院环境保护联席会议的成员单位、议事规则等，由国务院环境保护部门会同有关部门制订，报国务院批准后施行。县级以上地方人民政府成员单位、议事规则等，由县级以上人民政府环境保护部门会同有关部门制订，报县级以上人民政府批准后施行。

环境咨询委员会。关于建立环境咨询委员会的规定是《建议稿》的一个创造。环境咨询委员会的设立是为了落实科学发展观，深化政务公开，加强对行政权力的监督和制约，为政府有关环境事务的民主决策提供组织保障。环境咨询委员会是一个由非政府人士为主组成的咨询性委员会，其宗旨是参与政府有关环境的决策，为政府决策提供来自政府以外的方方面面如专家、学者、社会团体、居民等的意见和建议，使政府在决策时能够听到各种利益相关方的声音。它是一个民主程序。《建议稿》不仅规定环境咨询委员会有权列席国务院和省级人民政府的环境保护联席会议，而且有权参与政府环境与发展综合决策、重大决策建议的环境影响评估、有重大环境影响的行政决定和规划的备案、主体功能区划、环境功能区划和生态功能区划、重点区域流域生态保护规划和规划环评。

设立环境咨询委员会的好处，一是在事前（即政府决策之前）解决问题，而不是在事后（即政府决策之后）进行补救；二是在体制内解决问题，而不是在体制外解决问题。大量的环境污染或生态破坏事例证明，事后补救和体制外的解决所带来的社会成本大大超过事前解决和体制内解决所需要的社会成本。“在参与‘无门’，监督‘无路’的情况下，公众常常寻求非常规手段，如群体性‘散步’、‘静坐’、‘围攻’行政机关等，引发群体事件。”[①]现实中，当出现有关环境问题的群体事件时，当地政府往往召开会议，邀请当地的人大代表、政协委员、居民代表、企业代表和专家、学者等德高望重人士就有关问题发表意见，寻求各方利益的协调。问题在于，这种做法是事后的，没有预防的作用。与其让公众由于事前参与无门和采用“体制外”的非常规手段寻求问题的解决，不如在法律上做出制度安排，使之可以在事前和体制内表达意见，在决策阶段避免问题的出现。环境咨询委员会就是为了这种事前解决和体制内解决问题而设计的一种组织形式。我认为，环境咨询委员会是一个可以为执政党和政府所用的民主形式，为在党的领导下的公众参与的有序化和组织化提供了一个有益的途径。执政党和政府可以利用这个形式来保障公众（和所有利益相关方）的知情权、参与权、表达权和监督权。相关条文如下：

① 王曦，“环保事业基础法”：让特殊的《环保法》特殊起来！《绿叶》，2011 年第 1 期，第 18 页。

第 18 条 （环境咨询委员会）

国务院设立环境咨询委员会。

国务院环境咨询委员会是国务院的顾问机构，其职责主要有：

1. 对国务院提供关于国家环境状况和环境保护工作的意见和建议；

2. 参与国务院环境保护部门的环境区划工作和规划和建设项目的环境影响评价工作；

3. 应国务院或国务院环境保护部门的委托，对环境问题和事项开展调查研究，提出调查报告；

4. 列席国务院环境保护联席会议。

国务院环境咨询委员会由赞同本法，具有高度的社会公益心和社会责任感，具有丰富学识和经验，有能力对环境保护政策、法律、法规、规划、计划和项目做出评价和建议的德高望重之政府官员、专家、学者、社会团体代表和其他人士组成，其中政府官员不得超过委员会成员总数的三分之一。

国务院环境咨询委员会的委员人数、章程和议事规则，由国务院环境保护部门提出方案，经国务院批准后施行。

省、自治区、直辖市人民政府设立环境咨询委员会。省、自治区、直辖市人民政府参照本法关于国务院环境咨询委员会的规定规定本级政府环境咨询委员会的委员人数、章程和议事规则。

政策建议的环境影响评估。这里的“政策建议”是指关于拟由县级以上人民政府或县级以上人民政府部门的名义发布的政策或其他决策的建议，不包括《环境影响评价法》中规定的各种规划。做出这项规定的理由，主要是为了防止政府，尤其是地方政府，制定“土政策”，在执法上对辖区内的污染型企业违法环境资源法律的行为给予偏袒或放纵。环境执法方面的地方保护主义在不少地方发生过并仍在发生。因此有必要从立法上加以规范，为地方政府设立最低行为准则，禁止这类行为的发生。《建议稿》相关条文如下：

第 19 条 （政策建议的环境影响评估）

县级以上人民政府及其部门在提出政策的建议之前，应当由本级政府环境保护部门对该建议的环境影响进行评估，并提出环境影响评估意见。政策的环境影响评估意见应当抄送相应级别的环境咨询委员会并征求其意见。

政策建议的环境影响评估应当分析和说明该政策如付诸实施将会对环境带来的影响。政策建议环境影响评估意见应当作为政府和有关部门做政策决策时的参考依据。

政策建议的环境影响评估办法，由国家环境保护部门起草，报国务院批准后施行。

主体功能区划。主体功能区划是一项从从宏观上对有关环境的政府决策进行控制的重大措施。①党的十八大报告提出到 2020 年全面建成小康社会，其中一项目标是“主体功能区布局基本形成”。报告要求“加快实施主体功能区战略，推动各地区严格按照主体功能定位发展，构建科学合理的城市化格局、农业发展格局、生态安全格局”。主体功能区划实际上是对有关环境的政府决策的一个重大约束条件。政府在制定产业发展规划、招商引资时，必须按照主体功能区化办事。《建议稿》相关的条文如下：

第 21 条 （主体功能区划）

国务院发展与改革部门应当会同有关部门，编制全国国土主体功能区划。全国国土功能区划经国务院批准后施行。

县级以上地方人民政府应当依据全国国土主体功能区划，根据本地资源禀赋、环境容量、生态状况、人口数量以及国家发展规划和产业政策，明确本行政区内不同区域的功能定位和发展方向，分别实行优化开发、重点开发、限制开发和禁止开发。

县级以上地方人民政府应当邀请省、自治区、直辖市人民政府环境咨

① 参见周卫，完善各类环境生态区划和规划制度，《绿叶》，2011 年第 1 期，第 35-38 页。

询委员会参与本行政区主体功能区划的制定，并向社会征求关于本行政区主体功能区划的意见。

全国国土功能区划和县级以上地方人民政府国土主体功能区划应当向社会公布。

县级以上地方人民政府制定的国土功能区划，不得与全国国土功能区划相冲突。

全国国土功能区划和县级以上地方行政区域的国土功能区划应当作为国家和地方制定国民经济和社会发展规划和计划的依据。

政府公共咨询。这里的政府公共咨询指的是政府在做出有关环境的重要决策时向可能受该决策影响的利益相关方和公众征求意见。最近频繁发生的环境群体事件一再告诉我们这种公共咨询的重要性。《建议稿》的相关条文如下：

第 60 条 （公开听证会）

除依法需要保密的情形外，编制规划、制定政策和审批建设项目等与公众环境利益密切相关的重大决策，政府主管部门应当通过听证会等形式公开听取公众意见。听证会的结果应当对社会公布。

（二）建立政府环保履职监督制度

政府环保履职不力，尤其是环保执法不力，多年来一直为人们所诟病。政府环保履职不力的主要原因是在“唯 GDP”的发展观的指导下政府缺乏严格依照环境法办事的动机。“政府不履行环境责任以及履行环境责任不到位，已成为制约中国环保事业发展的严重障碍。”[①]解决这个问题的办法，一是靠对政府官员进行守法和严格执法的教育，二是靠有效的外部监督。事实证明，光靠教育是不够的。几乎每一部环境资源保护法律的出台，都

① 徐丰果，把确保政府勤勉履行环保职能的“达摩克利斯之剑”挂起来！《绿叶》，2011 年第 1 期，第 48 页。

伴随着对政府守法和执法的要求。对政府官员的普法教育一直包含这方面的内容。但政府环保履职始终没有做好。因此，在环保事业中，“第三方”主体的监督是不可或缺的。理论和实践都证明，缺了这个监督，政府不会勤勉履行环保职能。在政府不勤勉履行环保职能的情况下，企业一般也不会履行其环保社会责任。

就政府环保履职监督而言，现行《环保法》和其他环境资源保护类法律的规定非常薄弱。已有的规定，基本上只有《环保法》第六条和第十六条两条原则性的、不具可操作性的规定。[①]《环保法》的修改为解决政府环境执法不力这个“老大难”问题提供了一个难得的机遇。立法机关应当抓住这个机遇，通过修改《环保法》建立有效的政府环境履职监督制度，“在法律上把确保政府勤勉履行环保职能的‘达摩克利斯之剑’挂起来。”[②]为此，《建议稿》以第四章专门规定了“第三方”主体对政府履行环保职能的监督，主要的制度有人民代表大会监督、政府内部监督、政府环保履职考核和环境公民诉讼制度等。

人民代表大会监督。人民代表大会掌握着对行政官员的任免权和监督权。人民代表大会对政府的监督是法律监督，最为有力。在我国，政府掌握着大量的资源并且是经济发展的主要规划者、实施者和推动者。政府的行为稍有不慎就可能对环境甚至人民生命和健康带来大范围、长时期的危害。新中国在这方面教训深刻。因此，对政府这只“有形的手”必须加以有力的约束。而能够对政府进行有力约束的，莫过于它的授权者——人民代表大会。政府是人民代表大会的执行机关。我国虽然已有《人民代表大会常委会监督法》，但如何将人大对有关环境的政府行为的监督落到实处，仍然有很多工作要做。为此，《建议稿》一方面要求政府向人大报告环境管理工作并按照人大的整改建议进行整改；另一方面要求政府将此类报告和

---

① 《环保法》第六条规定：“一切单位和个人都有保护环境的义务，并有权对污染和破坏环境的单位和个人进行检举和控告。”《环保法》第十六条规定：“地方各级人民政府，应当对本辖区的环境质量负责，采取措施改善环境质量。”

② 徐丰果，把确保政府勤勉履行环保职能的“达摩克利斯之剑”挂起来！《绿叶》，2011 年第 1 期，第 48-49 页。

整改情况通报同级环境咨询委员会并向社会公开，将社会监督与人大监督结合起来。《建议稿》的这些规定是人大监督在环保事业中的合理延伸。相关的条文如下：

第61条 （人大监督）

县级以上人民政府应当每年向同级人民代表大会报告环境保护工作。人民代表大会闭会期间，县级以上人民政府应当根据同级人民代表大会常务委员会的要求向其报告环境保护工作，接受同级人民代表大会常委会的监督和检查。报告的内容包括环境保护目标的实现情况，环境保护规划、计划、预算的执行情况和环境保护法律、法规的执行情况。此报告应抄送相应级别人民政府的环境咨询委员会并向社会公布。

县级以上人民政府应当根据同级人民代表大会及其常务委员会关于改进政府环境保护工作的决议和建议，采取相应的整改措施。整改情况应当向同级人民代表大会及其常务委员会做出专门报告，并抄送相应级别人民政府的环境咨询委员会和向社会公布。

政府内部监督。政府，尤其是地方政府，在规划经济发展、招商引资、审批建设项目时，往往遇到发展经济与保护环境的矛盾。在很多情况下，由于政府的主要领导信奉“唯 GDP”发展观，政府环保部门的正确意见得不到采纳，从而导致政府决策失误。这种情况表明在政府内部，除了建立环境与发展综合决策制度以外，还有必要加强政府环保部门对于其他部门和上级环保部门对于下级人民政府有关部门的制衡。为此，《建议稿》结合实践中的成功经验，规定了行政约谈和上级政府督办和代办制度。相关的条文如下：

第62条（约谈和环保履职行政建议）

国务院其他部门和县级以上地方人民政府不依法履行环境保护职责或履行不力的，国务院环境保护部门应当及时了解情况，与有关部门或地方人民政府的负责人约谈，并提出环境保护履职行政建议。环境保护履职行政建议中应当包括适当的改正期限。环境保护履职行政建议应当抄送国务院公务员管理部门、行政监察部门和国务院环境咨询委员会。

国务院其他部门和县级以上地方人民政府在同国务院环境保护部门约谈并收到环境保护履职行政建议后，在改正期限内仍不履行环境保护职能或履行不力的，国务院环境保护部门应当将有关情况报请国务院公务员管理部门和行政监察部门处理。

地方各级人民政府除环境保护部门以外的其他部门不依法履行环境保护职责或履行不力的，同级人民政府的环境保护部门应当及时了解情况，与有关部门的负责人约谈并提出环境保护履职行政建议。环境保护履职行政建议中应当包括适当的改正期限。环境保护履职行政建议应当抄送地方人民政府公务员管理部门、行政监察部门和省、自治区、直辖市人民政府环境咨询委员会。

地方各级人民政府的其他部门在同级环境保护部门约谈并收到环境保护履职行政建议后，在改正期限内仍不履行环境保护职能或履行不力的，同级人民政府的环境保护部门应当将有关情况报请同级人民政府的公务员管理部门和行政监察部门处理，并抄送省、自治区、直辖市人民政府环境咨询委员会。

第63条 （上级政府督办和代办）

当出现以下情形之一时，上级人民政府环境保护部门应当单独或联合有关部门对管辖该区域的人民政府环境保护部门的执法工作实行督办：

1. 发生重大、特大环境污染事件或生态破坏事件；

2. 限期治理没有按期通过验收；

3. 经催告后，管辖该区域的环境保护部门仍不依法对环境违法行为进行处理。

督办必须明确办理责任人员、办理期限和方式。被督办的环境保护部门应当及时向督办部门报告办理进度和结果。

督办期满后，被督办的环境保护部门未能完成督办目标的，该部门的执法行为由督办部门代为执行，并依法对被督办的环境保护部门的办理责任人员给予处分。

督办的环境保护部门应当将督办通知和督办结果抄送相应级别人民政府环境咨询委员会并向社会公布。

政府环保履职考核。官员的政绩考核是影响官员行为的“指挥棒”。考核和问责，将政府环保履职的情况同政府官员的个人利益如名誉、晋升、收入等联系起来，是确保政府忠实、勤勉地履行环保职能的重要保障。《建议稿》将政府环保履职考核同《公务员法》和《行政监察法》相联系，把政府环保履职纳入公务员和国有企业领导成员工作实绩考核和问责。相关的条文如下：

第 64 条 （行政机关和国有企业领导成员环境保护工作实绩考核）

国务院和县级以上地方人民政府公务员管理部门和行政监察部门应当依法对国家行政机关领导成员和国有企业领导成员遵守和执行本法的情况进行监督、检查和考核。

国务院公务员主管部门应当制定行政机关领导成员环境保护工作实绩考核指标，将其纳入各级行政机关领导成员工作实绩考核方案，对国务院各部门和地方各级人民政府及其各部门的领导成员履行环境保护职责的情况进行考核。

国务院中央企业管理部门和地方人民政府国有企业管理部门应当制定国有企业领导成员环境保护工作实绩考核指标，将其纳入国有企业领导成员工作实绩考核方案，对国有企业领导成员履行环境保护职责的情况进行考核。

环境保护工作实绩考核指标包括贯彻执行环境保护法律、法规和标准的情况；环境质量改善情况；主要污染物排放总量控制指标完成情况；环境保护重点任务完成情况和人民群众对环境保护工作的满意度等。

国务院公务员管理部门和行政监察部门应当会同国务院环境保护部门

制定行政机关和国有企业领导成员环境保护工作实绩考核办法，报国务院批准后施行。

环境公民诉讼。公民诉讼（citizen suit）制度本是美国环境法的一个重要制度创新。它为督促政府勤勉履行环境保护公共职能和监督污染者遵守环境法提供了一种新的法律手段。资料表明，公民诉讼制度在这两方面都起到了很好的作用。美国的公民诉讼与环境影响评价制度一样，产生了广泛的国际影响，为很多国家所仿效。①在认真研究美国公民诉讼制度的经验之后，研究组根据我国的具体情况，设计了一个具有中国特色的环境公民诉讼制度。②

这项制度的目的是为我国公民和公民团体依法监督政府履行环保职能提供一个新的途径。它赋权公民和公民团体以行政诉讼为威慑，敦促政府勤勉履行环保职责。严格地说，诉讼不是它的目的。它更希望在不得不对政府提起行政诉讼之前，政府有关部门已经接受了公民或公民团体的意见，开始履行依法履行环保职责。这个制度的一个关键点是诉讼前通知期。原告只是在这个通知期到期之后，才会向将有关行政机关告上法庭。“我国的环境公民诉讼制度不以直接监督企业为目的，而是以监督政府的管理行为来达到监督企业的目的。这样设计的理由主要有三：一是我国现行的环境法律对企业的管制措施比较完备；二是现行的环境法律对政府行为的监督与制约比较薄弱，而政府勤勉履行环保职能在当前经济快速发展的情况下尤为重要；三是监督对象单一，突出重点，易于法律的实施。”③这个制度同现行的各种监督政府行为的制度不矛盾、不重复，是对现行各种制度的有益补充。我国《宪法》第 41 条第 1 款规定：“中华人民共和国公民对于任何国家机关和国家工作人员，有提出批评和建议的权利；对于任何国家

---

① 关于美国环境法中的公民诉讼制度，详见王曦、罗文君、张鹏、杨亚辉. 论创立中国环境公民诉讼制度，《上海交通大学学报（哲学社会科学版）》，2010 年第 1 期，第 5-9 页。

② 关于这个有中国特色的公民诉讼制度的初步设计，详见王曦、罗文君、张鹏、杨亚辉，论创立中国环境公民诉讼制度，《上海交通大学学报（哲学社会科学版）》，2010 年第 1 期，第 9-15 页。

③ 王曦、罗文君、张鹏、杨亚辉，论创立中国环境公民诉讼制度，《上海交通大学学报（哲学社会科学版）》，2010 年第 1 期，第 9 页。

机关和相关人员的违法失职行为，有向有关国家机关提出申诉、控告或者检举的权利……”《宪法》这一规定为创立环境公民诉讼制度提供了重要依据。“中国环境公民诉讼是这种‘批评、建议、申诉、控告或者检举’的变化了的形式，是一种以审判权来最后依托的对行政机关的‘批评、建议、申诉、控告或者检举’。它是我国公民所享有的这项宪法权利在新的社会经济条件下的合理的延伸和发展。”[①]《建议稿》的相关条文如下：

第65条（环境公民诉讼——督促政府履行环保职能的特殊手段）

公民、法人和其他组织如果有初步证据证明地方人民政府或其部门有疏于履行本法或者其他法律规定的应当由其履行的环境保护职责之嫌，可以对该政府或政府部门发出书面通知，告知其疏于履行职责的情况并要求其依法履行该职责。

如果被告知的政府或政府部门在书面通知送达60日内仍未依法履行有关职责，则公民、法人和其他组织可就该事项向人民法院提起行政诉讼，请求人民法院裁决其依法履行有关职责。

对本条规定的行政诉讼，不论原告胜诉与否，人民法院可以判决被告为原告支付适当的律师费用、监测鉴定费用或其他诉讼费用。

本条第 1 款所称“本法规定的”环境保护职责指的是本法规定的有关重大决策的环境影响评估意见抄送环境咨询委员会并征求其意见；在做出可能对环境产生重大影响的决策之前书面征求国务院环境咨询委员会的意见；可能对环境带来重大影响的行政决定和经批准的综合性规划或专项规划的备案和抄送；邀请环境咨询委员会参与主体功能区划的制定；邀请国环境咨询委员会参与环境功能区划和生态功能区划的制定，并向社会征求关于环境功能区划和生态功能区划的意见；邀请环境咨询委员会参与重点区域、流域生态保护规划的制订并征求其意见；规划环评、行政限批、工业开发区环境监管、政府信息公开和举行公开听证会的政府职责。

① 王曦、罗文君、张鹏、杨亚辉，论创立中国环境公民诉讼制度，《上海交通大学学报（哲学社会科学版）》，2010年第1期，第11页。

四、《环保法》特殊功能之三：规定一般性环境监管制度

环境监管制度是政府履行环保职能的主要途径。环境监管制度可以分为两类。一类是一般性环境监管制度；另一类是特殊性环境监管制度。一般性环境监管制度是指由《环保法》这样的“环保事业基础法”规定的，广泛适用于环境资源保护领域的环境监管制度，例如环境监测、政府环境信息公开、限期治理和环境污染事故处理等制度。特殊性环境监管制度是指由污染控制类、自然资源保护类和专门事项类环境法律规定的，适用于环境资源保护领域里特定范围、事项或活动的监管制度，例如《大气污染防治法》规定的二氧化硫控制区、《野生动物保护法》规定的禁猎期和《清洁生产促进法》规定的清洁生产审核制度等。[①]

自《环保法》施行以来，环境管理实践中涌现出很多适应新时代特点的一般性环境监管制度。其中得到广泛运用并取得良好效果的环境监管制度主要有行政限批、环保基础设施建设和监管、工业开发区环境监管、企业环保信用信息管理、公布严重违法者、会商改正方案、联合执法、环境污染风险与损害评估等。《建议稿》对这些制度做出规定，赋予其法律约束力和法律的稳定性，使政府更好地发挥环境监管职能。《建议稿》的这些规定主要体现在第三章（环境监管）中。主要的新监管制度有：行政限批（第38条）、环保基础设施建设和监管（第39条）、工业开发区环境监管（第40条）、企业环保信用信息管理（第45条）、公布严重排污者（第44条）、会商改正方案（第46条）、排污者与环保部门联合执法（第47条）、环境污染风险与损害评估（第49条）（由于篇幅所限，这里不列举具体条款）。

“政府履行环保职能的另一个主要途径是环保经济手段”（又称为“环保经济政策”），主要表现为运用各种环保经济手段，将环境保护的需要与市场主体对切身经济利益的追求联系起来，以市场这只“无形的手”，引导市场主体改变消费习惯，选择“绿色”消费，从而实现保护环境与生态这

① 王小钢，与时俱进，发展和完善一般性环境监管制度，《绿叶》，2011年第1期，第39-40页。

个公共物品与市场主体个人效用最大化的“双赢”。由于经济手段能够调动市场主体保护环境的积极性，它的环保效果往往比政府管制的效果更为广泛和持久。因此，环保经济手段是政府环境管制的重要补充。[①]自从 20 世纪 70 年代中期以来，环保经济手段在美国和欧洲逐渐得到应用。美国在 20 世纪 70 年代中期在空气污染控制中实施“泡泡政策”和“排放交易”等措施，取得了比较好的减少空气污染控制成本的效果。[②]在欧洲，欧盟在 20 世纪 80 年代提倡环保经济手段的运用，并在欧洲建立了温室气体排放交易系统。温室气体排放交易系统有力地增强了欧盟应对温室气体减排的能力。

“环保经济手段的运用需要法律为其提供制度环境。没有法律为其提供依据和秩序，环保经济手段难以得到广泛、长期和稳定的实行。这是因为环保经济手段的运用，需要法律的‘第一推动’，即做出初始的制度安排。”[③]《环保法》中没有关于环保经济手段的规定。这个缺陷对于不利于我国推行环保经济手段，应当在这次修改中予以弥补。《建议稿》根据改革开放以来我国运用环保经济手段的实践经验，在第四章中对排污交易（第 50 条）、“绿色信贷”（第 52 条）、“绿色证券”（第 53、54 条）、“绿色采购”（第 40 条）、“生态补偿”（第 57 条）和“绿色保险”（第 58 条）做了初步规定，从而为环境经济手段的应用做出了初始的制度安排（由于篇幅所限，这里不列举这些条文）。

五、结论

法律对于环保事业主体良性互动关系的保障程度，是衡量一个国家的环保事业和环境法制发展水平的重要指标。[④]现行《环保法》的功能已经落

---

① 张鹏，调动“无形的手”：为环境保护经济手段的运用提供法律基础，《绿叶》，2011 年第 1 期，第 45 页。
② 详见王曦著，《美国环境法概论》，武汉大学出版社，1992 年 9 月第 1 版，第 269-274 页。
③ 张鹏，调动“无形的手”：为环境保护经济手段的运用提供法律基础，《绿叶》，2011 年第 1 期，第 46 页。
④ 王曦，环保主体互动法制保障论，《上海交通大学学报（哲学社会科学版）》，2012 年第 1 期，第 5 页。

后于现实。党的十八大将加快建设生态文明作为“五位一体”的社会主义事业总体布局的有机组成部分，标志着我国环保事业和环境法制进入了加速发展阶段。在这个新的形势下，《环保法》的功能亟待改造和提升。这个改造和提升应当以补充和完善本文论述的四项特殊功能为方向。这四项功能都服务于我国环境法“为环保主体良性有效互动提供法律保障”这一总任务。经过这样的改造和提升，《环保法》将成为一部以为环保事业奠定基础和规范和制约有关环境的政府行为为主要功能的“环保事业基础法”。它将同其他的以管制污染者为主的环境资源保护类法律并行不悖，各司其职，共同保障我国环保事业的顺利发展。

论新时期完善我国环境法制的战略突破口[①]

王　曦[②]

改革开放30多年以来，我国建立了一个覆盖面相当广泛的资源环境法律体系。在资源环境领域里，立法空白点已经比较少。资源环境立法工作已经从以制定新法，填补立法空白为主，转向以修订现行法，提高现行法的质量和实施效果为主。在这种形势下，完善环境法制，关键要抓什么？战略突破口在哪里？这是当前国家立法机关、行政机关和环境管理工作者和环境法学研究者都十分关心的问题。本文试图回答这些问题。

一、方法论——从实际出发，实事求是

对上述重大问题的回答，首先要解决方法论问题。只有掌握和运用正确的方法论，才能从资源环境领域当前纷繁复杂的现实中，认清主要矛盾，发现和抓住对环境管理全局的改观具有决定意义的关键问题。

社会科学是研究人类社会及其发展规律的科学。法学是一门社会科学。法学研究必须联系实际，从实际出发，研究人类社会生活中的法律现象及其规律。环境法学是社会科学中法学的一个组成部分，是有关环境和资源的行为规范的理论体系。环境法制是运用法的理论和环境法律调整人们行为的政治过程。研究环境法制的完善应当针对环境法律在实施过程遇到的关键问题。解决了这种关键问题，其他问题往往可以迎刃而解。毛泽东同志在1941年《改造我们的学习》一文中对社会科学的方法论有一段很好的

① 本文原刊于《上海交通大学学报（哲学社会科学版）》，2009年第2期，第5-11页。
② 王曦（1952—），男，上海交通大学凯原法学院教授、博士生导师、环境资源法研究所所长。

阐释，他说："我们要从国内外、省内外、县内外、区内外的实际情况出发，从其中引出其固有的而不是臆造的规律性，即找出周围事变的内部联系，作为我们行动的向导。而要这样做，就须不凭主观想象，不凭一时的热情，不凭死的书本，而凭客观存在的事实，详细地占有材料，在马克思列宁主义一般原理的指导下，从这些材料中引出正确的结论。"[1]根据这个从实际出发，实事求是的方法论，探索完善环境法制的战略突破口，应当从考察我国资源环境管理的现状入手，从中发现影响环境法制效果的具有规律性的东西，并从客观事实中引出正确的结论。

二、对现实的考察之一 ——资源环境领域的"市场失灵"十分严重

考察环境法制，最重要的是看它的实际效果如何。换言之，我们要看环境法制所服务的目标——宏观环境和生态质量的改善——是否实现或者在多大程度上得到实现。经济学的一般原理告诉我们，资源环境法律存在的理由是克服资源环境领域里的"市场失灵"（market failure）。环境法制是对资源环境领域里的"市场失灵"的政府干预。看环境法制的实际效果，就是看在资源环境领域里的政府运用环境法律干预"市场失灵"的效果。这种政府干预又叫环境管理。干预得好或者有效，资源环境领域里的"市场失灵"就轻微；反之，资源环境领域里的"市场失灵"就严重。

当前，我国的资源和环境现状和发展趋势令人忧虑。2004 年 3 月，胡锦涛同志在中央人口资源环境工作座谈会上鲜明地指出我国面临严重的资源和环境问题。他指出我国在资源环境领域里的问题主要有："资源紧缺的矛盾日益突出，一些关系国计民生的矿产资源特别是石油严重短缺。一些地方乱批滥占滥用耕地和乱采滥挖矿产资源的现象依然存在。生态环境总体恶化的趋势尚未根本扭转，环境治理的任务依然相当艰巨。大江大河防洪体系尚不完善，农村水利基础设施比较薄弱。水资源供需矛盾十分尖锐，已成为影响经济社会发展和人民生活的一个突出制约因素"。[2]2005 年《国务院关于落实科学发展观加强环境保护的决定》指出："环境形势严峻

的状况仍然没有改变”。[3]

2007年10月党的十七大报告将我国在资源环境领域里面临的种种困难和问题总结为一句话：“经济增长的资源环境代价过大”，并将这个问题列为我国面临的七个重大问题之首。[4]“经济发展的资源环境代价过大”实际上是对我国资源环境领域里的资源配置失调的另一种表述。这种资源配置失调，就是经济学上所说的“市场失灵”。

资源环境领域里的“市场失灵”，可以用经济学的两条原理来解释。其一是“外部性”（externalities）理论。另一个是“公共”品（public goods）理论。①

“外部性”理论中的“外部不经济性”理论能够很好地解释环境污染和生态破坏现象的原因。外部性指的是“对他人产生有利或不利的影响，但不需要他人对此支付报酬或进行补偿的活动”。[5]“当私人成本或收益不等于社会成本或收益时，就会产生外部性”。[5]外部性有两种。一种是外部经济性，指的是对他人提供的不需他人为其支付费用的利益，例如养蜂场的蜜蜂为邻近的苹果园中的苹果树传播花粉而带来苹果产量的增加；另一种是外部不经济性，指的是对他人造成损失但自己却不必为之承担补偿费用的情况。正是这种“外部不经济性”，在我国几乎随处可见。我国的江河湖海、空气等环境客体正在受到来自企业生产活动和居民生活活动的严重污染，而企业和居民为之支付的补偿费用大大低于消除这种环境损害所需费用。生产者的生产成本和居民的生活成本中没有充分包括由于它们排放的污染物而导致的污染治理成本。这些成本没有进入市场价格体系，而由全部社会成员分担了。市场机制即价格规律在它们面前是“失灵”的。正是由于这种外部不经济性的广泛存在，我国的环境污染和生态破坏始终没有从总体上得到有效的遏制。

“公共品”理论从另一个角度解释环境污染和生态破坏现象的原因。“公共品”是与“私人品”或“私人物品”相对的一个概念。它指这样一种物

① 公共品（public goods），又称为“公共产品”、“公共物品”。

品，“其效用不可分割地影响整个公众，而不管其中任何个人是否愿意消费”。作为社会公共利益载体的环境和生态系统就属于公共品。[5]公共品具有与私人物品相对应的四个特性，即“非排他性”、“强制性”、“无偿性”和“不可分割性”。[6]作为社会公共利益的环境和生态就属于这种公共品。由于公共品的这四个特性，特别是其中的非排他性和无偿性，它极易受到滥用。作为“经济人”，公共品的消费者天然地倾向于最大限度地消费公共品，最终导致所谓“公地的悲剧”[7]，即公共品因遭到滥用或过度消费而同消费者的公共利益一道毁灭或消失。公共品的特性带来的另一个问题是所谓“搭便车者”现象。由于公共品是供免费消费的，且不具有排他性和不可分割性，人们天然地倾向于无偿享受公共品带来的利益并避免为维护公共品的完善性而支付费用。例如，作为公共品的环境，正在被生产者和居民用做免费的“垃圾坑”而遭到日益严重的污染和破坏。从江河湖海的污染，到城市空气质量的恶化，无不属于此列。在我国，作为公共品的环境和生态遭到滥用和破坏的现象不仅比比皆是，而且还在发展之中。国家的环境和生态正在陷入“公地的悲剧”。

在外部不经济性和公共品被滥用的问题没有得到有效遏制的情况下，高速的经济发展所带来的必然是资源的不合理耗损、环境污染的蔓延、生态系统的失调、人类健康水平和生活质量的下降等一系列问题。这些问题以一言以蔽之，即“经济发展的资源环境代价过大”或资源配置失调或“市场失灵”。

三、对现实的考察之二——环境管理中的“政府失灵”十分严重

怎样才能解决外部性和公共品遭到滥用这类市场机制无力解决的问题呢？经济学一般原理告诉我们：答案在于“政府干预”（government intervention）或“管制”（regulation），即通常所说的政府管理。对于资源环境领域里的外部不经济性问题，国家通过立法和制定标准，以税收、收费等手段来将企业的外部不经济性“内部化”（internalization），即通过管

制迫使外部不经济性的制造者承担起那些被“外部化”了的成本。对于在市场机制中得不到合理调节和保护的环境公共品，国家通过立法为环境的利用者规定行为规则如污染物排放限度并以政府部门检查其遵守情况。总之，国家以政府管制这只“有形的手”来纠正和克服市场这只“无形的手”的失灵。

法律是政府干预市场失灵的基本手段。政府运用法律手段保护环境与资源，就是环境法制。然而，如上所述，我国的环境污染和生态破坏状况从总体上尚未得到遏制，当前的资源环境状况离“资源节约型、环境友好性社会”和“生态文明”的目标有很大距离。由此我们可以推论：环境法制的效果离它所服务的目标——宏观环境和生态质量的改善——还有很大的距离。这就是说，我国的环境法律的实施效果是令人不满意的，在资源环境管理中存在着比较大的“政府失灵”（governmental failure）。

近年来，媒体披露的一系列事件，证明我国资源环境管理中的确存在比较严重的“政府失灵”。这种“失灵”的第一种表现，也是比较普遍的一种表现，是中央政府中有些部门和比较多的地方政府在规划经济发展，招商引资，审批建设项目的过程中，只看规划或项目的经济效益和对 GDP 的拉动效应，却忽视规划或项目可能带来的环境污染或生态破坏。这是一种由政府或者政府官员的“积极”行为导致的“政府失灵”。例如，国家环境保护总局（现环境保护部）于 2005 年 1 月 18 日责令停止金沙江溪洛渡水电站等 13 个省市的 30 个违法开工项目。这些停建的项目都是在环评报告书未获批准的情况下就开工建设的项目，其中有些工程已基本完成。这些项目的开工建设都违反了《中华人民共和国环境影响评价法》规定的建设项目环境影响评价程序。这 30 个项目的批准部门涉及水利部、多家大型国企和多个地方政府。国家环境保护总局依法责令立即停止这些项目的建设，并予处罚，对直接责任人员，建议有关部门依法给予行政处分。这个事件被称之为环保总局掀起的“环保风暴”。[①] 2007 年 1 月 10 日，国家环保总

① 详见新浪网，“国家环保总局通报 30 个违法开工项目(附名单)”，http://news.sina.com.cn/c/2005-01-18/21505590777.shtml，2008 年 12 月 28 日访问。

局再掀“环保风暴”，首次动用“区域限批”手段，通报了 82 个严重违反环评和“三同时”制度的项目。这些项目涉及大唐国际、华能、华电、国电四大电力集团和钢铁、电力、冶金等领域，投资达 1 123 亿元。同时，国家环保总局还通报了河北省唐山市、山西省吕梁市、贵州省六盘水市、山东省莱芜市 4 个行政区域，其境内的除循环经济类项目外的所有建设项目均被停止审批，直到违规项目被彻底整改为止。这 82 个项目是国家环保总局在建设项目环保“三同时”核查和新开工建设项目环评审批专项清查工作中发现的。其中 23 个严重违反“三同时”环保验收制度，59 个严重违反环评制度。①同第一次“环保风暴”中的情况一样，这次“环保风暴”仍然直指政府的违法审批行为。这种“政府失灵”往往是政府官员在“唯 GDP”发展观驱使下的积极作为。它的结果往往是在经济增长的同时造成严重的污染或生态破坏。政府这只“有形的手”在这里发挥了相反作用，不仅没有减少“市场失灵”，反而加重了“市场失灵”。

资源环境领域里“政府失灵”的第二种表现是“懈怠”。政府的懈怠，一般表现为政府或政府官员在履行政府职能上的消极和不作为。这种管理上的“懈怠”的一个典型例子是 2007 年的太湖蓝藻暴发事件。2007 年 5 月由于连续高温高热，太湖蓝藻在短期内积聚暴发，使无锡等太湖沿岸城市的饮用水水源受到严重污染。据无锡市政府公布的数据，除锡东水厂之外，其余占全市供水 70%的水厂水质都被污染，影响到 200 万人口的生活饮用水。[8]无锡市居民一度无法饮用自来水厂的水，饮用水全靠购买瓶装水维持。太湖蓝藻暴发的主要原因是太湖水体的富营养化。太湖是我国第三大淡水湖，面积 2 400 平方公里。面积如此大的水体发生如此严重的污染，不是一日之功，而是多年积累的结果。据报道，“国家早在 1991 年就启动了第一期太湖治理工程，十数年间投资逾百亿元。其间，国务院有关部委会同苏浙沪两省一市发动声势浩大的水污染治理运动，其中规模最大的就是 1998 年底的‘聚焦太湖零点达标行动’，并在 1999 年元旦钟声敲响之前宣布‘基

① 详见新浪网，“环保总局将四大电力集团等列入黑名单”，http://news.sina.com.cn/c/2007-01-10/155712001209.shtml，2008 年 12 月 28 日访问。

本实现阶段性的治理目标’。所谓的‘零点达标’，就是在1998年底，太湖地区1 035家重点污染企业必须全部实现达标排放。这1 035家企业中，江苏省占770家，浙江省占257家，上海市占18家。”[8]2007年太湖蓝藻暴发，表明此前的治理基本上是失败的。这个事件揭示政府积极履行环境管理职能的重要性。企业和居民的污水，总是要排的。关键在于怎么排。如果太湖沿岸政府从1991年就切实履行职能，为企业和居民的污水提供了接受和处理污水的管网和处理设施，污水就不会大量直排入湖，太湖就不会暴发蓝藻。显然，太湖流域各地政府多年来没有切实将人口集聚、经济发展同太湖的保护结合起来，管理不力，污染治理设施建设滞后，发展了经济，牺牲了太湖。甚至在太湖蓝藻暴发事件期间，仍然有官员疏于排污监管。据报道，“无锡市辖下的宜兴市 5 位政府官员因在对相关企业违法排污上‘工作不到位’或‘监管失责’，分别受到行政记过、行政记大过、行政撤职等处分。”[9]太湖蓝藻暴发，充分凸显政府勤政的重要性。政府存在的理由之一就是克服和纠正太湖污染这样的“市场失灵”。如果政府疏于环境保护公共设施的建设和管理，执法不严，懈怠政府环保职能的履行，其结果必然是太湖这样的“公共品”的毁灭。

以上两种形式的“政府失灵”，一种是“积极”的政府行为即为了追求经济发展而做出的规划和审批，另一种是政府的消极或不作为即在建设和管理污染处理设施上和执法上的懈怠，都导致一个相同的后果，就是资源环境状况的恶化。这两种形式的“政府失灵”不除，以企业和居民对环境排放污染物为表现的“市场失灵”是不会消除的。因此，当前完善我国环境法制的战略重点应当放在“政府失灵”问题上。我们必须寻找导致我国资源环境管理中“政府失灵”的原因。

四、“政府失灵”的原因——利益驱动和制度缺陷

从环境污染和生态破坏的种种悲剧中，我们很容易发现资源环境领域里“政府失灵”的一个重要原因是政府官员的个人利益或政府的部门利益

驱动在作祟。作为理性的人，政府官员在“唯 GDP 增长率”是瞻的政绩考核制度环境中，要么选择以牺牲环境和生态换取 GDP 快速增长，因为只有这样他才会得到比别人更多的职务升迁的机会；要么选择对于环境保护职能的懈怠，因为积极地履行环境保护职能对他个人而言不会带来好处，反而可能使他的 GDP 政绩落在别人的后面。

在发现个人和部门利益驱动这个原因后，我们不仅要问：这种利益驱动为什么可以大行其道？原因在于制度缺陷，即我国的资源环境法律没有为预防和遏制这种利益驱动规定监督和制约的制度。监督和制约是一种必不可少的促使政府官员保持勤政和清廉的外部力量。如果没有来自外部监督和制约，政府官员往往选择懈怠。在有的情况下，甚至选择寻租和腐败。在缺乏监督和制约制度的情况下，上述“积极”的和“消极”的“政府失灵”只会愈演愈烈。

如果我们对规定我国环境与资源保护基本制度的《中华人民共和国环境保护法》（以下简称为《环保法》）和其他资源环境法律做一个仔细的考察，就能够看到其中缺乏对于政府影响资源环境的行政行为的监督和制约的制度安排。这是我国资源环境法律乃至其他法律中普遍存在的一个重大缺陷。从法律条文看，我国的资源环境类法律都是以管制企业为主的法律。法律对企业影响环境与生态的行为如排污和资源开发行为，规定了比较系统的管制措施如建设项目环境影响评价、“三同时”、排污申报登记和法律责任等。但对于政府的有关资源环境的决策和执行行为，法律的规定却十分薄弱。在《中华人民共和国环境保护法》中，除了第 6 条（一切单位和个人都有保护环境的义务，并有权对污染和破坏环境的单位和个人进行检举和控告）、第 16 条（地方各级人民政府，应当对本辖区的环境质量负责，采取措施改善环境质量）和第 45 条（环境保护监督管理人员滥用职权、玩忽职守、徇私舞弊的，由其所在单位或者上级主管机关给予行政处分；构成犯罪的，依法追究刑事责任）涉及对政府行政行为的监督和制约以外，没有其他的针对政府的影响资源与环境的行政行为的条款。另外，这些条款本身都很笼统，法律中没有具体的制度设计来保障它们的实现。由于没有制度的监督和制约，“唯 GDP”的发展观可以大行其道，上述“积极的”和“消极的”政府失灵愈演愈烈。这是我国资源环境法律的内涵上的一个重大缺陷。

由此我们可以得出这样的结论：我国资源环境领域里的“政府失灵”是“现象”或“标”，而制度缺陷才是“原因”或“本”。从资源环境领域的市场失灵，我们看到了政府环境管理的“失灵”。从政府环境管理的失灵，我们看到了现行资源环境法律虽然在外延上已经有了比较广泛的覆盖面，但在内涵上却存在比较大的缺陷。

新中国成立以来的历史和当前的现实都告诉我们，政府的决策失误和管理缺位或失效往往比企业行为对资源环境的破坏更大、有害影响更深远。早在 20 世纪 50 年代，“大跃进”、“大办钢铁”等宏观决策的失误，对国家的自然资源和环境带来的巨大破坏性影响至今犹存。因此，现在到了从制度安排上解决资源环境领域里的“政府失灵”问题的时候了。抓住并解决了这个关键问题，将使我国政府在资源环境领域里的干预和管制大为增强，从而一方面大大减少由于政府的决策失误直接导致的环境和生态问题，另一方面大大减少由于政府管理不力而由企业和其他管理相对人的生产、生活活动导致的环境和生态问题。换言之，在制度建设这个问题上取得突破，将收到重要的“一石二鸟”之效果，既有助于克服“政府失灵”，又有助于克服“市场失灵”。

五、对策——以立法建立对政府环境行政行为的监督和制约

在找出了关键问题——制度缺陷之后，我们应当做的是通过立法来弥补这个缺陷。我们应当把弥补我国资源环境法律中缺乏约束环境行政行为[①]的制度这一重大缺陷立即提上立法议事日程。

① 在本文中，笔者在宽泛的意义上使用“环境行政行为”一词。本文中的“环境行政行为”，泛指政府行政部门做出的所有影响资源环境状况的行政决策和行政执行行为，包括对产业发展规划、区域发展规划等各种政府规划的审批、建设项目审批、环境行政执法行为等。

制度缺陷，只有通过立法才能得到最为有效和稳固的弥补。这是法律的特性所决定的。首先，法律是为规定制度而产生的。立法的主要任务是针对现实中需要由法律对付的问题作出制度安排，用严谨的制度解决现实中的问题。其次，法律是具有最高权威的行为规范。法律是国家权力机关制定的，以国家强制力做保障的行为规范。这种最高的权威使法律规定的制度比行政机关制定的制度或者其他来源的制度有更高的法律约束力。再次，法律是刚性的行为规范，具有稳定性和严肃性。法律的修订要经过法定的程序，要得到立法机关法定多数票的同意。法律的变更不是随意的。这一特性，决定了法律上规定的制度比较稳固、持久。这种稳固性和持久性带来对违法后果的明确预期，有利于保障法律制度得到遵守。最后，就弥补现行资源环境法律中缺乏约束环境行政行为的制度这一缺陷而言，以立法来弥补是最为恰当的。因为只有立法机关是既有权对行政机关进行授权，又有权对其进行监督的国家机关。对行政行为进行监督和制约的制度，应当首先由立法机关在法律上作出规定。

根据国外环境法中行之有效的经验，如美国等工业化国家的环境法经验，以及我国现阶段的国情，我国的资源环境法律需要建立两类监督和制约制度。一类是政府内的监督和制约制度（这里的“政府”，指的是行政机关，即国务院和地方人民政府）。这类制度包括行政机关在行政决策过程中的部门之间的制约制度。例如环保部门对于其他部门的环境行政行为的制约程序，以及上级政府对于下级政府的环境行政行为的制约程序，例如中央政府对地方政府在环境事务上的监督和制约制度。另一类是行政部门以外的力量对行政行为的监督和制约制度，例如来自人民代表大会、法院、政协、民主党派、群众团体和公民的对政府环境行政行为的监督和制约制度。只有建立了这两类监督和制约制度，我国政府的行政部门才能保持勤勉和清廉，从而对资源环境领域里的“市场失灵”给予有效的矫正和克服。如果缺乏这些制度，在资源环境领域里的“政府失灵”将会继续下去。

以上论证的逻辑，可以用下图表示。

现实："市场失灵"——发展的资源环境代价过高

↓

对策：加强环境管理

↓

问题：环境管理中的"政府失灵"

↓

对策：寻找环境管理"政府失灵"的原因

↓

发现：制度缺陷——法律上缺乏对环境行政行为的监督和制约制度

↓

战略突破口：通过立法建立对环境行政行为的监督和制约制度

六、结语

在新时期，我国环境法制建设的战略目标是使我国的环境管理达到这样一种状态，即以一个各部门和各级都按照科学发展观办事并处于有效的内外监督和制约之下的，勤政、尽职的政府，来管制企业和其他社会实体的影响资源环境的生产和消费行为，纠正资源环境领域里的"市场失灵"。在建立对政府环境行政行为的监督和制约制度这个关键问题上取得突破，将极大地从内涵上增强我国的资源环境法律，使其更好地保障政府环境保护公共职能的实现和克服资源环境领域里的"市场失灵"。

参考文献

[1] 毛泽东. 毛泽东选集（第 3 卷）[M]. 北京：人民出版社，1991.

[2] 胡锦涛. 在中央人口资源环境工作座谈会上的讲话[EB/OL]. http://news. xinhuanet.

com/ newscenter/2004-04/04/content_1400069_1.htm, 2004-04-04.

[3] 中华人民共和国国务院. 国务院关于落实科学发展观加强环境保护的决定（国发[2005]39 号）[EB/OL]. http://www.gov.cn/zwgk/2005-12/13/content_125680.htm，2005- 12-13.

[4] 胡锦涛. 高举中国特色社会主义伟大旗帜 为夺取全面建设小康社会新胜利而奋斗——在中国共产党第十七次全国代表大会上的报告[EB/OL]. http://news. xinhuanet. com/ newscenter/2007-10/24/content_6938568.htm，2007-10-24.

[5] 保罗 •A •萨缪尔森. 萨缪尔森辞典[M]. 陈迅、白远良译. 北京：京华出版社，2001：19-177.

[6] 曾艳玲. 英汉西方经济学辞典[M]. 北京：机械工业出版社，2003：656-657.

[7] Garrett Hardin. The Tragedy of Commons[J]. Science, 1968(162):1243-1248.

[8] 李艳. 蓝藻寓言：太湖治污 16 年功败垂成[N/OL]. http://www.thebeijingnews. com/ news/deep/2007/06-08/018@012453.htm，2007-06-08.

[9] 李克诚. 江苏宜兴 5 名官员因太湖排污监管失职被处分[N/OL]. http://news.sina. com.cn/c/2007-06-11/050211995984s.shtml，2007-06-11.

从环境基本法的立法特征论我国《环境保护法》的修改定位[①]

汪 劲[②]

一、引 言

第十届全国人大环境与资源保护委员会一经成立，就于2003年3月25日召集在京的部分环境法专家就本届人大环境与资源保护立法工作召开了专家座谈会。会上，部分专家、学者针对近20年来我国环境与资源保护法律体系不断完善的现状，就将我国《环境保护法》修改成为国家环境保护基本法提出了许多积极的建议。

实际上，无论是国家立法、司法还是行政机关，对《环境保护法》的修改都是非常关注的。据笔者调查了解，立法机关主要关注《环境保护法》在我国环境与资源保护法律体系中所处的地位及其应有的功能。[③]司法机关则关注《环境保护法》与其他单项环境与资源保护法律在法律效力以及法律适用上的相互关系。[④]

---

① 本文原刊于《中外法学》，2004年第4期（总第94期）。

② 汪劲，法学博士，时任北京大学法学院副教授。

③ 20世纪90年代中叶，受第八届全国人大环境与资源保护委员会的委托，原国务院法制局曾邀请国务院部分环境与资源保护部门官员以及环境法专家，就《环境保护法》在中国环境与资源保护法律体系中的地位、作用以及该法是否需要修改等问题进行了专门的研讨。组织召开这次研讨会的背景在于：随着国家单项环境与资源保护立法的不断完善，《环境保护法》在环境与资源保护法律体系中作为基本法的地位和作用已显露出严重的问题：其一是该法的立法理念、原则和基本制度已远远滞后于中国实行社会主义市场经济后制定或修改的新的单项环境与资源保护法律；其二是该法作为实施法，其原有可操作性的条款也落后于新制定的单项环境与资源保护法律。

④ 在审理环境污染案件的法律适用上，当单项环境污染防治法律的适用与《环境保护法》相矛盾时应当如何适用法律成为审判实践上经常出现的问题。例如，排污收费制度在1989年《环境保护法》中作为基本制度的一般规定是实行超标收费方式（该法只规定向水体排放污染除外）。而2000年修改制定的《大气污染防治法》则规定实行“排污收费、超标处罚”方式。另外，有关环境损害赔偿的免责条款规定在《环境保护法》与单项环境污染防治法律的规定也不一致。

鉴于环境与资源保护管理涉及诸多行政机关的参与，特别是涉及国家和地方经济的发展，各级政府与相关行政主管部门则基于它们的管理权限以及不同的利益需求关系，其关注点则更为广泛。在中国目前“行政主导立法”的现实状况下，各级政府与相关行政主管部门对《环境保护法》地位和作用的认识也直接影响和决定着对该法的修改。

例如，环保部门所关注的是如何通过修法来加强环境行政权，而从1989年修改的《环境保护法》到2002年新制定的《环境影响评价法》以及相关立法的实践看，环保部门认为国家每制定或者修改制定一部新的环境与资源保护法律，就会出现一次环境行政的倒退现象。因此，“宁可维持《环境保护法》立法的现状、也不希望修法造成的倒退”是环保部门对修法的心态。[①]而资源管理部门则关注如何通过修法来合理分配资源保护管理的权力，他们认为现行《环境保护法》是由环境保护部门主导制定的，因此如果依然由环保部门主导修法，就可能出现环境行政权会进一步扩张到自然资源管理领域的现象。另外，经济主管部门则关注环境行政权力的不断增强是否可能对国民经济的迅速发展造成不利影响，它们认为作为发展中国家，中国在现阶段不宜提倡“环境优先”，它们担心过度提倡环境保护会导致国家或地方经济增长速率的减低。[②]

我认为，修改制定新的《环境保护法》是国家实现可持续发展战略的需要，而明确《环境保护法》的修改目标以及对该法在我国环境与资源保护法律体系中的合理定位，是《环境保护法》修改成功的关键。

有鉴于此，本文首先拟对世界各主要国家和地区有关环境基本法的立法进行比较，以总结环境基本法立法的基本特征。在此基础上，就将我国《环境保护法》修改成为国家环境保护基本法提出自己的建议。

---

①据笔者2003年4月参加由国家环境保护总局主持召开的修改《环境保护法》座谈会所见，这种看法是来自部分省市环保部门的执法官员对近10年来国家环境与资源保护立法的普遍反映。

②据笔者从参加1995年修改《大气污染防治法》到2000年起草《清洁生产促进法》和《环境影响评价法》的立法实践看，国家经济行政主管部门和资源行政主管部门对加强环境与资源保护持认同感，对有关法律草案的反对意见主要集中体现在对环保部门行政权力不断扩张之上。

二、各国（地区）环境基本法的立法比较

（一）环境基本法的立法沿革

所谓环境基本法，是指在一国环境与资源保护法律体系内，由国家立法机关制定的与单项环境与资源保护法律相对应、处于最高位阶的法律。[①]

在西方国家某一部门法律体系内出现以基本法为首、以单项法律为补充的立法现象，是“二战”结束以后各国在经济发展过程中，针对社会问题的广泛化、多样化和复杂化，对它们的解决或处理需要多方位、多层次、采取综合对策调整而出现的新的立法形式。

20 世纪 50 年代以后，世界各主要国家大多确立了发展或振兴本国经济的政策目标，伴随经济开发政策的施行和工业化、都市化的进程，各国的环境污染现象也不断加剧。举世闻名的“八大公害事件”就在这个时期相继发生于欧、美、日等工业化国家。在依靠传统法律手段不能全面解决日益增多的环境侵害及其污染所造成人身、财产权益侵害的得不偿失的教训面前，各国纷纷开始大量制定环境与资源保护法律，试图通过事前的控制和预防措施消除环境污染和自然破坏。据笔者对西方主要国家在 20 世纪 50 至 70 年代的环境立法统计，各国分别在大气、水、噪声、废弃物、野生动植物、森林、土地、河流、海洋、草原、自然保护区与优美景观保护等环境与资源领域制定实施了大量的单项法律。以日本为例，在 1970 年第 64 届国会上一举制定和修改制定了 14 部公害和环境保护法律，以至于这届国会在日本被称为“公害国会”。

此外，为调整环境与资源保护法律与其他传统部门法律的关系，各国

①需要说明的是，这里所谓的环境基本法非指我国法理学分类上的“基本法”。因为我国法理学对基本法的解释源于我国《宪法》和《立法法》对国家立法机关按照不同程序制定效力不同法律的规定，即由全国人大制定和修改的法律属于“基本法”，而由全国人大常委会制定和修改的除基本法律以外的其他法律属于“一般法”。关于我国环境基本法与国家基本法的关系问题，笔者将在后面论述。

还制定施行了许多有别于传统法原则的特别法。例如，在行政立法方面，制定实施了环境税（费）负担法、环境影响评价法、环境纠纷行政处理法、环境规划法等；在民事或刑事立法方面，通过修改法典或者制定单项特别法确立了新的环境损害责任制度以及制裁危害环境犯罪制度。

然而，环境问题的产生是与人类社会进步和经济发展相互交织的，随着环境问题的日益深化，有关环境的科学延伸到政策、法律、经济、行政、管理、工程、医学、技术等各个领域，其结果造成对环境问题发展趋势的认识上出现不同的，甚至是针锋相对的主张。

对环境的法律控制也是如此。例如，针对环境污染因子和自然资源要素而制定单项法律的方法，不仅会因社会对法律执行效果的追求而造成立法、行政和司法机关的工作压力，而且因各单项法律制度在对策措施上的单一性也会因法律的实施而制造更多的社会成本。由于单一的环境保护对策与国家总体经济政策、发展计划、工业技术水平等现状的相对脱节，导致对环境的法律控制最终演变成为环境保护与经济发展相对抗的矛盾。这样，在经济发展功利的确定性与环境控制效果的不确定性面前，政府在决策时往往会出于企业对国家或地方经济贡献而考虑选择前者。

另外，由于环境保护行政、自然资源行政以及经济发展行政分属于政府各部门，鉴于它们之间的职能与行政目标的差异，也会造成大量单项环境与资源保护法律在实施上因部门利益冲突而大打折扣，难以从总体上达成国家的环境政策和目标。

西方国家在大量单项环境与资源保护立法并未全面奏效的现实面前总结出一个经验，就是在对涉及多方面法律调整的环境问题制定一系列预防性、控制性、管理性以及救济性的法律措施时，必须先在环境与发展的关系方面统一观念和采取综合性对策，将环境预防的各项原则渗透到各类计划性、综合性行政之中，从宏观调控的角度予以解决。

为此，各国（地区）纷纷在制定和实施大量单项环境与资源保护法律的基础上，新制定了高位阶的统筹各类环境与资源保护政策目标的环境基本法。

例如：联邦德国于1959年和1974年分别制定了《自然保护法》和《污染控制法》；前苏联于1960年制定了《自然保护法》；前苏联瓦解后，新成立的俄罗斯联邦又于1991年制定了《自然环境保护法》；瑞典于1964年和1969年分别制定了《自然保护法》和《环境保护法》；美国于1969年制定了《国家环境政策法》；日本于1967年和1972年分别制定了《公害对策基本法》和《自然环境保全法》，1993年又将二法修改制定成为《环境基本法》；荷兰于1979年制定了《综合环境法》，1993年将其修改成为《环境管理法》。另外，加拿大也于1997年制定了《环境保护法》。我国台湾地区在基本完善环境与资源保护法律体系之后，也于2002年制定了“环境基本法”。

我国自1972年6月参加出席了联合国人类环境会议之后，便开始着手解决中国的环境问题。1978年我国在新修改颁布的《宪法》第11条专门对环境保护作了规定：“国家保护环境和自然资源，防治污染和其他公害。”在中共中央的支持下，国务院有关部门于1978年底依据《宪法》的规定起草了《环境保护法（试行草案）》。制定该法的目的，一是把国家保护环境的基本方针和基本政策以法律的形式确定下来，二是为未来我国环境与资源保护法律体系的建立确立蓝图。立法的初步设想是“只规定国家在环境保护方面的基本方针和基本政策，而将一些具体的规定在将来制定大气保护法，水质保护法等具体法规和实施细则时解决。”① 1979年9月13日，全国人大常委会原则通过了《环境保护法（试行）》。②

与外国（地区）环境基本法立法在时机上滞后于单项环境与资源保护法律所不同的是，我国《环境保护法（试行）》的起草是在1979年国家基本法体系刚刚建立，其他任何单项环境与资源保护法律尚处于空白状态下

①李超伯：“关于《中华人民共和国环境保护法（试行草案）》的说明”，1979年9月11日。

②所谓“原则通过”，一般是指人大常委会委员虽然不对整个法律的具体条文全部表示同意，但对法律的基本精神表示同意，因此对该法律草案仍然予以通过的一种通过方式。所谓“试行法”，一般是指人大常委会虽然对法律草案感到不够充分或立法条件不够成熟，而实际生活却又需要该法律加以调整，因此而予以通过的法律。这种公布法律的方式，是在20世纪80年代以前中国人大常委会进行立法以及国务院制定行政法规时的习惯做法。与之相应的还有“暂行”的概念。参见袁建国著：《法律创制论》，河南人民出版社1989年版，177-179页。

完成的。[①]所以尽管制定环境保护法的设想是将其作为基本法、只规定国家环境基本方针和政策，但该法的制定依然必须面对我国日益严重的环境污染和自然破坏的现实，必须确立广泛的污染控制对策和自然保护措施。为此，在环境污染防治方面，鉴于我国的环境污染和其他公害主要是工业企业排放污染物和城市公用设施不足，特别是以直接燃煤的燃料结构所决定和造成的，该法重点对环境污染防治的行政法律制度作了一系列规定；在自然保护方面，鉴于中国的自然生态破坏情况也非常严重，并且认识到它的影响和危害比环境污染问题更加深远，该法还规定了自然环境保护的基本政策。并考虑将依此制定具体的法规，使自然环境保护逐步加强和完善。此外，为了促使该法的全面施行，该法还对环境保护机构和职责、科学研究和宣传教育、奖励和惩罚等也作出了规定。

20 世纪 80 年代初、中叶，我国对《环境保护法（试行）》进行了修改。当时修法是基于三个因素考虑的：一是中国的经济体制正在从计划经济向有计划的商品经济过渡，并且国家环境与资源保护法律体系还不完善；二是由于我国《宪法》在 1982 年作出了修改，因而立法依据发生了改变；三是由于《环境保护法（试行）》作为试行法本身存在的规范性和约束性不强、有些规定不够妥当、一些单项环境与资源保护法律和行政法规的规定已经超前、法律规定的体例也与后来的国家立法不一致等问题，使其作用逐渐下降。

值得一提的是，这次修法历时约七年，其间还经历了 1982 年和 1988 年国务院两次机构改革和国家环境保护行政主管部门的三次升迁。[②]随着国家环保行政主管部门权力的不断扩充，其他相关行政主管部门逐渐感到了环境保护的压力，特别是环境保护的崭新理念与旧的经济发展模式的矛盾。

在该法修改的过程中，围绕环保部门的职权范围、法律的调整范围、环境管理体制以及是否实行较为科学和严厉的法律制度诸问题，主要在环

---

①需要说明的是，虽然这个时期中国尚未制定单项环境与资源保护法律，但国务院及其主管部门仍制定实施有大量自然资源管理的行政法规和部门规章。

② 1982 年国务院进行机构改革，将国务院环境保护领导小组撤销，将领导小组办公室并入城乡建设环境保护部作为部内设的司局级机构，名为环境保护局；1984 年底，国务院将环境保护局升格为部委归口管理的国家局，并成为同年 5 月新成立的国务院环境保护委员会的办公机构；1988 年，国务院又进行机构改革，将国家环保局从原城乡建设环境保护部中独立出来，成为国务院直属局。

保部门与资源管理部门之间、环保部门与经济行政部门之间、环保部门与其他行政管理部门之间、环保部门与企业之间展开了激烈的争论。另外，一些地方政府也对加强环境保护可能导致经济利益受损而表示担忧。其结果是环境保护的基本国策向“以经济建设为中心”的发展政策作出退让，一些在国外环境法律实践中被认为是行之有效的法律制度如排污许可制度则以“不符合中国国情”为由而未予采纳。[①]

尽管如此，与《环境保护法（试行）》相比，修改以后的《环境保护法》不论在法律结构上，还是在法律条文、规范的具体内容上，都作了较大的修改。但是实质性的进展却未能从修改中看出。它也留下了一个现在不得不面对的问题：作为环境保护的基本法，我国《环境保护法》与单项环境与资源保护法律之间到底应当是一种怎样的关系呢？

（二）各国（地区）环境基本法的立法特征

1. 环境基本法在环境与资源保护法律体系中处于高位阶的指导地位。

虽然各国（地区）环境基本法的立法在立法时机上滞后于各单项环境与资源保护法律，但是各国（地区）在制定环境基本法之后都会通过各种形式强调环境基本法在国家环境与资源保护法律体系中的指导地位。因此有“环境宪法”之称。

例如，美国《国家环境政策法》第 4 条（《美国法典》第 4332 条）规定，国会授权并命令国家应当尽一切可能实现“美国的各项政策、法律以及公法解释与执行均应当与本法的规定相一致”。

加拿大《环境保护法》则开宗明义地宣布，保护环境是加拿大人民福利的基础，本法的首要目的在于通过污染预防以有助于实现可持续发展。

瑞典《环境保护法》第 2 条规定，除本法外，对环境有害的行为还可以适用公共卫生、建设、自然保护以及其他法律。

日本虽然未在《环境基本法》中对该法与其他相关法律的关系作出规

① 2000 年修改制定的《大气污染防治法》已将排污许可制度作为防治燃煤引起大气污染的一项重要制度予以确立。

定，但是在该法颁布的同时专门制定了《关于伴随环境基本法施行整备相关法律的法律》，由这部法律专门对诸多相关法律条文中与《环境基本法》所不符的规定进行了修改。

我国台湾地区在2002年“环境基本法”立法时也借鉴了美、日环境基本法立法的经验。在该法（草案）制定的总说明中，专门就该法与其他相关法律的关系做出如下说明：“为建立完备之环境保护法规体系，俾使各级政府、全体国民及各事业协同一致，有效推动各项环境保护工作，参酌美、日等国立法例，并衡酌国情需要，拟具《环境基本法》（草案），以为各环境保护相关法律制（订）定及修正之指导原则。”为此，台湾地区“环境基本法”第1条后半段特别规定：“本法未规定者，适用其他法律之规定。”

此外，在世界各国编辑的国家环境法律出版物中，也将环境基本法作为环境法律体系中的重要法律予以编排。例如，在由日本环境省编撰的《环境六法》中，将《环境基本法》收编于第一章“环境一般”之首，而其他单项环境法律则分别收编于之后各章。①在《美国法典》的编撰中，将《国家环境政策法》收编于涉及公民基本权利的“公众健康与福利”卷，而将《水污染控制法》收编于行政管理类的“航行与可航水域法律”卷。在《法国环境法典》的编撰中，将行政管理组织等环境保护的基本事项收编于该法典的第一部分。②

由此，我们可以看出，各国（地区）均通过明确的法律规定将其他现行政策、法律的原则统一到环境基本法的原则上来。因此，尽管西方议会立法一般没有国家基本法与国家一般法的区分，但环境基本法的效力实际上是高于单项环境与资源保护法律的。

2. 环境基本法的内容是确立国家环境基本政策和原则、政府环境责任以及与其他相关法律在适用上的关系。

由于在环境基本法制定之前，各国（地区）现实上已经制定了大量单项环境与资源保护法律，所以环境基本法立法在调整对象、调整范围以及

---

①参见日本环境省编集：《环境六法》（平成九年日文版），中央法规出版株式会社2001年版。
②参见法国环境部编：《法国环境法典》“目录”，王姤华译，国际文化出版公司1996年版，1-15页。

法律规范等的内容上的合理定位，是处理和解决好环境基本法与单项环境与资源保护法律相互关系以及在实施中正确适用法律的关键。

比较分析各国（地区）的环境与资源保护立法，总体上是将环境基本法定位于政策法和基本法的层面上，而将单项环境与资源保护法律定位于一般法和特别法的层面上。我认为这不仅可以从前述环境基本法在国家环境与资源保护法律体系中的地位中看出，而且还可以从各国（地区）环境基本法的内容上找到根据。

（1）从法律条文上考察，环境基本法的篇幅一般较为简短，目的主要在于确立国家综合性环境保护方针策略、调整环境与发展的关系、明确政府的环境责任、设立专门的环境问题对策委员会以及确立有关环境纠纷在处理上的法律适用问题。

例如，制定于1969年的美国《国家环境政策法》的目的在于“宣示国家政策，促进人类与环境之间丰富、舒适的和谐；努力提倡防止或者减少对环境与自然生命物的伤害，增进人类的健康与福利；充分了解生态系统以及自然资源对国家的重要性；设立环境质量委员会。”该法总共只包括“政策与目标”、“环境质量委员会”两章计 14 条。①主要内容是确立国家环境政策；明确提出联邦政府等各种活动均应当考虑对环境的影响并进行环境评价；明确联邦政府与机构的环境保护责任及其职权划分；明确联邦政府与机构实施环境政策的程序和方法；设立环境质量委员会并明确其地位与作用；确立环境决策的公众参与机制；规定环境保护费用与政府拨款保障。

制定于1969年的瑞典《环境保护法》的目的在于确立环境保护的基本原则和制度，控制对环境的有害活动和行为。该法共设有导则、许可制度、许可证的申请和审查、许可决定、个人诉讼请求等、监督管理、法律责任以及执行协助与申诉等、环境保护费用、总体防护措施中的环境保护、环境损害保险、公共机构工作费用等十一章计 69 条。主要内容是通过设立一个独立于立法和行政机关以外的高级别“许可证委员会”对所有对环境有

①与《国家环境政策法》的规定相比，美国《清洁水法》的规定则洋洋数十万言。详见赵国青主编：《外国环境法选编》第一辑（上），中国政法大学出版社 2001 年版，11-216 页。

害活动进行管理，在此基础上由国家行政主管机关实施执法监督。此外，根据环境侵害的特点，该法还确立了公民环境诉讼的诉权制度、环境损害保险制度以及确立了环境保护工作费用的负担。值得一提的是，瑞典在自然资源保护管理方面还制定有《自然保护法》（1964 年），目的在于规范人们利用自然资源的行为和政府保护自然的责任，特别是不至于在自然资源开发利用中造成对自然环境的破坏。该法共计十一章 43 条，分别对自然保护的政府责任、国家公园、自然保护区、自然遗迹、野生生物物种保护、户外娱乐设施保护、特殊自然环境保护、损害赔偿以及罚则等作出了规定。

制定于 1993 年的日本《环境基本法》在其立法理念上比美国《国家环境政策法》又进了一步。该法的目的是“在环境保全方面规定基本理念，并且明确国家、地方公共团体、企业者以及国民的责任，规定作为环境保全基本对策的事项，从而综合且计划的推进环境保全对策，以有助于确保现在以及将来国民健康、文化的生活，为人类的福利作贡献。”该法共设有总则、关于环境保全的基本对策、环境审议会共三章（未包括附则）计 46 条。主要内容是明确规定将日本社会建设成为减少对环境负荷的可持续发展的社会；明确规定国家、地方政府、企业以及国民的环境保护责任；明确将环境保全基本对策制定、环境基本计划制定、环境标准制定、公害防止计划制定、实施各项涉及环境影响活动对环境的特别关照、防止环境保全上的妨害、环境宣传教育、环境情报公开、圆满处理环境纠纷、促进地方政府实施环境对策、国际环境合作以及财政措施等事项规定为国家以及地方政府的责任；明确了环境保护的费用负担原则；为了促使政府和部门落实国家的环境政策措施，该法还规定在环境厅设立中央环境审议会以及在总理府设立公害对策会议。

制定于 1997 年的加拿大《环境保护法》，其立法理念是在可持续发展战略提出后确立的，因此，加拿大《环境保护法》在前言中就以 15 个方面的“鉴于”来宣示了其立法意图：

“鉴于加拿大政府寻求达到可持续发展，而这依赖于生态性地有效利用自然的、社会的和经济的资源，以及政府和私人实体在做出所有的决定时，认可将环境的、经济的和社会的因素综合予以考虑的必要性；鉴于加拿大政府承诺执行污染预防，将其作为一个国家目标和达到保护环境的优先途径；鉴于加拿大政府认可，有必要实际消除那些存在持久性的和生物聚积性的有毒物质；如果污染物质和废弃物排放进入环境是不可能被防止的，有必要对其予以控制和管理；鉴于加拿大政府认可生态系统途径的重要性；鉴于加拿大政府决意继续展示其在确定环境标准、生态系统目标、环境质量指导方针和行为准则方面的国家领导能力；鉴于加拿大政府承诺执行预防原则，一旦出现严重的危险或者不可逆转的破坏，缺乏完全科学确定性不得以延迟节省成本措施为理由来预防环境退化；鉴于加拿大政府认可，加拿大境内的所有政府具有的权力使得他们能够保护环境，认可所有政府所面对的环境问题可以通过合作解决获益；鉴于加拿大政府认可，通过与各省、地区和土著人民的合作，以尽力达到所有加拿大人民的最高环境质量水平和最终实现可持续发展的重要性；鉴于加拿大政府认可，有毒物质在环境中存在的风险成为国家关心的问题；有毒物质一旦进入到环境就不可能一直包含在某一地理区划内；鉴于加拿大政府认可，在作出与保护环境和人类健康相关的决定的过程中，科学所扮演的整体角色如同传统的土著居民的知识所扮演的角色，并且认可应当在该过程中考虑这种环境的或者健康的风险和社会的、经济的和技术的问题；鉴于加拿大政府认可，与有毒物质、污染物质和废弃物质相关的使用者和生产者的责任，并且已经采用‘污染者付费’的原则；鉴于加拿大政府承诺，确保其以一定方式在联邦的和土著的土地上实施的经营和活动，与污染预防和保护环境与人类健康的原则相一致；鉴于加拿大政府将致力于通过污染预防排除对生物多样性的威胁，对使用和排放有毒物质、污染物质和废弃物进行控制和管理，以及实际消除持久性的和生物聚积性的有毒物质时产生的任何不利影响的风险；鉴于加拿大政府认识到通过确保安全和有效地使用生物技术以保护包括生物多样性在内的环境，和保护人类健康的必要性；以及鉴于加拿大政府必须能够履行环境方面的国际义务。”

制定于 2002 年的我国台湾地区“环境基本法”，是各国、各地区进入

21 世纪以后制定的首部环境基本法。该法在制定过程中曾广泛考察了世界各国环境基本法的立法，并考虑到台湾地区已经制定实施的其他单项环境与资源保护法律，因此该法的功能定位是“明示环境保护制度、政策之相关基本方针，揭示环境保护个别法制、措施之基本方向与共通性质，导引具体制度、政策与环境保护相关法令之制（订）定，以落实实施达成环境保护之总目标。”①立法的目的在于“提升环境品质，增进国民健康与福祉，维护环境资源，追求永续发展，以推动环境保护”。该法共分总则、规划及保护、防制及救济、辅导、监督及奖惩、附则等五章计 41 条。值得一提的是，该法在确立了经济开发活动中的环境优先原则，各级政府以及公民、企业的共同环保责任原则等的基础上，从规划及保护开始到防制及救济、直到相关的辅导、监督及奖惩为止，用大量篇幅对中央和地方各级政府的环境保护管理责任以及对法院审理环境案件作出了明确的规定。

如果从法典化的角度看，环境基本法的内容则相当于环境法典的总则部分，而单项环境与资源保护立法则相当于法典的分则部分。这一点，《法国环境法典》就是一个典型的例证，而编撰《法国环境法典》的目的在于将分散于法国各传统部门法典（如《农村和林业法典》、《行政法典》、《城市化法典》、《民法典》、《刑法典》和《公共卫生法典》等）中零乱的环境条款与法国环境立法统合在一起。②

（2）从法的规范上考察，环境基本法立法对政府环境责任的规定较多，义务性、鼓励性和授权性规范也运用得较多，而很少对政府各职能部门的职权职责作出直接规定。

通过上述对各主要国家（地区）环境基本法立法条文的比较，我们不难看出，在环境基本法立法所运用的规范上，各国（地区）立法均大量运用了义务性、鼓励性和授权性规范，而禁止性、强制性规范运用得较少或者根本没有运用。其中，将各级政府的环境保护责任用义务性规范来表述的占环境基本法立法的多数，而对政府各职能部门的职权和职责则通过授

①参见我国台湾地区立法院公布：“环境基本法总说明”。2002 年 11 月 19 日。
②法国环境部：p266 注②。

权性规范由政府根据现实自由裁量。

由此我们也可以看出，与单项环境与资源保护立法相比，环境基本法的立法除了统一国家环境政策目标和确立环境保护的一般原则外，主要目的还在于通过义务性和授权性规范将环境责任明确赋予各级政府，以避免因政府各部门在环境与资源保护实践中存在的权力交叉和重叠问题而影响国家环境保护政策措施的圆满施行。

之所以将环境责任赋予政府而非政府各部门，是因为现代环境行政实际上包含环境污染行政与自然保护行政两个方面，而这两方面的行政权力又受到来自有关经济行政权力的牵制。例如，在工业污染（传统的“三废”）排放问题方面，控制措施与产业现有条件、技术现有状况、未来产业发展以及对国家或者地方的财税等有着密切的联系，因此除专门的环境管理机关外，管理职责还涉及经济、规划、工业以及公共管理部门。另外，在自然保护与资源开发利用的关系问题上也是如此。

所以，只有将环境责任明确赋予各级政府，才能真正促使政府及其责任长官在本地区有关环境与发展关系的问题上综合平衡，不至于顾此失彼。

为了促使各级政府在有关经济决策中能正确处理环境与发展的关系，各国（地区）环境基本法主要从如下两方面作出了保障性的规定：

第一，通过立法直接阐明政府在决策中如何处理环境与发展的关系。例如，美国《国家环境政策法》4331 条规定对环境质量具有重大影响的各项提案或法律草案、建议报告以及其他重大联邦行为均应当向决策者提供一份详细的说明以及替代方案；日本《环境基本法》第 19 条规定国家制定与实施涉及环境影响的对策时必须在环境保全方面予以关照；加拿大《环境保护法》前言规定，“政府和私人实体在做出所有的决定时，认可将环境的、经济的和社会的因素综合予以考虑的必要性”。台湾地区“环境基本法”第 3 条规定当经济、科技及社会发展对环境有严重不良影响或有危害之虞者，应环境保护优先。

第二，通过立法设立政府环境委员会以辅佐政府的决策。例如，美国《国家环境政策法》4342 条规定总统府设立环境质量委员会；日本《环境基本法》

第19条规定在中央和各级地方政府设立环境审议会和公害对策会议；加拿大《环境保护法》第6条规定由部长建立一个国家咨询委员会，以促使国家行动能够对影响环境的问题得到实施和采取协作以及避免政府间的管理活动相重复。台湾地区“环境基本法”第3条规定，行政院设置国家永续发展委员会，负责国家永续发展相关业务之决策，并交由相关部会执行。

综上所述，环境基本法是在一国环境与资源保护法律体系中具有统领地位的综合性、政策性法律。环境基本法的功能定位在于宣示国家环境政策、明确环境与发展的关系以及确立政府的环境责任，因此环境基本法一般不对具体环境与资源保护事项作出规定。至于具体的环境保护事务以及单项环境污染因子的规制措施与自然资源的保护性规范，则应当分别由各单项环境与资源保护立法予以具体规定。

三、关于我国《环境保护法》的修改定位

（一）我国现行《环境保护法》存在的问题

从1989年至今，我国先后制定（修改制定）了20余部单项环境与资源保护法律，可以说我国的环境与资源保护法律体系已初步建立。[①]与此相比，《环境保护法》显露出如下不适应之处：

首先，《环境保护法》是基于中国实行的有计划的商品经济体制制定的。现在我国实行的是社会主义市场经济体制，不仅所有制形式发生了重大改变，国家相关基本法和一般法的立法也已初具规模，社会主义法律体系已经基本形成。在这个背景下特别是在中国加入WTO以后有关贸易与环境的

①全国人大常委会通过的环境与资源保护法律中，除《环境保护法》外，在海洋环境保护方面制定有《海洋环境保护法》；在环境污染防治立法方面制定有《水污染防治法》、《大气污染防治法》、《环境噪声污染防治法》、《固体废物污染环境防治法》，目前全国人大常委会审议中的还有《放射性污染防治法》；在自然资源立法方面制定有《土地管理法》、《水法》、《渔业法》、《草原法》、《森林法》、《矿产资源法》和《煤炭法》；在自然与生态保护方面制定有《水土保持法》、《野生动物保护法》。此外，在环境行政管理制度方面制定有《环境影响评价法》；在企业环境管理制度方面制定有《清洁生产促进法》、《节约能源法》。在灾害防治立法方面还制定有《防洪法》、《防沙治沙法》。

国际规则尚未在我国环境与资源保护立法中确立的情况下，该法的许多基本规定不符合我国新时期社会、经济发展的需要和全球环境保护形势发展的需要。

其次，作为环境保护的基本法，现行《环境保护法》是由全国人大常委会审议的形式通过的。与全国人大常委会通过的、目标各异的单项环境与资源保护法律相比，因该法不是国家基本法，依其地位和效力都难以在宏观上对各单项环境与资源保护立法予以指导，对环境与发展的关系更不具有综合性、统一性和协调性的功能。

再次，环境与发展的关系在我国现实经济发展和社会生活中还存在着对立的一面，国家经济行政立法有关环境条款的相对不足，造成政府在依法进行具体的发展规划和宏观决策时难以统合考虑环境与发展的关系。①这种状况仅靠目标各异的单项环境与资源保护立法是不足以改善的。

最后，《环境保护法》的主要条文业已被后来制定（修改制定）的单项环境与资源保护法律所重申或者修改，与单项环境与资源保护立法相比，环境污染防治立法的规定比《环境保护法》更为具体、更有针对性；而在自然（生态）环境保护立法方面，《环境保护法》的规定要么存在着大量空白，要么还不如自然资源立法的有关规定。

通过对我国《环境保护法》与单项环境与资源保护法律的条文进行对比，笔者发现《环境保护法》所有47条规定中，除立法目的规定、立法解释规定、适用范围规定、对自然保护的原则性和准用性规定、对诉讼时效的规定以及国际环境条约在我国的适用规定、法的施行日期规定等固有规定外，其他具有实质性和可操作性的条款已全部重复规定于单项环境与资源保护法律之中（见表1）。

①从对20世纪90年代以来我国发生的众多环境与自然破坏事例的调研结果看，问题的根源大多指向于事前有关规划的决策与对环境的考虑相脱节。例如，南京市规划局于2001年批准某企业在紫金山顶兴建观景台，在兴建过程中因严重影响紫金山风景而被媒体披露，从而引起社会各界的质疑和关注。南京市政府在强大的舆论压力面前只好下令拆除了该建筑。该建筑的总投资为3 000万元人民币。此外，类似事件还有武汉市政府下令拆除位于长江河道上耗资1.6亿元兴建的“外滩花园”事件；洛阳市炸毁投资2 700万元的龙门石窟宾馆等建筑。参见黄小伟：“被迫拆除”，载于《新闻周刊》2002年第3期，13页。

表 1 中国《环境保护法》与单项环境与资源保护法律的总体比较

法律		《环境保护法》与各单项环境（资源）立法规定的重复（不含各法的目的、术语解释、附则等条款的规定）																											单项立法的共同性规定	
《环境保护法》的规定及其条文出处		总则			环境监督管理						保护和改善环境							防治环境污染和其他公害								法律责任				
		将环保规划纳入国经与社发计划	鼓励奖励以及检举和控告权	环境行政监督管理职权及其体制	环境质量标准与污染物排放标准	环境污染监测以及环境质量公报	环境保护规划制度	环境影响评价与三同时制度	现场检查制度	解决跨区环境纠纷	地方政府对本辖区环境质量负责	划定自然保护区域	资源利用与保护结合	农业环境保护	海洋环境保护	城市规划与环境	城乡园林风景名胜	企业环保责任制	最新技术与综合利用	排污申报登记制度	排污收费制度	限期治理制度	禁止引进不符环保要求的技术和设备	污染事故报告处理以及强制应急措施	防止污染转嫁规定	行政违法处罚	民事损害赔偿	刑事责任规定	淘汰落后生产工艺设备	1.国家所有权；2.企业经营申报登记；3.开发许可证；4.资源补偿费、税；5.纠纷处理；6.禁、限养育；（本栏数字为制度编号）
		4	5.6.8	7	9～10	11	12	13.26	14	15	16	17.18	19	20	21	22	23	24	25	27	28	29	30	31～32	34	35～40	41～42	43～45		
环境污染防治法	水	○	○	○	○	○?	×	○	○	○	×								○	○	○	○	×	○	×	○	○	○	◎	
	大气	○	○	○	○	○?	×	○	○	×	×								○	○	○	○	×	○	×	○	○	○	◎	
	噪声	×	○	○	○	○?	○	○	○	×	×								○	○	○	○	○	×	×	○	○	○	◎	
	固废	×	○	○	×	×	○	○	○	×	×								○	○	○	○	○	○	○	○	○	○	◎	
	海洋	×	×○	○	○×	○	○	○	○	○	○	○	○		○	○	○		○	○	○	○	○	○	×	○	○	○	◎	
	相关法规			#				○											○		○					○	○	○		
	相关规章						○	○												○				○		○				
自然资源与	土地			○			○						○	○		○										○	○	○		◎
	森林			○			○					○	○													○	○	○		◎
	草原			○			○						○													○	○	○		◎
	水			○			○					○	○													○	○	○		◎
	矿产			○			○						○													○	○	○		◎

法律	《环境保护法》与各单项环境（资源）立法规定的重复（不含各法的目的、术语解释、附则等条款的规定）																											单项立法的共同性规定	
	总则			环境监督管理						保护和改善环境							防治环境污染和其他公害								法律责任				
	将环保规划纳入国经与社发计划	鼓励奖励以及检举和控告权	环境行政监督管理职权及其体制	环境质量标准与污染物排放标准	环境污染监测以及环境质量公报	环境保护规划制度	环境影响评价与三同时制度	现场检查制度	解决跨区环境纠纷	地方政府对本辖区环境质量负责	划定自然保护区域	资源利用与保护结合	农业环境保护	海洋环境保护	城市规划与环境	城乡园林风景名胜	企业环保责任制	最新技术与综合利用	排污申报登记制度	排污收费制度	限期治理制度	禁止引进不符环保要求的技术和设备	污染事故报告处理以及强制应急措施	防止污染转嫁规定	行政违法处罚	民事损害赔偿	刑事责任规定	淘汰落后生产工艺设备	1.国家所有权； 2.企业经营申报登记； 3.开发许可证； 4.资源补偿费、税； 5.纠纷处理； 6.禁、限养育； （本栏数字为制度编号）
《环境保护法》的规定及其条文出处	4	5.6.8	7	9～10	11	12	13.26	14	15	16	17.18	19	20	21	22	23	24	25	27	28	29	30	31～32	34	35～40	41～42	43～45		
生态保护法 渔业			○			○						○													○	○	○		
生态保护法 水土保持			○			○						○													○	○	○		
生态保护法 野生动物			○			○					○	○													○	○	○		◎
生态保护法 相关法规											○					○									○				
相关规章	政出多门，不拟列举																												

编制说明：

①《环境保护法》中的“总则”章主要规定了法的一般原则以及政府主管部门的职权划分等；“环境监督管理”章主要规定了环境污染防治的基本制度；“保护和改善环境”章主要对自然保护作了原则性规定；“防治污染和其他公害”主要规定了防治环境污染的行政管理措施；“法律责任”章主要规定了行政、民事和刑事责任条款。

② 法律栏（纵向）中，水、大气、噪声、固废、海洋分别代表现行各类型污染防治法以及《海洋环境保护法》。

③ 各方格内，空白表示没有任何相关规定；“○”表示有相同内容的规定；“？”表示为未作规定或者规定不明确；“◎”表示单项环境与资源保护法律的共同性规定；“＃”为行政组织规则有规定，如国务院“三定”方案等。

④ 专门的行政法规、规章不包括实施细则或条例。

因此在各单项环境与资源保护法律不断完善的今天，《环境保护法》实际上已经名存实亡，失去了其应有的地位和作用，真正成为“不符合中国国情”的立法例证。这种状况事实上也将《环境保护法》的修改推到了我国环境与资源保护立法的最前沿。

（二）关于法律效力的修改定位

根据我国《宪法》和《立法法》的规定，国家立法机关制定的法律包括由全国人大制定和修改的基本法律（也称基本法）与由全国人大常委会制定和修改的除基本法律以外的其他法律（也称一般法）两大类。尽管它们均为立法机关制定的法律，但由于宪法赋予全国人大立法权的特殊地位，使得其制定的法律在效力上高于全国人大的常设机构常委会制定的法律。

然而，尽管我国法学界对某一部门法律体系的构成在结构上有基本法与单项法之分的理论，世界各国（地区）也有这方面的立法实践，但我国国家立法机关过去却未有过在某一部门法律领域制定综合性基本法的立法实践。

我认为，无论是从借鉴西方国家（地区）的环境立法实践出发，还是从环境与资源保护在国家社会、经济发展中的重要程度出发，我国都有必要制定一部高位阶的环境保护基本法来指导和统领单项环境与资源保护法律。具体的做法就是由全国人大将《环境保护法》作为国家基本法予以修改制定。

那么，怎样的法律才具备国家基本法律的性质呢？从立法学的观点结合我国的立法实践看，全国人大的立法权所调整的对象，是整个国家、社会和公民生活中带有根本性的、全局性的、基本的关系和问题，它们属于国家、社会和公民生活中特别重要的问题。[①]我认为，将《环境保护法》修改成为我国环境保护的基本法，符合全国人大制定的基本法的性质与特征。这是因为：

第一，党中央、国务院于1983年就明确提出“环境保护是我国的一项基本国策”。

所谓国策，就是立国之策，治国之策。只有那些对国家经济建设、社会发展和人民生活具有全局性、长期性和决定性影响的那种谋划和策略，

①周旺生：《立法论》，北京大学出版社1994年版，360页。

才可以成为国策。[①]国家目前推行的环境保护策略以及在此基础上提出的"可持续发展战略"正因为其符合基本国策的条件才为国家所确立、为《宪法》所规范。由于环境保护这项基本国策也同时符合全国人大制定基本法的性质特征，[②]因此将其以国家基本法的形式予以确立也是理所当然的。

第二，中国目前已经制定了20多部单项环境与资源保护法律，环境与资源保护立法是我国各法律部门中最为活跃、立法最多的领域。

从1979年以来国家立法机关所制定的200多部法律看，环境与资源保护法律就占有20余部，其数量约占国家法律总数的十分之一。在全国人大未来的立法中，还将制定大量单项环境与资源保护法律，它们既有环境污染防治类，又有自然资源保护和管理类，还有生态保护类。由于这些立法在具体和直接的立法目标上还存在着差异，因此需要有一部高位阶的基本法以一个综合性的整体理念和基本思想将它们统合起来，以达成立法总目标的一致。

第三，在《环境保护法（试行）》立法之初我国就该法其定位于国家基本法，从《环境保护法》立法思想的沿革与发展看目前通过修改将其上升为国家基本法的时机已经成熟。

从1979年制定《环境保护法（试行）》的立法设想、到1989年修改制定《环境保护法》的指导思想，我国对《环境保护法》的定位都是将其作为国家环境保护基本法。如前所述，因这个时期我国环境与资源保护法律体系还不完善、中央政府的行政管理体制较为庞杂、国家和地方环境监督管理权限还亟待加强，所以这时不可能考虑将《环境保护法》上升成为国家基本法。

如今，我国不仅已经完善了环境与资源保护法律体系，更为重要的是我国20多年来的经济飞速发展也为加强国家环境与资源保护管理奠定了坚实的基础。因此，比较西方国家（地区）环境基本法的立法实践，我认为我国制定实质意义上的环境基本法的时机已经成熟。全国人大环境与资源保护委员会或其他专门委员会应当按照立法程序，向全国人民代表大会提

①曲格平：《中国环境问题及对策》，中国环境科学出版社1984年版，137页。
②我国《立法法》第7条第2款规定："全国人民代表大会制定和修改刑事、民事、国家机构的和其他的基本法律。"

出修法的议案或者草案，将《环境保护法》以国家基本法的形式修改通过。

（三）关于政府环境责任的修改定位

从前述西方国家（地区）环境基本法的立法实践看，高位阶的环境基本法立法在法律关系主体的定位上，主要是将环境保护的职权职责直接委任给各级政府及其主要负责人来实现的。与单项环境与资源保护立法应当强调各行政主管部门的职责相比，环境基本法更为强调政府及其主要负责人的环境责任。只有政府及其主要负责人的责任明确，环境政策及其目标的实现才能真正受到政府的重视。

与外国（地区）环境立法不同的是，我国现行《环境保护法》对行政权务关系的责任正好定位于各级政府的环保部门和其他部门之上。[①]至于各级政府及其主要负责人的责任，除了在环境与资源保护方面宏观决策权力规定以及政府有权干预和限制环保部门的职权规定外，政府环境责任的规定相对较少。个中缘由，是《环境保护法》立法在征求各级政府的意见时因地方各级政府的强烈反对而未作出规定。

从单项环境与资源保护立法的角度考察，由于法律所具体调整对象和范围不同，在各单项立法中体现的保护价值也有所不同。例如环境污染防治立法是通过控制和减少污染物的排放保护生活环境，最终达成保护公民的人身权和财产权的目的；而自然资源立法保护的对象是自然资源对人类的经济价值，由于其立法意图是保护人类对自然资源的开发利用，尽管在保护自然资源的同时也保护了环境要素，但这并不意味着因保护而改变了自然资源立法的初衷；生态保护立法所保护的是人类赖以生存的环境条件以及生态系统中自然物个体和群体之间相互存在的独立于人类以外的内在（固有）的价值，这种价值的保护虽然具有很大的社会效益，但是与现实可得的经济利益相比却相形见绌、无法展现。

在《环境保护法》未将环境责任明确赋予各级政府，而只是授权委任各政府行政主管部门的情况下，政府各部门之间关于环境与发展问题的所

①见《环境保护法》第8条。

有矛盾或冲突最终将集中向政府及其主要负责人反映。如果政府的环境责任未通过立法予以明确，终将导致政府及其主要负责人在环境与发展关系的决策面前会出现“重经济增长、轻环境保护”的现象。

从我国环境问题的历史看，新中国成立以来我国所发生重大环境破坏问题几乎都与政府重大经济活动的决策失误有着密切的联系。以中央政府为例，20 世纪 50 年代“除四害”运动所导致的蝗虫泛滥和生态失衡现象、大办钢铁运动所造成的环境污染和自然资源破坏现象，以及 80 年代鼓励严重污染环境的生产企业在乡镇开办导致环境污染在全国农村各地泛滥成灾等，可以说都是政府决策失误所为。尽管后来国家都采取断然措施予以纠正，但是由此造成的环境破坏和经济损失却是长期和深远的。①

当前我国环境问题仍在恶化的现实告诉我们，如果不将环境保护的责任明确赋予各级政府而不是政府部门、不建立追究政府主要负责人的环境责任制的话，地方各级政府及其主要政府官员还将为追求本地区短期的经济利益而忽视长远的环境利益。那么环境破坏的悲剧还将在我国继续发生。②

为了加强政府的环境保护责任，就必须通过修改《环境保护法》、以国家基本法的形式明确规定中央和地方政府的责任。除由单项环境与资源保护法律将与资源保护的具体执行事务规定赋予政府职能部门外，应当将地方环境与资源保护事务的职权和职责统一赋予各级政府，并大张旗鼓地宣传鼓动，促使社会各界监督政府行为，真正实现各级政府对环境质量负责的目的。

（四）关于法律内容的修改定位

比较各国（地区）环境基本法，它们在内容与结构方面大体具有如下

①以国务院 1989 年制定实施的《关于当前产业政策要点的决定》为例，该决定将若干严重污染的行业或产业列入国家“重点支持”的项目，导致 20 世纪 90 年代初中全国各地因发展这些产业而造成严重的环境污染和自然破坏。国务院后于 1996 年公布了《关于环境保护若干问题的决定》，要求对上述曾重点支持过的行业或产业予以限期取缔和关闭。该决定的施行又造成中国农业银行无法回收贷款本息达 50 多亿元人民币。参见全国人大环资委法案室编：“政策、规划实施后造成不良环境影响的若干事例”，载于《中华人民共和国环境影响评价法立法资料汇编》，2002 年 11 月。
②本文的撰稿正值全国人民在党和政府的领导下开展抗击“非典”的斗争期间。“非典”在中国的流行以及后来得以有效的控制，恰好说明各级政府在处理具有全局性、重大性社会问题上的协调力和强制力。这一点仅靠卫生行政主管部门单方面的努力是难以做到的。

共同之处：

在内容方面，规定国家有关环境行政的目标、原则和环境政策，以及确立环境保护的基本制度和基本方法，有关国家、地方以及国民或团体的环境保护权利义务，环境保护事务与其他社会经济发展事务的协调，环境法律与其他法律在适用上的相互关系，环境行政组织体系及其构成、有关环境污染或自然破坏行为的法律责任等的基本事项。

在对策方面，以确立计划性、综合性的行政和行政目标为基础；以环境质量标准为依据；以事前的土地利用计划和预防性措施为手段；明确造成环境问题不同主体的责任；明确各主管部门的预防责任。

在结构方面，无论是否设立篇、章、节，对《环境保护法》的修改应当按照总则（立法目的、适用范围、环境保护主体的权务关系、环境保护的法律原则等）、分则（环境计划与规划、政府的环境职权与职责、环境组织体制与决策机制、环境保护法与其他法律在适用上的相互关系、环境保护的基本制度、环境责任与纠纷处理机制等）的顺序作出安排。

值得一提的是，在环境基本法中，几乎均未对有关法律责任规范作出具体规定。笔者研究认为，由于环境保护基本法属于政策法的范畴，它主要确立的是授权性规范、而不设定具体的环境保护事项，因此在法律规范的逻辑结构上未就消极的法律后果作出具体安排。这些则应当留待于单项环境与资源保护立法解决。

为此，按照我国全国人大基本法的立法模式、结合环境基本法的特点及其在环境与资源保护法律体系中的地位，我认为总体上可以考虑将《环境保护法》的修改草案分为七章。各章分述如下：

第一章为总则。主要内容应当包括：立法目的；适用范围；确立国家环境保护的基本方针、政策；明确国家对环境与发展相互关系的态度；确立国际环境保护理念和全球环境问题的应对措施；确立环境保护的法律原则，诸如预防原则、受益者负担费用原则、资源再生与循环利用原则、公民参与环境决策原则、高水平保护环境原则、国家环境责任原则等；明确国家、政府、企事业单位、个人有关环境保护的共同责任；确立国家鼓励环境宣传教育与技术进步。

第二章为政府环境保护管理的组织体制与决策机制。应当针对政府的责任确立如下内容：确立政府从宏观决策、编制计划、规划到项目实施相关的环境保护决策机制，将各类发展计划、规划与环境保护计划协调一致；以环境保护计划统合现行环境污染行政计划和自然保护行政计划；建立环境信息交流网络和信息公开制度；设立相关环境委员会（可为非常设机构，委员由专家、学者和官员以及各方代表等组成）以处理环境质量鉴定、重大经济活动的环境决策以及纠纷调查处理等事项；明确中央政府与地方政府的环境保护责任。

第三章为预防环境污染与自然破坏。主要内容应当包括：确立环境保护的基本制度，诸如环境标准、环境保护计划、环境影响评价、环境行政申报与审批许可、环境行政指导、环境保护费用负担、重大环境污染与自然破坏事故的报告与应急措施等；自然保护区与生物多样性保护，诸如保护方式、生态安全与外来物种入侵防止、自然资源开发利用中的保护措施等。

第四章为治理环境污染与自然破坏。主要内容应当包括：环境破坏的恢复责任；费用负担；各类制度措施；政府责任；基金建立；环境损害责任保险制度；环境行政补偿制度。

第五章为合理利用与节约使用自然资源与能源。主要内容应当包括：以清洁生产为目标，确立减废、回收、再生；鼓励措施。值得一提的是，这里不涉及单项环境与资源保护立法的具体管理问题。

第六章法律责任。主要内容应当包括：在行政责任方面只规定原则、程序与方法，不规定具体处罚措施，以统合指导单项环境与资源保护法律的行政处罚规定；另外，应当确立公民的环境行政诉讼。在民事救济方面，确立侵权的赔偿责任与相邻环境妨害的排除责任的原则与措施；在危害环境犯罪与刑事责任方面，扩大增设行为犯；另外，应当确立纠纷的行政处理方式。鉴于在经济发展进程中环境侵害的必然性，建立环境侵害的民事救济制度与排除妨害责任机制，强化环境纠纷的行政和司法处理机制，建立政府对环境损害的“兜底”责任。

第七章是附则。主要规定术语解释、法律生效的日期以及与国际环境条约在中国的适用。另外还可以就当国家各部门法律在适用上出现与本法原则不符合或者不明确的现象时如何适用法律作出明确规定。

需要说明的是，对《环境保护法》内容的修改将直接影响单项环境与资源保护立法的内容。我认为，未来单项环境与资源保护立法不应当像现在这样简单地对环境保护基本法的重要规定再次予以重申，而应当将重点放在对单项环境（资源）要素的保护或管理之上、针对环境（资源）要素的不同特点和保护管理措施确立可操作执行的条款，以免造成单项环境与资源保护立法中的法条资源的浪费。

四、结　论

环境基本法是确立国家环境政策、目标以及重要原则和制度的法律，目的在于综合协调国家环境政策与经济政策的关系，解决实践中可能出现的法律适用问题。因此，环境基本法的效力应当高于其他单项环境与资源保护法律和国家一般法律，其本质属于基本法和政策法的范畴。

目前我国环境与资源保护立法已日臻完善，单项环境与资源保护法律已经制定有 20 余部。而全国人大常委会于 1989 年作为环境基本法修改制定的《环境保护法》无论在效力等级，还是在调整对象和范围等方面已显现出严重的功能缺陷，应当予以修改。

鉴于我国立法机关对《环境保护法》的修改正在组织研讨，我认为《环境保护法》修改的目标应当是：第一，将其作为国家基本法由全国人大通过，以提高其法律效力，强化其对单项环境与资源保护立法和法律实施的指导作用；第二，顺应国际潮流，树立全球环境保护思想，增强国人对实施环境保护基本国策的决心和信心；第三，强化政府在实施可持续发展战略过程中的环境与资源保护责任，明确政府对环境质量负责的基本义务，在行政管理方面将环境污染防治与自然生态保护并重；第四，确立国家环境政策目标，宣示国家协调环境与社会、经济发展关系的基本理念；第五，明确推行清洁生产制度，将环境保护与企业技术进步协调一致；第六，在法的适用上协调单项环境与资源保护法律与国家其他法律，特别是有关民事法律、刑事法律以及程序法律的关系。

论有限修改《环境保护法》的有效性课题[①]

汪　劲[②]

一、问题的提出

早在 1993 年八届全国人大成立环资委之时，就雄心勃勃地将对 1989 年《环境保护法》的修改纳入修法的议事日程。尽管此后第九、十、十一届人大常委会均将修法纳入立法规划，并开展了数十次专题调研、执法检查以及专门组织法律专家和官员赴境外考察培训环境立法，但直到 18 年后的 2012 年年初，人大常委会才最终决定将《环境保护法》的修改作为 2011 年的立法工作，环资委也将修法草案的工作委托环保部进行。从修法动议的这一历程可以看出，修改《环境保护法》的难度是相当大的。

出乎很多学者、官员以及各界人士的意料，本次修法确定的总目标是“有限修改”，修法的基本原则是“有限目标、突出重点”、“稳定体制、固化职责”与“强化责任、完善制度”。根据我个人 1993 年以来多次参与全国人大环资委以及与有关部门有关修法工作研讨的理解，做出这种选择，一是因为 18 年来伴随环境污染和生态破坏的不断加剧，修法呼声日益高涨；二是因为修法作为环保法治的一项系统工程面临诸多现实课题，不仅理论分歧较大，而且因体制和机制问题导致实践难度很高。在这个背景下，人大常委会决定修法并将总目标定为有限修改，是特定历史条件下既高度肯定 1989 年《环境保护法》的地位与作用，又合理推动作为环保基本法的《环境保护法》与不断修改完善的有关环保单项法律法规在制度之间建立互动关系的两全之策。

---

① 本文原载于《清华法治论衡》，2012 年第 2 期。
② 汪劲，北京大学法学院教授。研究领域：环境法、核政策与法律。

摆在立法者面前的现实是：18 年来我国社会主义法律体系不断完善，环保单项法律制度不断健全，环保机构改革不断推进，公众环境意识不断提高，环境司法保障不断增强。如果再加上环保压力不断增大的现实背景，我认为本次修法成功的关键是要将“有限修改”的基本命题化为“有效修改”的立法行动。以下本文拟就“有限”与“有效”的关系结合我国环保法律实施的现状与问题，就修法工作涉及的十大立法课题及其应对策略作一基本论述。

二、有限修改《环境保护法》的十大课题

1．从有效协调修法思路和模式论有限修改。关于《环境保护法》的立法思路及其与我国环境法体系关系的研究，法学界一直存在着法典模式与“基本法—单项法”模式的不同认识。在两大模式之下还有更为细致与不同的分化，因此一直没有统一认识。这也是十多年来法学界影响《环境保护法》修改的重要因素之一。

本次人大常委会决定有限修改《环境保护法》，似乎从修法思路上回避了模式选择问题，但若修改不当，则会给未来构建环境法律体系或者法典化编撰带来更多麻烦，从而影响我国社会主义法律体系的进一步完善。因此有效协调修法思路和立法模式成为有限修改成功的第一个课题。

我认为，有效协调修法思路和立法模式，应当在保持《环境保护法》现有框架体系的基础上依旧将该法定位在国家环保基本法的范畴之上。据我观察，无论是法学界还是政府有关部门，他们对《环境保护法》作为国家环保基本法的认识与适法上对该法的“普遍尊重”是现实存在的。但是，除环境污染防治单项法律的结构与内容基本一致外，自然资源与能源、循环经济与清洁生产领域等的立法无论在管理模式、制度体系还是在执法方式等方面都大相径庭，很难形成目标一致、体系完整的广义环境法的体系。

因此，尽管修改有限，但在立法思路与模式上应当对既有自然资源保护、能源合理利用和清洁生产与循环经济等领域目标一致的法律制度在修

法中予以统一。同时此举也不影响未来我国环境法体系及其发展模式的构建与选择。

2．从有效解决《环境保护法》自身问题论有限修改。分析 20 多年前制定的《环境保护法》自身存在的问题，我认为主要表现在计划色彩浓厚（尽管在实行有计划的商品经济时期）、与单项环境与资源保护法律之间效力定位不清、全方位环保监管思路不明、政府责任缺失以及与其他国家基本法（如民法、刑法、程序法以及相关法律）在适用上关系混乱等问题方面。因此有效解决《环境保护法》自身存在的问题成为有限修改成功的第二个课题。

虽然不能指望对《环境保护法》的有限修改能够一一解决上述问题，但本次修法必须确立几个相对明确的原则和操作指引。如明确政府依公权力实施环保监管与环境利用行为人主动积极地通过市场自主、自愿调控的关系、确立与污染防治条款同等的生态环境领域开发与保护目标和方法、创立环保执法的联动与纠错机制、借鉴《水污染防治法》修改确立的环保目标责任制和考核评价制度，等等。

3．从有效衔接其他环保单项法律法规与国家有关基本法律论有限修改。有限修改《环境保护法》成功与否的第三个课题，是修法是否能够有效衔接《环境保护法》与其他环保单项法律法规以及国家有关基本法律的问题。

本文已在前一修法课题中提及这两个问题。首先，自 1989 年《环境保护法》颁行以来，我国先后颁布实施或者修改了 20 多部环境与资源保护、循环经济与清洁生产以及节约能源等方面的单项法律和行政法规。其次，也更为重要的是，国家民事、刑事和规范行政行为的基本法律也在不断制定或者修改完善，环境法治的氛围和条件已经基本形成。

我国环境与资源保护单项法律法规的不断完善，特别是国家民事、刑事与行政立法不断健全，已将作为环保基本法的《环境保护法》推向一个越来越尴尬的境地。首先，论法律调整的环境资源要素或者法律关系领域，它的制度建设不及环境与资源保护单项法律法规广泛、具体和具有可操作性；其次，论涉及环保的传统实体法责任与程序法规则，它较之于国家民事、刑事与行政立法要么点到为止、要么因效力不及而影响实施，我们也从未看到国家司法机关对《环境保护法》规定的司法条款作出解释；最后，这两类法律未作规范、需要由《环境保护法》解决的法律空白，却在《环境保护法》文本中找不到任何根据，自身也是空白。所以我十多年来一直对《环境保护法》的存在价值表示怀疑，也曾多次提及若不作出有针对性的修改还不如将其废止的主张。

鉴于《环境保护法》的修改涉及诸多环境与资源保护单项法律法规的效力及其范围，同时还涉及部分国家基本法有关环保与资源，能源开发利用的原则规定以及有针对性的实体规定或者程序规定，因此从有效衔接其他环保单项法律法规与国家有关基本法律上看，修法还应当对《环境保护法》与这两方面法律法规在适用上的关系、法条竞合及其适用等作出特别规定，以免今后出现各个法律在具体适用上可能出现的麻烦与混乱。

同时，此举还可以为今后国家进行环境法律体系的整理和清理或者编撰环境法典奠定立法基础。

4．从有效完善公众参与途径论有限修改。环保公众参与，一直是我国环保立法的一项基本原则。而现行《环境保护法》和其他单项法律法规，包括《环境影响评价法》及其相关法规规章至今也没有切实解决这个问题，所以说有效完善公众参与途径是有限修改成功的第四个课题。

我们常说，环保法在部门法分类上既不属于行政法，也不属于民法。限于环境和资源的多元价值，环境法律关系在构成上往往兼具公权与私权性质，一个看似简单的行政许可开发行为，法律关系的主体一定会涉及诸多对环境多元价值进行本能性利用的公众和群体，即使是司法机关在处理环境民事权益纠纷时也会拿公权力的环境标准来衡量是非。这也是为什么会有环境权的概念的根本原因，因为不当的环境与资源开发利用行为，会侵害广大公众的环境权益。

从这个意义上讲，我们应当顺应全国人大提出的建立有中国特色的社会主义法律体系的模式，将以往《环境保护法》的行政管制法本位朝向社会法本位的方向推进。

这一点，立法者应当多听法学者的建言和公众、环保团体的诉求，他们才真正代表民意。我们绝不能为了便利政府及其主管部门“好管”或者抱怨增加他们的麻烦而将公众参与条款原则化、教条化。因为《环境保护法》绝对不只是政府及其有关部门实施环境管制的工具，也是所有公众和个人拿法律说事并据以保护自身合法权益不受侵害的来源和准据。

修法时有效完善公众参与途径最简单的方法，就是将公众环境权益包括知悉权、建言权、受尊重权以及救济权等权利在现有条文的基础上进一步明确，特别是在行使权利和谋求救济的程序上要具有可操作性。

5．从有效明确政府官员环保责任论有限修改。无论是作为环境法体系中的环保基本法还是环境法典，各国环保立法无不将政府主要官员作为环保责任的首要对象。

或许是受限于“党管干部”的原则，我国环保立法对政府官员责任的规定一直呈躲躲闪闪之势，或者干脆只规定行为模式、不规定法律后果，导致《环境保护法》缺乏起码的责任追究机制。加上党组织制定的领导干部政绩考核机制缺乏公民环境福祉考量目标、中央和地方财政“分灶吃饭”体制，以至于引导地方政府官员热衷于“招商引资”和搞“短平快”的固定资产投资项目。我国环境质量状况20多年来一直呈“局部有所好转、总体还在恶化”之势的最重要的原因，在我看来应当归咎于地方政府官员没有依法对环保负起责任。所以有效明确政府官员环保责任是有限修改成功的第五个课题。

我国“十一五”规划中节能减排等约束性指标的完成情况表明，只有将环保责任与政府官员的政绩考评挂钩，才能使对政府官员保障环境质量不断改善的环保指标和责任落实到位。本次修法应当总结这一经验并利用《国家主体功能区规划》的实施，明确将政府官员的环保责任与政绩考评联系起来，实行环保目标责任制和考核评价制度，将环保目标完成情况作为对地方政府及其负责人考核评价的主要内容。

6．从有效突破环保行政外部制约论有限修改。实际上，环保行政的主要外部制约因素来源于地方党政主要领导干部。这一问题及其解决方法前文已述。这里所讲的有效突破环保行政外部制约，是指来自其他与环保相关的政府部门的制约因素，它是有限修改《环境保护法》是否有效的第六个课题。

《环境保护法》规定了环保统管与分管相结合的管理体制，十多个政府主管部门与环保部门统管职能都有直接交叉。尽管30年来环保部门经历了从国务院机构管理部门到国务院组成部门的演变，但因各部门职能交叉导致环保执法监督体制不畅、“统管管不了、分管管不到”的现象比比皆是，呈现出高消耗、低效能、低产出。

诚然，修法不应回避体制不顺所带来的矛盾和问题，而体制问题并非修法所能解决的。为避免修法过程中容易引发相关部门因不同认识而发生的争议，在有限修改的同时我们应将20多年来政府机构改革的成果和国务院“三定方案”已确立的环保职权职责关系在修法中一并考虑，将重点放在落实部门责任上，才能使修法实现既照顾现状，又为未来政府实行大部制改革、理顺环境管理体制提供模本的作用。

7．从有效强化环保监管论有限修改。“环保执法难”是当前我国环保法律实施的真实状况。我曾经专门对此做过调查，发现环保执法难的主要根源是环保执法权受限于地方政府的经济增长政策，因为政府部门中只有环保部门扮演着环境公益推动者和经济发展衡平者的角色，恰恰这些都有悖于地方政府官员的短期发展政绩。因此过去在环保立法中政府常常会向立法机关施加压力，以“不切合中国的实际为由”尽量让法律法规减少赋予环保部门更多有强制力的执行权，从而使环保部门有责无权，实践中降低了环保执法的有效性。

最近五年，随着环保机构改革的深入、司法保障作用的加强以及修改单项环保法律时与时俱进地固化环保执法权限，各级政府在加强环保执法权能工作方面已取得了很多突破。因此，能否在本次修法中将分散在各个单项法律法规以及国务院机构改革方案等文件中强化环保监管的内容纳入修法之中，是有限修改《环境保护法》能否有效的第七个课题。

从内容上看，如下几个方面的条文应当在修法中予以固化。第一，建立中央与地方环保部门分别管辖的监管体制，如建立跨地区的污染联防体制并设立区域性国家环境督察机构，由他们代表国家环保部门行使执法权和生态破坏索赔权；第二，与制定中的《行政强制法》内容相一致，赋予环保部门在一定执法范围和领域的强制执行权，引入执行罚手段（如按日连续处罚制）让环保行政命令能够令行禁止；第三，引入人大执法检查制度与环保执法报告制度，从立法监督的角度保障环保执法的有效性。

8．从有效完善环保基本法律制度论有限修改。本次有限修改《环境保护法》的实质，是对包括环评、排污收费、限期治理、公众环境权益、环境标准、环境监测、跨行政区污染防治协调、人民政府环境质量责任等在内的环保基本制度进行完善。因为原本出于《环境保护法》的这些制度在后来的立法与执法实践中，它们的程序、方法、内容与效力等都已发生了重大改变，而且目前还在不断变化。

以我参加国家立法的经验，在环保基本法中重申污染防治单项法律法规已经规定得更为具体的条款是比较困难的，因为从法律适用上看写了也等于白写。因此，有效完善环保基本法律制度是有限修改成功的第八个课题。

那么，修法应当如何找到重申这些基本法律制度的突破口以保有效、成功呢？

首先，在修法时应当做到“固化既有、拓展前沿”，即将已改革完善的制度内容作概括性与衔接性重申，同时应当为制度的进一步完善或创新留出立法空间；其次，在修法时应当重点关注并解决“制度本质相同但权务关系不同”的问题，即将不同时期针对不同环境要素制定或者修改的单项法律法规对同一制度作出规定的不同在修法时予以统一并澄清；最后，在修法时应当“轻行为模式、重法律后果”，即在制度明晰的前提下将重点放在切实保障制度得以有效执行的措施方面。

例如，环评制度应当关注设立“补办”的条件与“三同时”监管以及政府有关项目审批部门违反程序操作的责任，排污收费制度应当关注并与未来中国税费改革措施相衔接，限期治理制度更要强调制度的行政强制属性确保令行禁止，公众环境权益规定更应当关注权利的行使与救济保障，环境标准制度则需要强调编制标准的民主性以及适时修改和补充标准内容，环境监测制度应当在考虑现有国家环境监测网络和体制下各部门的配合分工与市场化并明确统一发布环境信息机关的权力及其效力，跨行政区污染防治协调必须建立相邻行政区域的联防互动机制与利益分配机制，人民政府环境质量责任制度则更应当关注政府官员任期的质量目标和要求。

特别需要指出的是，本次修法有关环保法律制度的完善不仅要考虑执法主体在法律适用上的有效性，还需要考虑引入信息公开和公众参与机制。因为环保立法的任何一项制度的实施都必然涉及公众环境权益的各个方面，因为环保行政法律关系的构成绝不仅仅是环保部门与相对人之间那么简单。

9. 从有效解决“违法成本低”论有限修改。目前，企业通过违法获取利益的行为主要表现在如下几个方面：第一，在项目环评阶段，项目建设单位不理睬环评程序或未经环评批复先建，在环保部门发现后通过“补办”环评手续弥补，此举既可以赢得项目建设时间，又可以倒逼环保部门事后予以批复同意；第二，在项目建设“三同时”阶段，利用环保监管密度不高故意逃避环保设施建设与运营义务，或者在竣工验收时骗取环保部门获得许可，达到减少环保投入的目的；第三，在排污申报或者登记、现场检查等阶段，故意瞒报或者编造虚假数据骗取环保部门的信任，达到少缴或者免缴排污费、超标排污费以及逃避违法处罚的目的；第四，故意私设暗管偷排污染物，或者拒不执行环保部门依法做出的责令限期改正、限期整改或者限期治理命令，持续获取违法收益。

尽管违法企业在事后会有很多借口推脱责任，但是故意钻法律的漏洞或者主动规避法律制度的企业仍不在少数。因此，有效解决企业“违法成本低”问题是有限修改成功的第九个课题。

实际上，解决这个问题的立法方法很简单，除了在完善环保法律制度的法律后果方面规定与行为模式要求相匹配、得以填补制度规范性与实效性不强等漏洞的处罚条款外，还应当通过修法确立统一、共通的追究环保违法行为责任的条款。这一点，各国与各地区目前通行的将按日计罚作为

确保行为模式与行政命令得以彻底遵守的执行罚措施，应当成为本次修法所重点考虑的、可以有效解决“违法成本低”的手段与方法。

10．从有效运用环保司法手段论有限修改。综观30年来我国的环保立法，强调政府环保行政作用的指导思想远远高于重视并运用司法手段保护环境的理念。因此，当环保行政遇到司法审查问题时，当污染被害人需要司法救济时，以及当人们认为对严重污染环境行为应当给予刑罚制裁时，环保立法给出的司法条款总是欠缺得很多。所以，能否在法律责任章尽可能多地将完善法律后果规定，引导今后更多地运用司法手段保护环境，理所当然地成为修法是否成功和有效的第十个课题。

在委托环保部修法的文件中，全国人大环资委特别提出“要在形成中国特色社会主义法律体系的新起点上”开展修法工作。这里的“法律体系的新起点”，是指全国人大对我国现行部门法律体系类别所作的最新划分，这一划分已将我国环保法律体系纳入社会法体系的范畴。因此，这一点一定要引起参与修法的官员、学者与其他立法参与者的注意。

本文已多次指出，鉴于环保有关法律行为涉及诸多不同性质的法律关系，因此我们不应当简单地套用环境政策所倡导的“环保靠政府”思想将环保法律也定位于国家行政管制类立法之中。这一点，过去由环保部门主导的环保法律在立法指导思想上总是存在着偏差。

作为环境与资源保护领域的基本法律，《环境保护法》所确立的基本法律制度及其体系应当表现出浓厚的社会法属性，也即在改革现行环保行政管制制度措施的同时，在管制行政之外注重在立法本位上突出权利而非义务，增加以公民合法环境权益对抗开发利用环境行为的条款。

最近几年，环保法庭与环保审判庭的建立初步实现了补强行政与专业判案的目的，最高人民法院还发布了关于支持污染被害人起诉和支持环保部门代表国家索赔诉讼的意见，因此修法还应当在诉讼法和民法之外确立特别法规范，规定诸如环保部门和其他环保监管部门可以代表国家提起污染致生态破坏的索赔诉讼以及公民、环保团体或者检察机关为主体的环境公益诉讼。

三、小结

总之，尽管本次修法的总体思路是有限修改，但修法的目标仍必须在形成中国特色社会主义法律体系的新起点上，应对环保法律法规实施亟待解决的执法课题，以提高环保法律法规实施的有效性。我认为，在这个背景下，与完善环保法律制度体系相比，修法的意义更应理解为一种昭示与释放国家环保法治信念与发展路径的信号。结合《环境保护法》在环保及其相关领域的基本法地位，只要将目前环保部门已经实施或者实践证明行之有效的做法以及各部门已就环境与资源保护达成一致的意见予以规范化、制度化，在此基础上做出一定突破并统一适用到环境与资源保护领域，《环境保护法》的有限修改还是可以获得圆满成功的。

参考文献

[1] 汪劲. 对构筑我国环境法律体系框架若干问题的思考[J]. 环境保护，1995（2）.

[2] 汪劲. 论环境立法的价值[J]. 环境保护，2001（8）.

[3] 汪劲. 论我国《环境保护法》的现状和修改定位[J]. 环境保护，2003（6）.

[4] 汪劲. 从环境基本法的立法特征论我国《环境保护法》的修改定位[J]. 中外法学，2004（4）.

[5] 汪劲. 环保法治 30 年：中国的成就与问题[J]. 环境保护，2008（21）.

[6] 汪劲. 序二：环境法的法典化：迷思与解迷//彭峰. 法典化的迷思：法国环境法之考察[M]. 上海：上海社会科学院出版社，2010.

[7] 汪劲. 环境法治的中国路径：反思与探求[M]. 北京：中国环境科学出版社，2011.

[8] 汪劲，等. 环保法治 30 年：我们成功了吗——中国环保法治蓝皮书（1979—2010）[M]. 北京：北京大学出版社，2011.

公民环境权入法符合时代潮流[①]

李静云[②]

中国环境保护领域的“基本法”——《环境保护法》终于迎来了大修。对《环境保护法》的修改应该抓住关键、突出重点，彰显这部基本法是保护人民切身利益，即关乎民生的法、维护公民基本权利的法，其关键在于确认公民的环境权。制定具体的环境法律制度可以循序渐进，而明确公民环境权是《环境保护法》修改中最重大、最关键的问题。

公民环境权入法有利于控制污染、加强执法、改善环境、促进环保事业发展，并且符合国际社会潮流。我国《宪法》中已经写入了人权，而环境权本身就是人权的一个重要组成部分，在修订《环境保护法》时应当明确公民环境权，即“公民有享受良好环境的权利和保护环境的义务”。

一、环境权的形成和发展

环境权理论的思想萌芽可追溯到20世纪初。早在1902年，日本学者宫崎民藏就在其撰写的《人类的大权》一文中提出“地球为人类所共有”的观点，他主张“土地公平享有”，认为地球为“天下生存的全人类所共有”。宫崎民藏关于地球共有权的主张对环境权理论的发展产生了深远的影响。

进入20世纪60年代，环境问题日趋严重，逐步成为威胁人类生存、制约经济发展和影响社会稳定的直接因素。在发达国家公害事件不断发生、污染严重，发展中国家贫困与人口压力巨大、资源破坏严重的形势下，世

① 本文原载于《中国环境报》2012年10月29日。
② 李静云，环境保护部政策法规司法规处处长。

界各国一方面致力于探索治理环境污染的科学技术方法，另一方面也在努力寻求解决环境问题的理论依据和法律依据。

20 世纪 60 年代，国际社会也展开了关于环境权法律依据的讨论。1966 年，联合国大会第一次辩论人类环境问题，在各成员国充分发表意见的基础上，大会取得共识，认为有必要召开一次专门会议共商环境保护大计，这就是 1972 年联合国人类环境会议的由来。

日本是环境权理论的重要发祥地。“二战”后的日本经历了快速发展，也遭受了严重的环境公害，并先后发生了一系列环境公害诉讼。20 世纪 60 年代以来，大阪府西淀川区公害受害者在抵制公害和寻求救济过程中，成立了公害患者联合会，大阪律师协会在代理受害者的诉讼过程中，组建了公害诉讼辩护团。大阪律协深刻认识到承认和保护公民环境权的极端重要性，开展了环境权研究，成立了环境权研究会，并产生了很大影响。

1970 年 3 月，国际社会科学评议会在东京召开了“公害问题国际座谈会”，会后发表的《东京宣言》明确提出：“我们请求，把每个人享有的健康和福利等不受侵害的环境权和当代人传给后代的遗产应是一种富有自然美的自然资源的权利，作为一种基本人权，在法律体系中确定下来。”由此，更为明确地提出了环境权的要求。

1970 年 9 月，日本律师协会召开“日本律师联合会第 13 回人权拥护大会”，大阪律师团发表了将防治公害作为极其重要的人权的建议，并表决通过了关于推进公害对策的宣言。会后，大阪律师团在对其提交的报告进行总结后将各种有关环境的权利称为“环境权”，并于 1971 年 5 月在日本期刊《法律家》第 479 期正式发表了《对确立环境权的建议》；1973 年又在日本评论社出版了《环境权》专著，标志环境权理论在日本的诞生。

20 世纪 70 年代初，著名国际法学者、诺贝尔奖获得者雷诺·卡辛向海牙研究院提交了一份报告，提出要将现有的人权原则加以扩展，将人类享有免受污染和在健康和良好的环境中生存的环境权包括在内。

欧洲人权会议经过 10 多年的讨论和研究后，终于在 20 世纪 70 年代初，接受了环境权的观点，并组织了 80 人的专家委员会，致力于将“人类免受环境危害的在这个星球上继续生存下去的权利”作为新的人权原则进行国际法编纂。

1972 年 6 月联合国在斯德哥尔摩召开了人类环境会议，113 个国家和国际机构的 1 300 多名代表参加了会议。联合国人类环境会议通过了《人类环境宣言》。宣言第 1 条庄严宣告：“人类有权在一种能够过着尊严的和福利的生活环境中，享有自由、平等和充足的生活条件的基本权利，并且负有保证和改善这一代和世世代代的环境的庄严责任。”

1982年召开的内罗毕人类环境特别会议和1992年召开的联合国环境与发展大会所发表的《内罗毕宣言》和《里约宣言》，都重申了《人类环境宣言》中关于环境权的观点。

近年来，关于防止臭氧层破坏、保护海洋环境资源、保护南极环境资源、保护生物多样性、保护月球和其他天体等国际公约，大多亦包含有承认公民、法人及其他组织和国家的环境利益和保护环境的义务、全人类的环境利益、人类子孙后代的环境利益等内容的条款。

二、其他国家关于环境权的立法概况

自 1972 年联合国人类环境会议通过的《人类环境宣言》郑重提出环境权，相继被一些国家在其国家根本大法——宪法中予以明确。据统计，目前已有 53 个国家在宪法中明确了环境权，有 60 多个国家在其环境保护法律中明确了环境权。

（一）宪法明确规定

通过宪法明确规定公民的环境权，是确认环境权的最理想方式。目前，在宪法中明确环境权的主要以发展中国家为多，尤其以非洲最为突出。

世界上最早在宪法中确认环境权的国家是原南斯拉夫。1974 年《南斯拉夫社会主义联邦共和国宪法》第 192 条规定：“人有得到健康的生活环境的权利。社会共同体为行使这一权利保证条件。”

在 1992 年联合国环境与发展大会召开后，不少国家在制定或者修改宪法时增加了有关环境权的条款。在宪法中确认环境权的最有影响力的是法国制定的《环境宪章》。

（二）环境保护法律明确规定

虽然迄今为止，无论是国际社会，还是各国立法对于环境权的定义并不完全一致，但总体来说，其内涵都是一样的，即公民享有健康、良好的环境，以及合理利用环境资源的基本权利。环境权在法律中予以明确，表明环境已不再被视为无主物，而被广泛确认为人类共同享有的基本权利。

美国和日本关于环境权的立法实践，对于环境权的发展也起到了极大的推进作用。迄今为止，世界上已有 60 多个国家在其环境保护法律中明确了环境权，从而使环境权成为一项新生的基本法律权利。现在有越来越多的国家，特别是发展中国家、处于经济转型时期的国家，正在将环境权或环境资源保护方面的基本权利和义务写入其宪法或者环境保护法律中。

三、关于中国环境权的立法建议

（一）以人为本应有之义

中国政府高度重视保障公民的环境权利。在 2012 年 4 月 25 日举行的斯德哥尔摩+40 可持续发展伙伴论坛上，温家宝总理提出要“保障人人享有平等的环境权利”。温总理明确表示：“人不仅有基本的政治、经济和发展权利，还应当有基本的环境权利，有权获得良好的生活环境，有权不遭受污染的危害，有权参与对影响环境行为的监督管理。要提高公民的环境权利意识和责任意识，加强对公民环境权利的保障，以更加合理地利用环境，更加自觉地保护环境，为可持续发展注入强大而持久的动力。”

经国务院批准并授权，国务院新闻办公室 2012 年 6 月 11 日公布了《国家人权行动计划（2012—2015 年）》。此计划明确环境权利为一项重要的基本人权，要求“采取积极措施，更有效地保障全体社会成员的工作权利、基本生活水准权利、社会保障权利、健康权利、受教育权利、文化权利、环境权利，努力使全体人民学有所教、劳有所得、病有所医、老有所养、住有所居，使发展成果更好地惠及全体人民”，并进一步详细论述通过修改《环境保护法》、有效防治重金属污染、加大水污染防治力度、改善大气质量、推进生态建设、加强海洋生态保护、加强放射性污染防治、严格监管危险化学品、完善环境监察体制机制等措施，以“加强环境保护，着力解决重金属、饮用水源、大气、土壤、海洋污染等关系民生的突出环境问题，保障环境权利”。

在现代社会权利法定原则下，公民环境权的法律化是使公民环境权得到保障的前提条件，也是国家担当环境管理职责的法律依据。在“以人为本”的和谐社会语境下，环境立法应以保障公民环境权为起点和归宿。

我国《宪法》中已经写入了人权，《国家人权行动计划（2012—2015年）》也将环境权利作为一项重要的基本人权。因此，公民环境权是人权的一个重要组成部分，是公民所享有的一项基本人权，理应入法。环境保护法作为国家环境保护的基本法，实际上具有“母法”的地位，是单项法以及相关立法的根基之所在。因此，应当将环境权作为公民基本权利在《环境保护法》中予以明文规定。

（二）有利解决环境问题

环境问题的产生及恶化，使公民产生了对环境予以保护的权利要求，环境科学以及经济的发展使国家具备了保护环境权的技术手段和物质基础。及时将这一应有权利确定为法律权利，有利于解决环境问题，促进环境质量得以改善。美国和日本的立法实践证明了这一点。

20 世纪 60 年代的日本，也正是一方面享受经济高速发展之乐，另一方面饱受公害泛滥之痛，公众反对污染的环境运动也是此起彼伏。在此背景下，日本大阪律师会在反污染公害的国内法律实践中，率先提出了公民享有不受污染损害和争取救济的“环境权”主张。

20 世纪六七十年代，是美国经济的高速发展时期，同时也是公害泛滥时期，公害事件所引起的痛苦和不安让公众产生了严重的“生存”危机。公众为了安全和健康，掀起了一场声势浩大、席卷全国、历时久远的反对污染的环境运动。在持续不断的请愿、游行、示威、抗议中，公众强烈要求在法律上赋予公民环境权。在此压力下，1969 年，美国国会通过的《国家环境政策法》中明确了公民环境权。

美国、日本为什么会如此的同出一辙呢？理由很简单，环境资源的使用具有典型的经济学上的外部性的特征，行为人享有其活动的利益，如果管制失灵，其不利后果由全社会承担。我们的环境法律体系是以政府管制构成环境法律基本内容的，通过这么多年的实践发现，打击环境违法行为总感到力不从心，环境质量总是难以改善到群众满意的程度。这固然与我国经济发展规模不断扩大有关系，但是根本原因是，在人力资源、信息收集、执法成本等问题的制约下，政府管制也会失灵。这并不是中国独有现象，这是世界各国政府管制中的普遍规律。美国的能源管制就是始终难以跳出政府管制—管制失灵—市场管制—市场失灵—政府再管制的循环圈。

我国环境立法基本上与工业化时代同步，这是比发达国家优越的地方，但是，环境质量总体上仍是局部有所改善、总体尚未遏制，环境群体性事件也呈增多发趋势。在此背景下，在法律中赋予环境权势在必行。因为政府永远不可能拥有足够的执法资源在全国范围内监测每一个污染源，而居住在污染源附近的公民常常是违法排污行为最经济、最有效的监控者。在《环境保护法》中明确公民环境权，赋予公民对违法排污者的排污行为以及对未履行法定义务的行为进行监督的权利，为公众参与环境保护监督管理、提起环境公益诉讼、开展环境维权行为奠定法律基础，对于有效打击环境违法行为、控制污染、加强执法、改善环境，将起到不可估量的作用。

（三）昭示保障人权态度

在《环境保护法》中明确环境权，对于我国开展环境外交也有着重要意义。首先，在《环境保护法》中明确环境权，将向国际社会昭示中国保护和改善环境的决心，在中国环境保护的基本法——《环境保护法》中明确环境权，则表示作为基本权利的环境权将是一切主体需要遵从的准则。

其次，在《环境保护法》中明确环境权是我国履行国际义务的体现，国际条约和国际法规范大多不能在国内直接适用，而需要经由国内立法予以明确。《环境保护法》作为最高地位的环境法律，直接反映我国履行国际义务的态度。在《环境保护法》中明确环境权，可以显示出中国作为一个大国的责任担当。

最后，某些国家常以人权状况攻击我国，而我国奉行生存权为最大人权，将作为生存权和发展权之基础与保障的环境权在法律中予以明确，将向世界昭示我国人权保障的积极态度。

（四）地方环境立法已有实践

近年来，我国地方立法对于环境权已有立法实践。《上海市环境保护条例》、《福建省环境保护条例》、《宁夏回族自治区环境保护条例》、《深圳经济特区环境保护条例》、《吉林市环境保护条例》，都明确规定了公民（或者单位和个人）的环境权。这些地方的环境保护工作实践也说明，赋予公民（或者单位和个人）环境权，对于加强环境保护工作、加大对环境违法行为的监督、改善环境质量是有积极作用和意义的。

值得一提的是，在1990年7月10日中央军委发布的《中国人民解放军环境保护条例》总则中就明确规定："军内一切单位和个人，都有保护和改善环境的义务，都有对污染、破坏环境的行为进行监督、检举、控告和在符合国家规定标准的环境中工作与生活的权利"。在修订后于2004年9月16日颁布实施的《中国人民解放军环境保护条例》中，进一步将环境权予以细化，明确规定"军队所有单位和人员都有保护和改善环境的义务，都有在符合规定标准的环境中工作和生活的权利、对环境质量知情的权利以及获得环境损害补偿的权利，并有权对污染和破坏环境的行为进行监督、检举和控告"。

附：地方立法和相关立法中环境权立法条款摘录

名称	制定或修改时间	所在章节	具体内容
上海市环境保护条例	2005 年 10 月 28 日	第一章 总则	第八条：一切单位和个人都有享受良好环境的权利，有权对污染、破坏环境的行为进行检举和控告，在直接受到环境污染危害时有权要求排除危害和赔偿损失
福建省环境保护条例	1995 年 7 月 5 日	第一章 总则	第九条：公民有享受良好环境的权利和保护环境的义务
宁夏回族自治区环境保护条例	2009 年 11 月 19 日	第一章 总则	第七条：任何组织和个人有享受良好环境的权利和履行保护环境的义务，有权检举、控告违反环境保护法律法规的行为，有权对环境保护工作提出意见和建议
深圳经济特区环境保护条例	2009 年 7 月 21 日	第六章 公众参与	第六十条：单位和个人享有在良好环境中生活、获取环境信息、参与环境监督管理以及得到环境损害赔偿的权利
吉林市环境保护条例	1987 年 9 月 19 日	第一章 总则	第八条：公民有享受良好环境的权利和保护环境的义务
原来的解放军环境保护条例	1990 年 7 月 10 日	第一章 总则	第六条：军内一切单位和个人，都有保护和改善环境的义务，都有对污染、破坏环境的行为进行监督、检举、控告和在符合国家规定标准的环境中工作与生活的权利
最新修改的解放军环境保护条例	2004 年 9 月 16 日	第一章 总则	第六条：军队所有单位和人员都有保护和改善环境的义务，都有在符合规定标准的环境中工作和生活的权利、对环境质量知情的权利以及获得环境损害补偿的权利，并有权对污染和破坏环境的行为进行监督、检举和控告